Decision-Making and Problems
of Incompetence

Decision-Making and Problems of Incompetence

Edited by Andrew Grubb

Reader in Medical Law, Executive Director
School of Law and
Centre of Medical Law and Ethics,
King's College London, UK

JOHN WILEY & SONS
Chichester · New York · Brisbane · Toronto ·
Singapore

Other Wiley Editorial Offices

John Wiley & Sons, Inc., 605 Third Avenue,
New York, NY 10158-0012, USA

Jacaranda Wiley Ltd, 33 Park Road, Milton,
Queensland 4064, Australia

John Wiley & Sons (Canada) Ltd, 22 Worcester Road,
Rexdale, Ontario M9W 1L1, Canada

John Wiley & Sons (SEA) Pte Ltd, 37 Jalan Pemimpin #05-04,
Block B, Union Industrial Building, Singapore 2057

Library of Congress Cataloging-in-Publication Data
.

Decision-making and problems of incompetence / edited by Andrew Grubb.
        p. cm.
    "Papers presented at the first Annual Conference of the UK Forum
on Health Care Ethics and the Law held . . . in April 1991"—Pref.
    Includes bibliographical references and index.
    ISBN 0 471 94236 7
    1. Informed consent (Medical law)—Great Britain.   2. Sick—Legal
status, laws, etc.—Great Britain.   3. Right to die—Law and
legislation—Great Britain.   4. Medical care—Decision making.
I. Grubb, Andrew.   II. UK Forum on Health Care Ethics and the Law.
Conference (1st : 1991 : King's College)
KD3410 . I54D43   1994
344 . 41'04197—dc20
[344.1044197]   93–6187
                                                                      CIP

British Library Cataloguing in Publication Data

A catalogue record for this book is available from the British Library

ISBN 0 471 94236 7

Typeset in 10/12pt Garamond by Tradespools Ltd., Frome, Somerset
Printed and bound in Great Britain by Biddles Limited, Guildford.

Contents

Contributors

Mylène Beaupré is a graduate of the Centre of Medical Law and Ethics and a member of the Quebec Bar Association in Canada.

Dan Brock is Professor of Bio-Medical Ethics and Director of Center for Bio-Medical Ethics, Brown University, Rhode Island, USA.

Will Cartwright is a lecturer in the Department of Philosophy, University of Essex, UK.

Maureen Eby is a lecturer in the Department of Nursing Studies, University of Birmingham, UK.

H. E. Emson is Professor of Pathology, Royal University Hospital, Saskatoon, Canada.

Dieter Giesen is Professor of Law and Dean, Law Department and Working Centre for Studies in German and International Medical Malpractice Law, Free University, Berlin, Germany.

Andrew Grubb is Reader in Medical Law and the Director of the Centre of Medical Law & Ethics, King's College London, UK.

Christopher Heginbotham is Chief Executive, Riverside Mental Health Trust, formerly Fellow in Health Services Management, King's Fund College, London, UK.

Brenda Hoggett is a Recorder of the Crown Court, a Queen's Counsel and Law Commissioner of England and Wales in charge of the

Commission's project on mentally incapacitated adults.

Jennifer Jackson is Director of the Centre for Business and Professional Ethics, University of Leeds, UK.

Ronald Link is Professor of Law, School of Law, University of North Carolina at Chapel Hill, USA.

Eric Matthews is Head of Department, Department of Philosophy, University of Aberdeen, UK.

The Terrence Higgins Trust Advice Centre provides legal, welfare rights and housing advice to people affected by HIV and AIDS. The Living Will project is composed of volunteer and staff solicitors at the Advice Centre.

Preface

This is the eighth volume of essays on medical law and ethics published by the Centre of Medical Law and Ethics at King's College. It is a special volume since it consists of the papers presented at the first Annual Conference of the UK Forum on Health Care Ethics and the Law held under the auspices of the Centre at King's in April 1991.

The theme of the Conference and the title of this volume reflect the central importance in medical law and ethics of decision-making and the incapacitated patient. The volume addresses the issues in relation to both children and adults. The courts have in a series of cases confronted the problems of deciding who, if anyone, may consent (or refuse consent) to medical treatment when a patient is incompetent and on what basis that decision must be made: *Re B (a minor) (wardship: sterilisation)* [1988] AC 199, *Re F (a mental patient: sterilisation)* [1990] 2 AC 1; *Re T (adult: refusal of treatment)* [1992] 4 All ER 649 and *Airedale NHS Trust* v. *Bland* [1993] 1 All ER 821. The papers examine these issues from an English perspective and from the experiences of abroad. They raise profound and fundamental questions about how society deals with and protects its vulnerable members.

As ever I am grateful to those at John Wiley who worked on this volume with me, in particular Lucy Jepson and Lesley Winchester.

Andrew Grubb
Centre of Medical Law and Ethics
King's College London

Introduction

Andrew Grubb

Until recently it was a widely held view, not least within the medical profession, that the next of kin or relatives of an incapacitated adult patient could consent to medical treatment on his behalf. Some judges even repeated this assumption,[1] although there seemed to be no legal basis for it.[2] Nevertheless, the assumption was convenient and arguably served a valuable purpose. It provided (so it was thought) a legal justification for carrying out desirable medical treatment when the patient was himself unable to consent. Parents, after all, have always been recognised as having the power to make decisions on behalf of their children.[3] Other legal notions were prayed in aid so as to provide a commonsense solution to a practical problem; for example, that the patient impliedly consented or that an emergency permitted treatment.[4]

The law was unclear and, if for no other reason than this, unsatisfactory. It was not until the House of Lords' decision in *Re F (a mental patient: sterilisation)*[5] that the courts clearly faced up to the issue of whether, and if so on what basis, treatment of an incapacitated adult patient could be justified. It is well known that the Law Lords sought refuge in the doctrine of necessity. Consequently, a doctor could act in the patient's "best interests" where the patient was unable himself to consent.[6]

In one sense, the case of *Re F* provided a legal solution to a practical problem. It had, however, four consequences worth noting here. First, it drew attention to the fact that the relatives of an incapacitated patient have no formal legal role in decision-making although as a matter of practice the patient's health carers would be likely to consult them. Secondly, the judges in *Re F* confirmed that the court did not have a protective jurisdiction (as *parens patriae*) to care for inca-

Decision-Making and Problems of Incompetence. Edited by A. Grubb.
© 1994 John Wiley & Sons Ltd.

pacitated adults, perhaps for no other reason than historical accident. Thirdly, the Law Lords confirmed that there were some medical interventions, such as contraceptive sterilisations, which it was desirable to bring before the court for its "approval" before being carried out.[7] Fourthly, as a result of *Re F* the uncertain legal position of incapacitated, and therefore necessarily vulnerable, adults was highlighted. What decisions could be made about their treatment? Who could make them? Should the court have greater powers to protect them, particularly if the proposed intervention was a sterilisation of an intellectually disabled woman or a decision that would have the consequence of the patient dying?

While the courts can make some progress, legislative intervention might be more desirable. Thus, the Lord Chancellor referred the matter to the Law Commission for their considered view on this relatively unexplored area. In 1991 the Law Commission published its Consultation Paper No. 119 on *Mentally Incapacitated Adults and Decision-Making: An Overview.*

Both the Law Commission's Paper No. 119 and the chapters in this volume address the following central questions:

1. When in law should a patient be considered incapacitated and unable to make a treatment decision for himself?
2. If incapacitated, who should be able to make a decision concerning medical treatment for that patient and on what basis should the decision be made?[8]

The subsequent case of *Airedale NHS Trust* v. *Bland*[9] has further focused public and professional attention on decision-making and the incapacitated patient. A Select Committee of the House of Lords was set up in the wake of the *Bland* decision to

consider the ethical, legal and clinical implications of a person's right to withhold consent to life-prolonging treatment, and the position of persons who are no longer able to give or withhold consent:

and to consider whether and in what circumstances actions that have as their intention or a likely consequence the shortening of another person's life may be justified on the grounds that they accord with that person's wishes or with that person's best interests:

and in all the foregoing considerations to pay regard to the likely effects of changes in law or medical practice on society as a whole.

In the spring of 1993 the Law Commission published a series of three further Consultation Papers.[10] The second in the series, Consultation Paper No. 129 on *Mentally Incapacitated Adults and Decision-Making: Medical Treatment and Research*, together with the recommendation of the Select Committee are likely to serve as the basis for legislative action.

The Law Commission's proposals go a long way to creating a framework for medical decision-making in respect of incapacitated adults and which seeks to affect the decision the patient would make. First, to this end, a statutory recognition of "anticipated decisions" is proposed which would bind doctors. A patient could, as a consequence, for example, refuse life-sustaining medical treatment at a time prior to becoming incompetent. The common law has reached a somewhat similar position in the Court of Appeal decision in *Re T (adult: refusal of medical treatment)*[11] and as acknowledged by a majority of the Law Lords in *Bland*.[12] Secondly, the Law Commission proposes that a patient be entitled to appoint a "medical treatment attorney" to make decisions on the patient's behalf when he becomes incompetent. However, this is perhaps the extent of the Law Commission's unreserved support for creating a legal framework to effect an incapacitated patient's choices. If a patient has not made an "anticipated decision" or appointed a "medical treatment attorney", the patient's doctor is to be empowered to make decisions, after consulting the patient's relatives, in the patient's "best interests" — a sort of statutory *Re F*. Finally all these mechanisms for decision-making are to be subject to judicial control through a new statutory jurisdiction confirmed upon a "judicial forum".

It could be argued that while the Law Commission has gone a long way to providing a framework for enhancing an incapacitated patient's autonomy, the proposals do not go far enough. This, I suspect, will be at the heart of the policy debate in the future.

To this end, we might gain useful insight by casting an eye abroad. Some of the papers in this collection draw our attention to developments in America and Canada. It is remarkable how jurisdictions in these countries and in New Zealand and Australia have in the last few years acted to create a legal framework for, *inter alia*, medical decision-making and incapacitated adults. The developments in America at a state level are well documented in Ron Link's chapter and at the federal level by Maureen Eby. It might, therefore, be of interest here to look at some developments in Canada, particularly in Alberta, Manitoba and Ontario. In the latter two provinces comprehensive legislation was enacted in 1992 in the Health Care Directives Act (Manitoba) and the Consent to Treatment Act and Substitute Decisions Act (Ontario). A final Report of the Alberta Law Reform Institute published in March 1993 recommended similar legislation.[13] These reforms have a number of important pointers for policy-makers in England when considering a legislative framework for the future.

First, the Manitoba and Ontario legislation and the Alberta proposals provide for an "anticipated decision" by a patient prior to incompetence and for the appointment of agents or attorneys to make decisions on the patient's behalf.[14]

Secondly, the Ontario legislation and the proposals in Alberta, however, go further and provide for decision-making by members of the patient's "family" if the patient has not made a prior decision or appointed an agent. The Ontario legislation is very widely drawn in defining "family" and confers decision-making power on, for example, a patient's spouse or partner; the latter arises if the patient and "partner" have "lived together for at least one year and have a close personal relationship, that is of primary importance in both persons' lives" (s.1(2)). "Family" decision-making has been rejected by the Law Commission in its Consultation Paper No. 129.

Thirdly, the Manitoba legislation and the Alberta proposals require the decision-maker, whether agent, proxy or court, to act in order of priority:

1. on the basis of the patient's clearly expressed prior decision;
2. in conformity with patient's wishes and to determine the decision the patient would make; and
3. in the patient's best interests.

Hence, these reforms give effect sequentially to the patient's actual (albeit anticipated) decision, the decision the decision-maker believes that the patient would make and only in default of either of these possibilities do they require the decision-maker to act in the "best interests" of the patient. Hence, in appropriate cases the reforms adopt the "substituted judgment" test if it can be applied by the alternate decision-maker. Ontario, like the Law Commission, rejects that approach, favouring instead the "best interests" test but making the patient's wishes relevant in applying the test. I have argued for reform along the lines of these Canadian proposals elsewhere and I do not repeat them here.[15] It is surely more than a curiosity that reform in other common jurisdictions has been more sympathetic to a "family" decision-making approach, provided always that a mechanism exists to exclude or at least minimise the dangers of abuse or impropriety by the "family" decision-makers. And, of course, a mechanism must exist as a fall-back to permit treatment if there are no "family" members able or willing to decide.

The debate has certainly begun in England. Legislation of some sort will undoubtedly follow. The chapters contained in this volume address and confront the analytical framework and policy decisions that will have to be made.

Notes and references

1. See, for example, *Wilson* v. *Pringle* [1986] 2 All ER 440 at 447 per Croom-Johnson LJ.
2. P. D. G. Skegg, *Law, Medicine and Ethics* (1984) at 72–3.
3. Even it would seem on behalf of their *competent* children: *Re W (a minor) (medical treatment)* [1992] 4 All ER 627 and commentary (1993) 1 Med L Rev 87 at 89–92.
4. See P. D. G. Skegg, *op cit*, ch 5.
5. [1990] 2 AC 1.
6. See the discussion in Grubb, "Medical Law" [1989] All ER Rev 200–6.
7. Subsequently, the courts have restricted this "special category" of case to procedures intended to sterilise the incompetent woman: *Re GF* (1991) 7 BMLR 135 (hysterectomy not carried out for "therapeutic" reasons); *Re SG (a patient)* (1990) 6 BMLR 95 (not an abortion); *Re H (mental patient)* [1993] 4 Med LR 91 (not a diagnostic procedure). But contrast, *Airedale NHS Trust* v. *Bland* [1993] 1 All ER 821 (discontinuing artificial hydration and nutrition from a PVS patient should come before the court).
8. While I concentrate in this introduction on the position of the incapacitated *adult* patient, the position of children should not be overlooked.
9. [1993] 1 All ER 821.
10. *Mentally Incapacitated Adults and Decision-Making: A New Jurisdiction* (Consultation Paper No. 128); *Mentally Incapacitated Adults and Decision-Making: Medical Treatment and Research* (Consultation Paper No. 129); *Mentally Incapacitated and Other Vulnerable Adults: Public Law Protection* (Consultation Paper No. 130).
11. [1992] 4 All ER 649 and commentary (1993) 1 Med L Rev 83 at 84–7.
12. [1993] 1 All ER 821 at 860 per Lord Keith, at 866 per Lord Goff, at 892 per Lord Mustill.
13. *Advance Directives and Substitute Decision-Making in Personal Healthcare* (Report No. 64).
14. See also, for example in Australia, Medical Treatment Act 1988 (as amended by Medical Treatment (Enduring Power of Attorney) Act

1989) (Victoria).
15. A. Grubb, "Treatment Decisions: Keeping It in the Family" in A. Grubb (ed.), *Choices and Decisions in Health Care* (John Wiley, 1993) 37 at 37–48.

Comparative legal developments

Dieter Giesen

Comparative law is not just an agreeable way of satisfying the curiosity of a generous and elevated mind, as Samuel Johnson would rightly have us believe.[1] It also offers fresh arguments from other jurisdictions which may shed new light on specific ethical and legal issues and suggest new directions for domestic law which has lost its way.

Decision-making

Proficiency in diagnosis and therapy, as a general rule, is not the only measure of a medical doctor's legal responsibility. A physician must not treat or even touch a patient without the patient's valid consent. Any *competent* person may refuse to accept medical attention, however foolish he may be in doing so, even if he dies as a result. No physician may impose medical care on a person against his or her will, no matter how beneficial or necessary it may be. These statements form the general legal principle[2] to which there are only a very few exceptions such as emergencies.[3] Any medical intervention not covered by the patient's valid consent is, therefore, unlawful[4] unless it falls within such exceptions.[5] Generally speaking then, consent is an essential prerequisite of all medical treatment. Consent is not the mere satisfaction of some legal formality,[6] which physicians might like to brush aside.[7]

What is frequently overlooked, however, is that within the patient–physician relationship expectations and realities both on the side of the patient and that of the physician are much more complex than is generally assumed, and that patients, to a much greater extent

Decision-Making and Problems of Incompetence. Edited by A. Grubb.
© 1994 John Wiley & Sons Ltd.

than physicians normally think, do want to be told.[8] "What may be beneficial to an individual's physical well-being may be harmful to his dignity as an autonomous person".[9] The autonomy principle justifies the patient accepting *greater* risks than others would choose for him.[10] In other words, "turning physicians loose on society to do what they think may benefit their patients"[11] can be a dangerous concept which does not find any justification in the legal systems, which emphasise an individual's interest in the integrity of his body[12] and the law's preference of patient autonomy over paternalism.[13] Indeed, in the words of Mr Justice Kirby:[14]

> The days of paternalistic medicine are numbered. The days of unquestioning trust of the patient also appear numbered. The days of complete and general consent to anything a doctor cared to do appear numbered. Nowadays doctors, out of respect for themselves and for their patients (to say nothing for deference to the law) must increasingly face the obligation of securing informed consent from the patient for the kind of therapeutic treatment proposed . . .

Honesty and truthfulness on both sides of a patient–physician relationship worth the name then means that the patient becomes responsible for his own destiny and the physician accountable for what he does.[15] Suffice it here to quote with approval what Professor Somerville has said of the modern duty of the physician to inform his patient:[16]

> There is a positive duty on the part of the physician to inform the patient. This type of duty is sometimes described as one of trust, confidence and conscience. It arises when the law recognizes an imbalance in power or status or position between the parties to a relationship, such that the person in the position of authority must prove that he did not abuse this authority. In the medical relationship the physician would abuse his authority if he failed to accord sufficient respect to the patient's rights to autonomy and inviolability. The rights of the patient require, if it is all possible, that the patient be placed in a situation where he can make his own decisions regarding medical treatment.

It is today no longer so much the duty to inform which is the centre of controversy, but the standard to be applied[17] and the extent to which information must be given by the physician in each individual case.[18]

Problems of incompetence

However, once the communication process between patient and doctor has reached the stage where decisions have to be made, it is the patient of adult years and sound mind who has the responsibility of deciding what, if anything, shall be done with his or her own body.[19] In the present context, this means it is the patient, not the physician, who has the final right to make treatment or no-treatment decisions.[20] Thus, the physician may act only within the fair limits of the patient's consent.[21] A consent will, however, be valid only if given by a patient who has the legal *capacity* to give it. The capacity to give a legally effective consent depends upon the capacity to understand and come to a decision on what is involved, and the capacity to communicate that decision. The law presumes that adults of sound mind have this capacity.[22]

Minors

In a considerable number of legal systems, the patient's consent may be valid even if the patient is *under age*, provided, of course, that he or she is capable of appreciating the reason for, and the significance of, the proposed treatment or operation, and of making up his or her mind correspondingly.[23] While it would not normally require any evidence beyond the tender age of a child to convince a court that the child was incapable of consenting,[24] some children under the age of, say 12, will probably be quite capable of consenting to relatively minor therapeutic procedures such as the binding up of a wound.[25] It would, however, be very unwise of a physician to assume, in the absence of statutory authority, that minors not yet well into their teenage years are capable of consenting to major therapeutic (let alone non-therapeutic) procedures.[26]

Today, the legal world distinguishes between consent to the medical *contract* (which a minor may not have the legal capacity to give) and consent to medical *care* (which may not depend on the minor's age alone).[27] The proper criterion then is not age as such[28] (which will, however, be decisive where expressly stipulated by statute),[29] but whether, for the purpose of consent to medical *care*[30] intended for his benefit, the minor is still "to young to exercise a reasonable discretion in such a matter",[31] or old enough "to exercise a reasonable discretion in the matter",[32] or to make "a wise choice in his or her own interests".[33] This, *mutatis mutandis*, is also the prevailing position in civil law jurisdictions where distinctions are also made between consent to the medical contract and consent to medical care,[34] and between a minor who can already appreciate the medical care issues involved and decide accordingly and is, thus, capable of giving an effective consent to therapeutic treatment (*mineur émancipé*), and a minor who is not yet capable of doing so and, therefore, needs the protection of the law, normally in the form of his or her parents' consent to both the medical procedures proposed and the medical contract itself.[35]

Cases from various jurisdictions illustrate the "mature minor" or the "emancipated minor" tests,[36] and they do so with a tendency that reminds one more and more, in the words of Lord Denning, that even during the age of minority and the difficult formative transitional experiences of adolescence, the law considers the rights of parents with regard to their children as "a dwindling right" which "starts with a right of control and ends with little more than advice".[37]

Apart from age and maturity of the minor, the degree of necessity of treatment, the urgency of treatment, the degree of risk involved and the gravity of harm to the patient should risks materialise will all be factors to take into account. Thus in one German case the court refused to accept the consent of a 16-year-old minor as valid because the cosmetic operation concerned was not urgent and carried with it considerable risks.[38] So where the treatment is not therapeutic, there are strong arguments for making the medical decision-maker pay heed to parental wishes, rather than automatically proceeding with treatment that the medical decision-maker considers to be in the patient's "best interests". However, the House of Lords in *Gillick* v. *West Norfolk Area Health Authority*[39] held that a physician may, without parental knowledge or consent, give non-therapeutic contraceptive advice and treatment to a girl under 16, the statutory age for consent to medical treatment. This transfer of decision-making power from parents to doctors is discouraging, to say the least, and it is particularly surprising that it was supported by Lord Scarman, whose reviews in this case are hard to reconcile with his vigilance against a "doctor knows best" approach in his dissenting judgment in *Sidaway* v. *Bethlem Royal Hospital Governors*.[40] As Fox LJ said in the Court of Appeal in *Gillick*,[41] "if the parents' wishes *are* to be overridden, *that should be done by the court* in relation to the particular circumstances of the time". The wholesale surrender of the decision-making process to doctors means the sacrifice of the values of particular families, and one may well ask in this context and after *Gillick* whether personal values as well as professional accountability are now to be determined by the medical profession. Commenting on the *Helga Wanglie* case from Minnesota in 1991, in which the hospital sought to *discontinue* the use of mechanical ventilation and other forms of life-sustaining treatment against the determination of Helga Wanglie's family to continue with such treatment, Daniel Callahan,[42] the director of the Hastings Center in New York, reflected that one should not override the moral values of the Wanglie family, whose judgment was different from both his own and that of the Hastings Center. Callahan argued that to allow the judgment of the Medical Center and its staff to triumph over that of the Wanglie family before a joint lay–medical process had been developed to make the combined medical–moral judgments was at least unwise, and perhaps unfair. "If the Wanglie family loses", the argument ran, "they may well feel that they were run over by the power of medical prestige, by a unilateral medical judgment now enlarged to include a moral evaluation. Why should they feel otherwise? Neither they nor families like them will have had any role in developing appropriate standards. Others will have done that, whether the hospital or the courts. The political dimension, as crucial as the medical and the moral, has just disappeared here."[43]

Problems such as these are all the more delicate in the case of minors, where the primary decision-makers are clearly the parents. As a general rule, parents may be presumed to have the best interests of their children at heart and act accordingly,[44] at least until the children acquire the natural capacity to make what an English judge once called a "wise choice" in their own best interests.[45] Parental rights and their collateral duties[46] are subject to limitation only in extreme cases when the health, safety[47] or best interests of the child are threatened. Such cases require the state's intervention. So long as the parents' decision is not grossly unreasonable, it is no part of the function of the state, as exercised through the courts,[48] to overturn it simply because it reflects value commitments outside those of the main stream of society.[49]

Incompetent persons

Just as minors *below* the age when they can form a "wise decision" in their own best interests, an adult patient who is incompetent, too, cannot give a valid consent to *treatment* proposed or thought necessary;[50] indeed, his incapacity is in general defined as his inability to do so. In cases of doubt, a physician must determine capacity to consent, so as to ensure that a patient who is in fact capable of directing the course of his treatment is not deprived of his basic human right of self-determination and, conversely, that an incompetent patient is protected from possible harmful effects of his own decisions.[51] But it *is* important to note that "[d]ecision-making incapacity is not a medical or diagnostic category",[52] and there is no *necessary* correlation either in law or in fact between incapacity and mental illness,[53] or retardation.[54] Nor should lack of capacity be assumed because, for instance, an elderly patient who has displayed symptoms of senility makes what in her doctor's professional judgment is an unreasonable decision.[55]

A determination of incapacity does not, however, mean that a physician may dispense with the requirement of consent and proceed with treatment in what he considers the patient's best interests. The law does not allow any person to control the life of another adult, however incapacitated, without express court or statutory authority.[56] As a general rule, consent must be obtained from a substitute with legally invested authority to consent on the incompetent patient's behalf,[57] usually a court-appointed guardian or curator[58] or family member.[59] There is no general rule of law whereby the nearest relative of a mentally disordered adult is authorised to consent to medical treatment on his or her behalf,[60] but such authority is widely assumed to exist, both by institutional regulations[61] and the courts.[62] In the words of the United States President's Commission Report on *Making Health Care Decisions*, "the proper presumption is that the family, defined to include closest relatives and intimate friends, should make health care decisions for an incapacitated patient".[63]

It has been suggested, however, by a leading authority that where no guardian exists, and the patient's incapacity is likely to be permanent, "a doctor should be justified in doing whatever good medical practice dictates should be done in the interests of the patient's health".[64] It is submitted though, that this flies in the face of all legal principles regarding consent, and could only be justified in an emergency, when a physician may in any case proceed without consent where it would be unreasonable (and not merely inconvenient) to postpone treatment[65] until consent can be obtained. Apart from emergencies, further exceptions to the rule of consent prior to the treatment of incompetent patients may be found in statute law. Mental health legislation in most if not all jurisdictions under review dispenses with the need for consent in respect of persons brought within its scope.[66] In some jurisdictions, an incapacitated person in need of medical treatment may be involuntarily committed so as to secure authorisation for such treatment,[67] while in others treatment without consent is limited to the mental disorder which rendered the patient liable to be detained.[68] And an incompetent patient may of course be treated without consent on the same basis as any other adult under, for example, statutory provisions for compulsory vaccination,[69] or treatment of venereal diseases.[70]

Although a guardian's consent is as a general rule a pre-requisite to treatment, it does not follow that he has the same discretion in making medical decisions on behalf of an incompetent ward as a competent adult enjoys on his own account.[71] He may only consent to interventions in the ward's "best interests".[72] It follows that he is not free to make a martyr of an incompetent ward who cannot make an informed and considered decision about whether to submit to procedures for the benefit of third parties or mankind in general which might have adverse consequences for himself. A guardian has therefore no power, in the absence of express statutory authority, to consent to any intervention of a non-therapeutic nature, such as participation in medical procedures for research or experimental purposes of no direct benefit to the ward himself,[73] or the donation of blood, double organs or other human tissue.[74] After all, no competent adult person may be compelled to submit to non-therapeutic interventions or to surgery for the removal of tissue for transplant; and it is wrong to oblige an incompetent person, who by definition cannot give an informed consent, to do so.[75]

Another problem of decision-making and incompetence is the *refusal* of medical treatment. Of course a patient of adult years and *sound* mind has the right to refuse medical treatment[76] "however unreasonable or foolish this may appear in the eyes of his medical advisers".[77] In a nutshell, the medical profession must *neither* usurp the right of the patient to consent *nor* ignore his refusal to do so.[78] After the *Sidaway* decision in England,[79] it is perhaps appropriate not only to refer with approval, in the present context, to Lord Scarman's "powerful dissenting approach"[80] respecting the doctrine of informed consent and the patient's inalienable right of self-determination,[81] but also to adduce some sentences from Lord Reid's speech in *S* v. *S* which serve as a clear warning against all encroachments upon that right by whatever philosophy: "English law goes to great lengths to protect a person of full age and capacity from interference with his personal liberty. We have too often seen freedom disappear in other countries not only by coups d'état but by gradual erosion; and often it is the first step that counts. So it would be unwise to make even minor concessions".[82] It would appear that other jurisdictions under review here tend to follow similar principles by applying a rule in favour of the capacity of adult persons and by resisting with increasing alertness all paternalistic attempts to defend a professional discretion which is quite capable of swallowing the principles of self-determination and shared decision-making whenever the clinician decides the occasion requires it.[83] The presumption of adult *capacity* is the legal bulwark against both blunt and more surreptitious acts of paternalism; this presumption cannot be taken too seriously.

This right to *refuse* treatment, even where this may be life-saving or life-sustaining, also extends to *incompetent* patients.[84] Neither mental illness nor involuntary commitment, without more, constitute a sufficient basis for concluding that a patient is incapable of making treatment decisions.[85] In the words of the Supreme Judicial Court of Massachusetts: "To presume that the incompetent person must always be subjected to what many rational and intelligent persons may decline is to downgrade the status of the incompetent person by placing a lesser value on his intrinsic human worth and vitality."[86]

Where a previously competent patient has made his or her wishes known before the onset of incapacity, whether in writing or by means of clear and unequivocal verbal assurances, these should be respected.[87] Where the evidence is less clear, or where an incompetent patient is able to express his views, they should nonetheless be given due consideration.[88] Furthermore, as was observed by Brennan J in his impressive dissenting opinion in the *Cruzan* case,[89] "[t]he testimony of close friends and family members . . . may often be the best evidence available of what the patient's choice would be".

In an emergency context, where a doctor has reason to believe that the patient *would* refuse treatment, he should be particularly careful to avoid doing anything which he could reasonably postpone until consent can be obtained.[90] Where, before the onset of incompetency, the patient has authorised a third party to make medical decisions on his behalf, refusal of consent within the scope of the authority given has the same effect as refusal by the patient himself.[91]

It may be, however, that the patient's previous views are unknown, or that he has never possessed the requisite capacity, in which case a decision must be made on his behalf, either by the court in its jurisdiction as *parens patriae* or by a legally authorised surrogate such as a court-appointed guardian or family member.[92] The new German law on (adult) incompetents may serve as an example, as it states that a guardian has to take care of his ward in accordance with the ward's welfare, but the incompetent's wishes, whether expressed before or after the onset of incompetency, are to be respected as long as they do not interfere with his welfare.[93] In addition to these requirements, the new German law provides that in medical decision-making the guardian's decision has to be confirmed by the wardship court when the incompetent is in danger of dying or of suffering severe and lasting damage, laying the guardian's decision more open to judicial scrutiny and control.[94]

Surrogate decision-makers do not, however, enjoy complete discretion in refusing treatment on behalf of incompetent patients: as in any other treatment decision, they are bound to act in the patient's "best interests".[95] Thus, although a guardian may choose from reasonable treatment alternatives,[96] he may not deny all treatment for a life-threatening condition where the treatment method is established and any inherent risks are reasonable in relation to comparatively certain benefits.[97] In the absence of firm statutory or case law, the doctor is best advised to continue treatment,[98] pending an application to the courts to clarify the legal position.

To be distinguished from cases where the incompetent patient is terminally ill from an incurable condition,[99] however, are those where appropriate medical or surgical treatment would ensure the continuation of life, but because of the severe nature of the incompetent's underlying handicap, the quality of such life is so low as to be, in the opinion of some at least, not worth living. In an English case, the Court of Appeal overruled parental refusal of consent to surgery to remove a life-threatening intestinal blockage from a newborn baby girl suffering from Down's syndrome. The court had to decide whether, in this particular instance, "the life of this child is demonstrably going to be so awful that in effect the child must be condemned to die, or whether the life of this child is still so imponderable that it would be wrong for her to be condemned to die ... The evidence in this case only goes to show that if the operation takes place and is successful then the child may live the normal span of a mongoloid child with the handicaps and defects and life of a mongol child, and it is not for this court to say that the life of that description ought to be extinguished."[100] The presumption of the court is thus emphatically in favour of life.[101] In the words of the Supreme Court of British Columbia, similar to those used by the German Federal Supreme Court in a comparable case,[102] "[t]he laws of our society are structured to preserve, protect and maintain human life. [I]n the exercise of its inherent jurisdiction, this court could not sanction the termination of a life except for the most coercive reasons."[103]

Where physicians are uncertain as to the scope of a guardian or other surrogate's legal right to *refuse* consent in a particular case, application should generally be made to the *court* for a ruling as to the incompetent patient's best interests. Where this would lead to unacceptable delay, however, a leading authority on English law has suggested that a physician *should* be afforded justification for proceeding in the face of surrogate refusal in the following circumstances where: (i) it is not reasonable or in the time practical to take action so that someone else is empowered to authorise performance of the procedure; (ii) the procedure is necessary to save life or prevent permanent injury to health or prolonged pain and suffering; and (iii) in spite of all reasonable efforts, consent has been unreasonably withheld.[104] It is submitted that in the narrow circumstances prescribed, a physician should be authorised to effect the minimum intervention required until the ultimate authority of the court can be invoked.

The extension to incompetents of the right to refuse treatment as an aspect of the right of self-determination has led in a number of American jurisdictions and, more recently, also of English cases,[105] to the application by the courts of a new standard of proxy decision-making, that of *substituted judgment* to replace the traditional "best interests" concept. The purpose behind the use of "substituted judgment" was set out in a leading case by the Supreme Judicial Court of Massachusetts: "[T]he decision in cases such as this should be *that* which would be made by the incompetent person, *if* that person were competent, but taking into account the present and future incompetency of the individual as one of the factors which would necessarily enter into the decision-making process of the competent person."[106] While this approach may well advance the rights of incapacitated persons who were once competent, it has been aptly criticised on the grounds that "[t]he very notions of self-determination, and hence a right to self-determination, only apply to a being who possesses, or has the potential for developing, certain complex cognitive functions, including the ability to conceive of the future, discern alternative courses of action, and make judgments about his own good".[107] This criticism has apparently influenced the Supreme Court of New Jersey in a recent case[108] in which it issued guidelines for termination of life-sustaining treatment in cases involving incompetent patients. The court held that a guardian should effectuate the decision the incompetent ward would himself have made if competent.[109] In England, the House of Lords held that whether medical treatment *was* to be carried out was to be governed by the *best interests* approach. But again: who is to determine what the "best interests" of the patient are? Is an effort to be made to find out what the patient would consider them to be? Are the courts allowed to determine this important question? According to the House of Lords in *F* v. *West Berkshire Health Authority*,[110] neither the presumed views of the patient nor the views of the court prevail. Instead, the *Bolam*[111] test is to be applied, putting the definition of the patient's best interests into the hands of doctors — a somewhat curious result considering the tentative attempt of the Law Lords earlier in their judgments to bring decision-making to the courts by requiring an application to be made to them for consent in such cases, albeit merely "as a matter of good practice".[112]

Conclusion

The application of the *Bolam*[113] test in this context received criticism from the Court of Appeal in *F* v. *West Berkshire Health Authority*. However, the alternative solution their Lordships proposed below was equality tied to medical opinion. The dependence of the law upon any responsible body of medical opinion was simply replaced by a test which subjects the patient to the views of the *majority of medical experts* (according to Neill and Butler-Sloss LJJ) or to the views of *any significant minority of them* (according to Lord Donaldson MR).[114]

Judicial approaches like these show clearly that even some of the highest courts seem willing to abdicate to doctors the power to define health and decide questions of competence, with the result that it is predominantly defined in terms of illness, mental illness or incompetence and deviant behaviour. And as long as it *is* accepted that health and mental competence is the exclusive preserve of doctors, something only they, or a majority of medical experts, or even a significant minority of them, have competence in, this state of affairs will continue, and the power is once again with the professional[115] who then by adopting some practice could legislate himself out of legal responsibility to the community by adopting or continuing what was an obviously legally unacceptable practice.[116] Where refusal of consent is seen not as an assertion of will, but rather as a symptom of unsoundness of mind and deviant behaviour, the endorsement of medical expertise as *conclusive* clearly shows the vulnerability of the principle of self-determination, contrasted with, as Professor Ian Kennedy put it, "the persuasive power of paternalism".[117] But clearly, too, the law and courts cannot "stand idly by if the profession, by an excess of paternalism, denies its patients a real choice"[118] and, with the highest judicial endorsement, makes all these decisions for and on behalf of those considered to be incompetent to take part in the decision about their own treatment and, as Sir John Donaldson MR (as he then was) once said, to play God.[119] No profession is above the law and the courts on behalf of the public are not there to rubber-stamp the medical me-thinketh of a majority of medical experts or even that of any significant minority of them. The courts have a critical role to play in monitoring and precipitating changes where required in professional standards and views.[120] That doctors may truly be motivated only by concern for incompetent patients makes no difference. As one of the most prominent American jurists warned us decades ago: "Experience should teach us to be most on our guard to protect the liberty when . . . purposes are [meant to be] beneficent . . . The greatest dangers to liberty lurk in insidious encroachment by men of zeal, well meaning but without understanding."[121] Therefore, and with great respect to the courts in England, a better approach would be the *legally* rather than medically determined standard of care which has won the day in other Common Law and Civil Law jurisdictions — a test which would put control back into the hands of the courts, allowing *them* to lay down the law after weighing the arguments for and against treatment, with the patient's perceived concerns playing a leading role in their deliberations. One is reminded, also in the present context, of the powerful reasoning of King CJ in the leading South Australian case of *F* v. *R*[122] which he gave when refusing to follow the *Bolam*[123] test in Australia.[124] Speaking of the evidence of the medical profession he said: "I am unable to accept . . . that such evidence can be decisive in all circumstances . . . [P]rofessions may adopt unreasonable practices. Practices may develop in professions . . . not because they serve the interests of the clients [or patients], but because they protect the interest or convenience of members of the profession. The court has an obligation to scrutinise professional practices to ensure that they accord with the standard of reasonableness imposed by the law."[125] Whether medical opinion conforms to the standards demanded by the law clearly "is a question for the court and the duty of deciding it cannot be delegated to any profession or group in the community".[126]

Notes and references

1. Boswell's *Life of Johnson I* (ed. Hill and Powell, Oxford, 1934) 89.
2. *Slater* v. *Baker* (1767) 2 Wils 359, 95 ER 860 (Common Pleas); *Chatterton* v. *Gerson* [1981] 1 All ER 257; *Hills* v. *Potter* [1983] 3 All ER 716; *T* v. *T* [1988] 2 WLR 189 (FamD; medical case); A. M. Dugdale and K. M. Stanton, *Professional Negligence* (London, 1982) at sections 17.01–22 (no longer in 2nd edn, London, 1989); J. Salmond and R. F. V. Heuston, *The Law of Torts* (19th edn, London, 1987) at section 187 (1); *Smith* v. *Auckland Hosp Bd* [1965] NZLR 191 (CA); *Battersby* v. *Tottman* (1985) 37 SASR 524 (FC); *F* v. *R* (1983) 33 SASR 189 (FC); Aust Torts Rptr section 90–980 at 15, 102; *Coughlin* v. *Kuntz* (1987) 17 BCLR2d 365 (SC); *Hopp* v. *Lepp* (1980) 13 CCLT 66 (SCC); *Mulloy* v. *Hop Sang* [1935] 1 WWR 714 (Alta CA); *Murray* v. *McMurchy* [1949] 1 WWR 989 (BC SC); *Reibl* v. *Hughes* (1980) 14 CCLT 1 (SCC); A. M. Linden, *Tort Law in Canada* (5th edn, Toronto, 1992) 61–2; E. I. Picard, *Legal Liability of Doctors and Hospitals in Canada* (2nd edn, Toronto 1984) at 46–53; *Canterbury* v. *Spence*, 464 F 2d 772, 781 (DC Cir 1972); *Crain* v. *Allison*, 443 A 2d 558 (DC 1982) (with earlier case law); Rest 2d sections 892, 892A (comment d); A. H. McCoid, "A Reappraisal of Liability for Unauthorized Medical Treatment" (1957), 41, *Minnesota Law Review* 381; *Stoffberg* v. *Elliott*, 1923 CPD 148; 17 LSA 191–2 (at 146–7, D. McQuoid-Mason, S. A. Strauss); G. Mémeteau and L. Mélennec, *Le contrat médical; La responsabilité civile du médecin* (Paris, 1982) 29 ff; X. Ryckmans and R. Meert-van de Put, *Les Droits et les Obligations des Médecins*, 2 vols (2nd edn, Bruxelles, 1971–72) i.438 ff (33 570–573); BVerfG, 25 July 1979, BVerfGE 52, 131 ff, 171 ff; BGH, 28 Nov 1972, VersR 1973, 244 (246); 12 Feb 1974, VersR 1974, 752 (753); 22 Jan 1980, NJW 1980, 1333 (1334); 24 June 1980 NJW 1980, 2751 (2753); 7 Feb 1984 (VI ZR 174/82) BGHZ 90, 103; MünchKomm (H. J. Mertens) 370 ff to section 823 BGB; BG, 12 Jan 1982, BGE 108 II 59; OGH, 19 Dec 1984, JB1 1985, 548 (550).
3. For which cf D. Giesen, *International Medical Malpractice Law (Tübingen, Dordrecht, London and Boston 1988) at section 27 (hereafter "D. Giesen")*.
4. *Chatterton* v. *Gerson* [1981] 1 All ER 257 (Bristow J at 265); Aust Torts Rptr section 9–080; R. L. Deutsch, "Medical Negligence Reviewed" (1983) 57 ALJ 674 at 677, J. G. Fleming, *The Law of Torts* (7th edn, Sydney, 1987) at 73; E. I. Picard, *Legal Liability of Doctors and Hospitals in Canada (2nd edn, Toronto, 1984) at 67–115; M. A. Somerville, "Structuring the Issues in Informed Consent" (1981) 26 McGill Law Journal* 740 at 788.
5. *Truman* v. *Thomas* (1980) 165 Cal Rptr 308 at 311 (Cal Sup Ct); *Crain* v. *Allison* (1982) 443 A 2d 558 at 562 (DC); *Scott* v. *Bradford* (1979) 606 P 2d 554 at 556–7 (Okla).
6. M. D. Kirby, "Informed Consent: What Does it Mean?" (1983) 9 *Journal of Medical Ethics* 69; BGH, 21 Sept 1982, VI ZR 302/80 VersR

1982, 1193 (1194); D. Giesen, Arzthaftungsrecht. Die Zivilrechtliche Haftung aus medizinischer Behandlung in der Bundesrepublik Deutschland, in Österreich und der Schweiz (3rd edn, Tübingen 1990) 105–112 (refs).

7. D. Giesen, *op cit*, at section 20 I para 486.

8. "The misattribution of the desire for information is one of the most common errors in clinical practice. Several studies point to the discrepancies between what patients want to know and what doctors *think* they want to know. These studies have examined attitudes both to clinical trials and to routine medical treatment. With regard to clinical trials, a recent British survey of 1022 adults aged between 16 and 70 found a strong response in favour of being given information about randomised clinical trials of cancer treatment. Ninety per cent of this sample also said they would want to be told if they had a major illness. Yet only 24 per cent said that their doctor had ever discussed with them the merits of different treatments before prescribing one. Although there was a greater tendency for older people in the lower social classes to want to leave the decisions to their doctors, there was still a substantial majority who wanted information. The fact that they may be reluctant to vocalise this need should not be interpreted as a lack of desire for information. In the context of treatment the most important study highlighting differences between doctors' and patients' views . . . [revealed that] in 65 per cent of the encounters [between patients and physicians] doctors underestimated the desire for information and underrated its clinical usefulness" — *Institute of Medical Ethics Bulletin* Supplement No. 3 (Dec 1986) at 4 (with a survey of recent empirical studies).

9. J. E. Giles, *Medical Ethics. A Patient-Centered Approach* (Cambridge, MA, 1983) at 8.

10. T. L. Beauchamp and J. F. Childress, *Medical Ethics. A Clinical Textbook and Reference for the Health Care Professions* (Cambridge, MA, 1983) at 3 ff; M. M. Shultz, "From Informed Consent to Patient Choice: A New Protected Interest" (1985) 93 *Yale Law Journal* 219.

11. R. M. Veatch, *A Theory of Medical Ethics* (New York, 1981) at 10; but cf B. Gert and C. M. Culver *Medical Ethics. A Clinical Textbook and Reference for the Health Care Professions* (Cambridge, MA, 1983) at 13 ff, who appear to conclude that a paternalistic attitude may be justified when a patient's reaction of medical advice is not rational. It is submitted that in the case of a competent adult this is never the case, cf D. Giesen, *op cit*, at sections 30 III c, 35 I, 36 I, and that in the case of minors and incompetent persons safeguards have to be insisted upon to guard against medical paternalistic excesses or what Dean Savatier called impérialisme médiale sur le terrain du droit (cf G. Mémeteau and L. Mélennec, *Le contrat médical; La responsabilité civile du médecin (Paris, 1982) at 34; for details, cf D. Giesen, op cit*, at sections 35 II–III, 36 II–III (refs).

12. Cf A. Grubb, "A Survey of Medical Malpractice Law in England: Crisis? What Crisis?" (1985) 1 *Journal of Contemporary Health Law and Policy* 75 at 113–14.
13. Cf J. Salmond and R. F. V. Heuston, *The Law of Torts* (19th edn, London, 1987) section 187.1 (at 557); cf D. Giesen, *op cit*, section 53 I.
14. M. D. Kirby, "Informed Consent: What Does it Mean?" (1983) 9 *Journal of Medical Ethics* 60 at 74–5.
15. M. Phillips and J. Dawson, *Doctors' Dilemmas. Medical Ethics and Contemporary Science* (Brighton, 1985) at 176; MünchKomm (H. J. Mertens) 426 to section 823 BGB.
16. M. A. Somerville, "Structuring the Issues in Informed Consent" (1981) 26 *McGill Law Journal* 740 at 753–754.
17. Cf D. Giesen, *op cit*, at sections 21–23.
18. Cf *ibid*, at sections 24–25.
19. Cf *ibid*, at section 20 II–III.
20. Cf *ibid*, at sections 21–23.
21. Cf *ibid*, at sections 20 III, 24–25.
22. Cf *ibid*, at sections 20 III, 24–25, 35 II (para 895).
23. *Gillick* v. *West Norfolk Gillick* v. *West Norfolk Area Health Authority* [1986] AC 112, [1985] 3 WLR 830, [1985] 3 All ER 402 per Lord Fraser at 411; further comparative refs in D. Giesen, *op cit* at section 35 II (para 895 n 21).
24. B R B v. *J B* [1968] 2 All ER 1023 (CA) per Lord Denning MR at 1025.
25. P. D. G. Skegg, *Law, Ethics and Medicine* (Oxford, 1984) at 54; S. R. Speller, *Law Relating to Hospitals and Kindred Institutions* (6th edn, London, 1978) at 194 n 1.
26. In *Gillick* v. *West Norfolk Area Health Authority* [1986] AC 112, [1985] 3 WLR 830, [1985] 3 All ER 402 [1985] 3 All ER 402, Lord Fraser stated at 412: "Nor do I doubt that any important medical treatment of a child under 16 would normally only be carried out with the parents' approval."
27. P. D. G. Skegg, *Law, Ethics and Medicine* (Oxford, 1984) at 47 ff, 53, 55; J. G. Fleming, *The Law of Torts* (7th edn, Sydney, 1987) at 73; *Johnston* v. *Wellesley Hosp* (1970) 17 DLR 3d 139 at 144–5 (Ont HC).
28. Cf B. Landau, "Barriers to Consent to Treatment: The Rights of Minors in the Provision of Mental Health Services" (1979) 2 *Canadian Journal of Family Law* 245; D. Giesen, *International Medical Malpractice Law op cit* at section 35 II (para 899 ns 33–41), for further refs.
29. E.g. *Carter* v. *Cangello*, 164 Cal Rptr 361 (App 1980) (parents' action based on lack of consent by 17-year-old daughter dismissed where daughter's consent valid under terms of state law permitting self-supporting minors over the age of 15 to consent to medical treatment); B. Werthmann, *Medical Malpractice Law* (Lexington, MA, 1984) at 229 (refs).
30. As distinct from consent to the medical *contract*; cf M. A. Somerville, *Consent to Medical Care. A Study Paper for the Law Reform Commis-*

sion of Canada (Ottawa, 1980) at 71 ff.

31. Minors (Property and Contracts) Act (NSW) 1970 s 49 (it is clear that in such cases the rule applies that the parents or guardian will have to consent to medical treatment: Aust Torts Rptr section 9–080 at 15, 103).

32. Tasmanian Crim Code 1924 s 51; also cf J. G. Fleming, *The Law of Torts* (7th edn, Sydney, 1987) at 73; *Johnston* v. *Wellesley Hosp* (1970) 17 DLR 3d 139 at 144–5 (Ont HC); Rest 2d (Torts) section 59; BGH, 5 Dec 1958, BGHZ 29, 33 (36); OGH, 19 Dec 1984, JB1 1985, 548 (550).

33. *Gillick* v. *West Norfolk Area Health Authority* [1986] AC 112, [1985] 3 WLR 830, [1985] 3 All ER 402 [1985] 3 All ER 402 per Lord Scarman at 423.

34. D. Giesen, *International Medical Malpractice Law* (Tübingen, Dordrecht, London and Boston, 1988) section 35 II (para 899 n 37).

35. *Ibid*, at section 35 II (para 899 n 38).

36. *Ibid*, at section 35 II (para 900).

37. *Hewer* v. *Bryant* [1970] 1 QB 357, [1969] 3 WLR 425, [1969] 3 All ER 578 (CA), per Lord Denning MR at 582, quoted with approval in *Gillick* v. *West Norfolk Area Health Authority* [1986] AC 112, [1985] 3 WLR 830, [1985] 3 All ER 402 per Lord Fraser at 412.

38. BGH, 16 Nov 1971, VersR 1972, 153; cf also BGH 13 Jan 1970, NJW 1970, 511.

39. *Gillick* v. *West Norfolk Area Health Authority, supra.*

40. *Sidaway* v. *Bethlem Royal Hospital Governors* [1985] AC 871, [1985] 2 WLR 480, [1985] 1 All ER 643.

41. *Gillick* v. *West Norfolk Area Health Authority* [1986] AC 112 at 146, [1985] 2 WLR 413 at 442, [1985] 1 All ER 533 at 556 (CA) (emphasis added).

42. Daniel Callahan, "Medical Futility, Medical Necessity. The Problem-Without-A-Name", (1991) 21 *Hastings Center Report* 30–34.

43. *Ibid*, at 34.

44. *Parham* v. *JR*, 442 US 584 (1979); United States President's Commission for the Study of Ethical Problems in Medicine and Biomedical and Behavioral Research Reports: Deciding to Forego Life-Sustaining Treatment (Washington, 1983) 212 (stating the presumption to be strong but rebuttable); Article 6 (2) German Constitution; BVerfG, 29 July 1959, 1 BvR 205, 332, 333, 367/58, 1 BvL 27, 100/58 BVerfGE 10, 59 (76); 3 Nov 1982, 1 BvR 25, 38, 40/80, 12/81 BVerfGE 61, 358 (371–372) = JZ 1983, 298 (D. Giesen); for a discussion cf D. Giesen, *International Medical Malpractice Law (Tübingen, Dordrecht, London and Boston, 1988) at section 32 III para 843, section 36 II paras 955, 956, 961.*

45. *Gillick* v. *West Norfolk Area Health Authority* [1986] AC 112, [1985] 3 WLR 830, [1985] 3 All ER 402 per Lord Scarman at 423.

46. Parents' constitutional rights are duty-bound in the best interests of the children; the German Federal Constitutional Court emphasises

the "parental right to act as a responsible parent", BVerfG, 29 July 1968, 1 BvL 20/63 BVerfGE 24, 119 (143–144); 15 June 1971, 1 BvR 192/70 BVerfGE 31, 194 (208); also cf D. Giesen, *op cit* section 36 II paras 955, 956, 961, 974.

47. *Wisconsin* v. *Yoder* 406 US 205 at 234 (1972).

48. A decision of the court is necessary, if the parents have no common opinion or the decision is grossly unreasonable and dangerous for the health of the child (cf section 1666 BGB [German Civil Code]).

49. D. Giesen, Ehe, Familie und Erwerbsleben (Paderborn 1977) 39–67; BGH, 5 Dec 1958, VI ZR 266/57 BGHZ 29, 33 (36–37); 28 June 1988, VI ZR 288/87 BGHZ 105, 45 (48) = JZ 1989, 93 (94) (D. Giesen); in Austria OGH, 11 Sep 1984, 9 Os 121/84 JB1 1985, 304 (306).

50. P. D. G. Skegg, *Law, Ethics and Medicine* (Oxford, 1984) at 56; E. I. Picard, *Legal Liability of Doctors and Hospitals in Canada* (2nd edn, Toronto, 1984) at 90; D. Giesen, *International Medical Malpractice Law* (Tübingen, Dordrecht, London and Boston, 1988) at section 35 III para 917.

51. United States President's Commission for the Study of Ethical Problems in Medicine and Biomedical and Behavioral Research Reports: Deciding to Forego Life-Sustaining Treatment (Washington, 1983) 122; BGH, 9 Dec 1958, BGHZ 29, 46 (51).

52. *Ibid*, at 123.

53. D. Giesen *op cit*, at para 917 (refs).

54. S. C. and R. Hayes, *Mental Retardation, Law, Policy and Administration* (Sydney 1982) 54; *In re Moe*, 432 NE 2d 712 (Mass 1982).

55. *Lane* v. *Candura*, 376 NE 2d 1232 (Mass App 1978); D. Giesen, *International Medical Malpractice Law* (Tübingen, Dordrecht, London and Boston, 1988) at section 35 III (para 917).

56. *Kirby* v. *Leather* [1965] 2 QB 367, [1965] 2 WLR 1318, [1965] 2 All ER 441 (CA); *D. Giesen, op cit*, at section 35 III para 921 (n 129 with further refs).

57. P. D. G. Skegg *op cit*, at 106; E. I. Picard, *op cit*, at 61; *Clites* v. *Iowa* (1982) 322 NW 2d 917 (Iowa).

58. In England under the *Mental Health Act* 1983 c 20; for a comparative survey cf *D. Giesen, op cit*, at section 35 III para 922 (n 131 with further refs).

59 D. Giesen, *op cit*, at section 35 III para 922 (refs).

60. P. D. G. Skegg, *op cit*, at 73; BGH, 9 Dec 1958, BGHZ 29, 46 (51–52).

61. Cf D. Giesen, *op cit*, at section 35 III para 922 n 131 (further refs).

62. *In re Dinnerstein*, (1978) 380 NE 2d 134 (Mass App); *In re Nemser*, (1966) 273 NYS 2d 624; also cf *D. Giesen, op cit*, at section 35 III (para 922 n 131).

63. United States President's Commission for the Study of Ethical Problems in Medicine and Biomedical and Behavioral Research Reports: Making Health Care Decisions, 3 vols (Washington, 1982) at vol i, 182.

64. P. D. G. Skegg, *op cit*, at 105.
65. *Marshall* v. *Curry* [1933] 3 DLR 260 (NS SC); *Murray* v. *McMurchy* (1949) 2 DLR 442 (BC SC); *Parmley* v. *Parmley* [1945] SCR 635.
66. D. Giesen, *op cit*, at section 35 III 925 (refs).
67. For references, cf D. Giesen, *op cit*, at section 35 III para 925 n 141.
68. P. D. G. Skegg, *op cit*, at 71–72; H. Göppinger, "Betrachtungen zur Unterbringung psychisch Kranker", FamRZ 1980, 854–865; H. Rüping, "Therapie und Zwang bei untergebrachten Patienten", JZ 1982, 744–749.
69. For details: D. Giesen, *op cit*, at section 27 I (refs).
70. D. Giesen, *op cit*, at section 27 I (refs).
71. D. Giesen, *op cit*, at section 35 III (para 926).
72. E. I. Picard, *op cit*, at 61; BGH, 28 Apr 1967, IV ZB 448/66 BGHZ 48, 147 (157 ff).
73. E. I. Picard, *op cit*, at 121.
74. Australian Law Commission Report on Human Tissue Transplants (ALRC 7, 51) section 113; E. I. Picard, *op cit*, at 125–126; D. Giesen, *op cit*, at section 35 III para 926 (refs).
75. Zelman Cowan, "Organ Transplantation: The Legal Issues", (1968–1969) 6 *University of Queensland Law Journal* 13; Australian Law Commission Report on Human Tissue Transplants (ALRC 7, 51) at section 112.
76. D. Giesen, *op cit*, at section 36 para 932 (refs).
77. *Smith* v. *Auckland Hospital Board* [1965] NZLR 191 (CA) per Gresson J at 219.
78. P. D. G. Skegg, *op cit*, at 76–81; J. G. Fleming, *op cit*, at 73–74; D. Giesen, *op cit*, at section 36 para 932 (refs).
79. *Sidaway* v. *Bethlem Royal Hospital Governors* [1985] AC 871, [1985] 2 WLR 480, [1985] 1 All ER 643.
80. *Brain* v. *Mador* (1985) 32 CCLT 157 (Ont CA) per Lacourcière JA at 165; also cf *Haughian* v. *Paine* [1987] 4 WWR 97, (1987) 55 SaskR 99, (1987) 37 DLR 4th 624, (1987) 40 CCLT 13 (Sask CA) per Sherstobitoff JA at 32.
81. *Sidaway* v. *Bethlem Royal Hospital Governors* [1985] AC 871, [1985] 2 WLR 480, [1985] 1 All ER 643 per Lord Scarman at 649, 652.
82. *S* v. *S* (sub nom *S* v. *McC*) [1970] AC 24, [1970] 3 All ER 107 per Lord Reid at 111; also cf D. Giesen, *op cit*, at section 36 para 932 (refs).
83. D. Giesen, *op cit*, at section 36 (para 932).
84. D. Giesen, *op cit*, at section 36 III (para 975).
85. D. Giesen, *op cit*, at section 36 III para 975 (refs).
86. *In re Saikewicz* (1977) 370 NE 2d 417 at 428 (Mass).
87. P. D. G. Skegg, *op cit*, at 116; E. I. Picard, *op cit*, at 48.
88. D. Giesen, *op cit*, at section 36 III para 977 (refs).
89. *Cruzan* v. *Director, Missouri Department of Health* (1990) 111 L Ed 2d 224 at 271 (SC).
90. P. D. G. Skegg, *op cit*, at 105.

91. P. D. G. Skegg, *op cit*, at 106; D. Giesen, *op cit*, at section 36 III para 978 (refs).

92. For a detailed discussion, cf D. Giesen, *op cit*, at section 36 III para 978 (refs).

93. Sections 1901 (1), 1904 (2) BGB (German Civil Code); cf M. Coester, "Von anonymer Verwaltung zu persönlicher Betreuung", Jura 1991, 1 at 7–8.

94. E. Deutsch, Arztrecht und Arzneimittelrecht (2nd edn, Berlin, Heidelberg, 1991) at 243.

95. This is the traditional standard for surrogate decision-making in the case of incompetent patients, and is designed to protect the patient's welfare in accordance with objective criteria; for a discussion cf D. Giesen, *op cit*, at section 36 III paras 980 ff.

96. For details see D. Giesen, *op cit*, at section 36 III 980 n 156 (refs).

97. B. Werthmann, *Medical Malpractice Law* (Lexington, MA, 1984) at 217.

98. D. Giesen, *op cit*, at section 36 III para 982 (refs).

99. D. Giesen, "Law and Moral Dilemmas Affecting Life and Death: Law and Ethical Dilemmas at Life's End", Report presented to the XXth Colloquy on European Law, Glasgow, 10–12 September 1990, Council of Europe Document, 13 June 1990, CJ-DW/XX (90) 2, 1–30, for a comprehensive discussion of the text-related problems in this context.

100. *Re B (a minor) (wardship: medical treatment)* [1981] 1 WLR 1421 per Templeman LJ at 1424; D. Giesen, *International Medical Malpractice Law* (Tübingen, Dordrecht, London and Boston, 1988), section 36 III para 983.

101. D. Giesen *op cit*, at section 36 III para 983 (refs).

102. BGH, 18 Jan 1983, VI ZR 114/81 BGHZ 86, 240 (254), cf Art 1I, 2II GG.

103. *Superintendent of Family and Child Services* v. *R D & S D* (1983) 42 BCLR 173 per McKenzie J at 183; BGH, 18 Jan 1983, VI ZR 114/81 BGHZ 86, 240 (254; emphasising the rule, *obiter dicens*, that a human being has to accept life as given to him by nature).

104. P. D. G. Skegg, *op cit*, at 109.

105. *Re C (a patient)* [1991] 3 All ER 866 (ChD).

106. *In re Saikewicz* (1977) 370 NE 2d 417 at 431 (Mass); D. Giesen, *op cit*, at section 36 III para 985.

107. A. E. Buchan, "The Limits of Proxy Decision-Making for Incompetents" (1981–2) 29 *University of California Los Angeles Law Review* 386; United States President's Commission for the Study of Ethical Problems in Medicine and Biomedical and Behavioral Research Reports: Deciding to Forego Life-Sustaining Treatment (Washington, 1983) 132–136; United States President's Commission for the Study of Ethical Problems in Medicine and Biomedical and Behavioral Research Reports: Making Health Care Decisions, 3 vols (Washington,

1982) at vol i, 177–181.

108. *In re Conroy* (1985) 486 A 2d 1209 (NJ).

109. It is submitted that this is the soundest approach; cf D. Giesen, *op cit*, at section 36 III para 987.

110. *F* v. *West Berkshire Health Authority* [1990] 2 AC 1, [1989] 2 WLR 1025, [1989] 2 All ER 545.

111. *Bolam* v. *Friern Hospital Management Committee* [1957] 1 WLR 582, [1957] 2 All ER 118 (McNair J and jury).

112. *F* v. *West Berkshire Health Authority* [1990] 2 AC 1, [1989] 2 WLR 1025, [1989] 2 All ER 545 per Lord Brandon at 552.

113. *Bolam* v. *Friern Hospital Management Committee* [1957] 1 WLR 582, [1957] 2 All ER 118.

114. The text-related tests were referred to and quoted by Lord Brandon in *F* v. *West Berkshire Health Authority* [1990] 2 AC 1, [1989] 2 WLR 1025, [1989] 2 All ER 545 per Lord Brandon at 559–560.

115. Cf Ian Kennedy, *The Unmasking of Medicine* (London, 1981) at 18.

116. Cf *Anderson* v. *Chasney* [1949] 4 DLR 71 (Man CA) per Coyne JA at 85, affd [1950] 4 DLR 223 (SCC); D. Giesen, *op cit*, at section 10 II (para 150); as to the consequences of this, cf D. Giesen, *ibid*, at section 10 VI.

117. Cf Ian Kennedy, *Treat me Right. Essays in Medical Law and Ethics* (Oxford, 1988) at 337, 347.

118. *Sidaway* v. *Bethlem Royal Hospital Governors* [1984] 1 All ER 1018 (CA) per Sir John Donaldson MR at 1028.

119. *Sidaway* v. *Bethlem Royal Hospital Governors* [1984] 1 All ER 1018 (CA) per Sir John Donaldson MR at 1028.

120. Cf *Hajgato* v. *London Health Association* (1982) 36 OR 2d 669 (HC) per Callaghan J at 693, affd (1983) 44 OR 2d 264 (CA).

121. *Olmstead* v. *United States*, 277 US 438 at 479 (Brandeis J, dissenting); *Cruzan* v. *Director of Missouri Health Department*, 111 LEd2d 224, 274 (Brennan J, dissenting).

122. *F* v. *R* (1983) 33 SASR 189 (FC South Aust).

123. *Bolam* v. *Friern Hospital Management Committee* [1957] 1 WLR 582, [1957] 2 All ER 118.

124. The *Bolam* test was also held not to be applicable in Australia in *Rogers* v. *Whitaker* (1992) 67 ALJR (High Ct). For a comprehensive discussion cf D. Giesen and J. Hayes, "The Patient's Right to Know: A Comparative View" (1992) 21 *Anglo-American Law Review* 101–122.

125. *F* v. *R* (1983) 33 SASR 189 (FC) per King CJ at 193–194.

126. *F* v. *R ibid*, per King CJ at 194.

Mentally incapacitated adults and decision-making: the Law Commission's project

Brenda Hoggett[1]

The project

The Law Commission is a statutory body set up to promote the reform of the law in England and Wales.[2] In 1989 the Lord Chancellor approved a new item in our programme of law reform: "an investigation of the adequacy of legal and other procedures for decision-making on behalf of mentally incapacitated adults".[3] I have been asked in this chapter to explain the work we are doing in this area and the stage we have reached in our deliberations.[4] We prefer to talk of "incapacity" rather than "incompetence" and not only because the latter has a transatlantic ring: in ordinary language, I may well be incompetent at doing something which I am nevertheless quite capable of doing. Our project is concerned, not with people who are able to do things for themselves, however badly, but with those who are unable to do things at all. Inability is, however, of two types: a person may in fact be unable to do something or the law may deem what he does invalid because he is considered legally unable to do it.[5]

Our normal method of working is to research the relevant law, discover what people think is wrong with it, devise some criteria or objectives against which any reforms might be judged, and then develop some provisional ideas about how the law might be changed. At this point we usually publish a consultation paper, which

---

Decision-Making and Problems of Incompetence. Edited by A. Grubb.
© 1994 John Wiley & Sons Ltd.

is sent to all the individuals and organisations who are likely to have a particular interest in the subject and made available to the general public through HMSO. Once the results of that consultation have been analysed, we go on to formulate recommendations for reform and to prepare a draft Parliamentary Bill to implement them. Our report, with the Bill annexed, is then presented to the Lord Chancellor, who lays it before Parliament. The Government will then consider whether to accept our recommendations and promote legislation: our success rate is the envy of many comparable bodies at home and abroad but varies from time to time and from subject to subject.[6]

Our consultation paper on *Mentally Incapacitated Adults and Decision-Making: An Overview*[7] was published at the end of April 1991. To date, more than 120 responses have been received from a wide variety of organisations and individuals, including representatives of government bodies, the health and social services authorities and professional bodies, voluntary organisations, lawyers and legal organisations, academics and members of the public, including carers and clients. We have also held meetings with several groups representative of the various interests involved.

That paper was not quite in our usual style. We recognise that the subject is huge, difficult and diffuse. Our first object, therefore, was to draw a map of the area, to identify the problems, the range of possible solutions and the various approaches which might be adopted to reforming the law, and to establish practicalities and priorities. The response has convinced us that there is a consensus on the need for reform but no consensus as to precisely what reforms are needed. We have divided the subject into a series of discrete but interlocking projects on particular topics, which could eventually be combined in a single coherent piece of legislation. We are now engaging in a further round of consultation based on more concrete proposals for reform.[8]

Why now?

A number of factors has led to the greater visibility of problems and an expectation that these will increase. They include demographic changes, resulting in larger numbers of very old people; medical advances which not only increase longevity but also present more difficult choices for practitioners and patients alike; the policy of community care which has presented many people with choices and challenges which they would never have faced in the old days of institutional care; and a greater concern with the rights and status of all individuals.

There was pressure for reform from a number of quarters, including the Law Society.[9] There was also much concern from professionals and carers during the Re F[10] litigation, although their concern may have declined since the decision in the House of Lords, which authorised doctors to act in the best interests of their incapable patients. However, the law is still so unclear, particularly in relation to carers, that there is a danger that people will do nothing when something should be done, or that they will do too much when the person concerned is in fact capable of acting for himself.

The subject is also under review in many other parts of the world,[11] including Scotland. In September 1991, the Scottish Law Commission published their own discussion paper on *Mentally Disabled Adults: Legal Arrangements for Managing their Welfare and Finances.*[12] They have been considering the subject for longer than us and their paper therefore contains more concrete proposals for reform. Our legal systems are still very different: they do not, for example, have a formal body equivalent to the Court of Protection, but they do have a procedure for appointing curators which can be used not only for financial affairs but also for personal matters. Nevertheless, it is clear that the problems and concerns are very similar both north and south of the border and we hope that the solutions which we eventually recommend will not be inconsistent in principle with one another, even if the methods of implementation will have to respect our different legal traditions.

The problems

Put simply, the problem is that there is no clear test or method of establishing a person's incapacity and no comprehensive machinery for making lawful decisions on his behalf. However, this masks an enormous range of problems. First, there is the diversity of people who may be legally incapacitated because of their mental state or functioning. "Mental incapacity" is a different concept from "mental disorder". Many mentally disordered or disabled people are quite capable of taking all or at least some decisions and acting upon them. They only become mentally incapacitated when they reach a mental state at which they are either actually unable to take and act upon the decision or the law deems that whatever decision they purport to take is invalid. This will affect different types of people in different ways.

There are those with fluctuating capacity, those whose capacity is deteriorating, and those for whom there is a possibility of improvement.

Secondly, there is a wide range of decisions involved. These are not just medical (or dental) decisions but also decisions about a person's "property and affairs", about where a person lives, how he should spend his time, whom he should see and otherwise how he should lead his day-to-day life. Our project is not just concerned with the "important" decisions. Much attention has been focused on the sterilisation of mentally disabled young women but this will be dealt with in other papers. Removal of a person's teeth, however, may be just as significant for that person as the removal of her womb.

Thirdly, there are the limitations of law reform. Not all problems can be solved by the law or in the courts. Many may be better solved by professional guidance, which is not our province. Law does have advantages of accessibility and public accountability. It can also be cumbersome and expensive. In England and Wales there has been a culture of informality, with decisions governed by professional judgment rather than the law and legal procedures. In relation to hospital admission, for example, the law deliberately does not insist that this be genuinely "voluntary", merely that the patient does not actively object. No one wants to establish a system under which formal procedures have to be invoked before any decision can be taken on behalf of any incapacitated person. So the first question must be whether the law should be changed at all, since there is always the "do nothing" option. Most of our respondents did not take this view.

If there is to be reform, the next problem is whether we should adopt a "minimalist" approach, tackling only those limited areas of major concern; or an "incremental" approach, targeting particular areas one by one; or an "overall" approach, aimed at devising a complete code of law and practice.[13] The minimalist and incremental approaches undoubtedly lead to quicker results which are much more likely to be implemented but it is the Commission's duty to promote the systematic reform and codification of the law.[14] So we are now trying to have the best of all worlds: "minimalist" in the sense that we should not seek to disturb the existing balance between formal and informal solutions whenever possible; "incremental" in that we propose to proceed with three separate although interlocking projects; and "overall" in that we hope that the individual solutions will be compatible with one another, so that they could eventually be combined in a coherent whole.

Finally, there is the perennial conflict of values, between freedom and protection, liberty and paternalism. Here, there does seem to be a consensus in favour of the broad values or policy aims set out in our consultation paper:[15]

1. that people should be enabled and encouraged to take for themselves those decisions which they are able to take;
2. that where it is necessary in their own interests or for the protection of others that someone else should take decisions on their behalf, the intervention should be as limited as possible and concerned to achieve what the person himself would have wanted; and
3. that proper safeguards be provided against exploitation, neglect, and physical, sexual or psychological abuse.

The areas of concern

We now think that the main areas of concern about the existing law can be grouped in the following way.

Private law

By the private law, we mean the law which gives decision-making powers to private individuals, rather than to public authorities or their professionals. Here, the main concern is the present rigid distinction between financial matters and personal care. While there is at least some machinery available for concerned individuals to take charge of an incapacitated person's property and affairs,[16] there is now no legal machinery for taking charge of their personal care and welfare.[17] Of course people do this all the time, but there is much uncertainty about what they can and cannot do and no way of resolving their disputes. Foreign systems solve this by appointing personal guardians. However, clarification of what carers and others may do without resorting to such formal measures would probably go a long way towards solving the problem, with a fall-back procedure for disputes and particularly difficult issues upon which people would prefer an independent judgment.

For financial matters, something like the Court of Protection is clearly needed for large and complicated estates, but for smaller estates or simpler dealings a different approach may be more appropriate. The social security appointeeship system presents a good model but at present is so unstructured that it is riddled with possibilities for abuse. If there were to be a new jurisdiction for resolving problems about personal care, it might well combine the functions of the Court of Protection, so that the same body could decide, for example, where an incapacitated person was to live and how the bills should be paid.

The same distinction between financial affairs and personal care applies in the field of proxy decision-taking by someone appointed by the individual affected while he was still capable. There is a case for expanding the concept of the enduring power of attorney into areas of personal and even health care, by some form of advance directive. There are two distinct types of such directive: appointing someone to take decisions for you at the time they have to be taken, and making the decision yourself maybe a very long time in advance. Extending and modifying the enduring power of attorney system could, of course, be a discrete project or combined with a wider overhaul of the private law area.[18]

Public law

By the public law, we mean giving powers and duties to public authorities and the professionals employed by or contracted to them. Unlike the private law, there exists here a large body of law covering a much wider range of people than the mentally incapacitated. Obviously, there is a problem of deciding whether the procedures which are appropriate for young adult mentally ill patients can possibly be appropriate either for mentally disabled adults or for the elderly mentally infirm, who present very different problems.

Here the main concern is a general feeling that the existing procedures for intervening to protect people from abuse and neglect are in need of reform. These are divided between the National Assistance Acts[19] and the Mental Health Act,[20] with no clear allocation of responsibility for invoking and implementing them, a limited range of options available, and procedures which are thought too Draconian.[21] Consequently they are rarely used.

Also very rarely used is Mental Health Act guardianship.[22] Although private individuals may be appointed guardians, in practice this also operates in the public law field. The main purpose is to provide "essential powers" for the social services in a very limited number of cases. Even for this purpose it seems inadequate and inappropriate for the people we have in mind. The question is whether any longer-term procedures are needed to protect such people, other than the power to intervene to protect them from abuse and neglect in their own homes, and if so whether these should be specially tailored to their needs,[23] leaving the younger adult mentally ill to be covered by Mental Health Act procedures.[24]

Medical law

The appropriate ways of providing for substitute decision-making and resolving disputes could of course be different for different types of decision. There is support for this in the medical area. I propose to discuss the issues here in a little more detail, partly because they are of particular interest in this forum but also because they may be a useful illustration of some general problems.

Issues in medical law

A separate system?

The first issue is whether medical decisions should be treated differently from others. Some people feel that *Re F* went too far in turning the question of incapacity, and of the appropriate treatment, into a purely medical decision. It is argued that some decisions are so important that they should be made by a court or at least an independent forum of some sort. There is a concern that leaving medical decisions solely to the medical profession might imply that they were to be taken solely on medical criteria. There is also support for the creation of a unified "one-stop" procedure for all types of decision, such as exists in some of the Australian and Canadian systems. Some feel that it is not possible to differentiate between medical and financial decisions since many decisions about medical care depend upon whether or not there is the money to pay for it.

In England and Wales, however, this argument may not apply with such force to decisions about medical as opposed to other forms of care. Usually the financial consequences to the individual patient will not play a part. It has also been put to us that treatment decisions are for the most part "one-off" decisions for individual incidents of disease, whereas running someone's life or finances is necessarily a continuing process. We are not sure that this argument holds good, because many other personal and financial decisions could be regarded as "one-off", and to encourage this approach would be consistent with the philosophy of "least restrictive" intervention mentioned earlier. But we are also conscious that there are ways of developing and encouraging interdisciplinary decision-making, with machinery for referring difficult or disputed cases elsewhere, which do not involve resort to the courts or other judicial bodies. The legal process is not necessarily the best adapted to some of the most sensitive judgments which have to be made.[25]

Defining incapacity

Defining incapacity is of course a problem for all types of decision. We start from a presumption of capacity, but how is it to be rebutted? Three different approaches were canvassed in our consultation paper:[26]

1. A "status" test has the advantage of certainty: this concentrates upon whether the person falls within particular categories, which might for example be defined according to diagnosis. The difficulty is that it can easily include many who are quite capable of taking the decision in question and might exclude some who are incapable of doing so. The law used to apply a "status" approach to the compulsory treatment of patients detained in hospital but, rightly in my view, does so no longer.

2. An "outcome" test depends upon the quality of the decision taken. It enables competent professionals to protect their patients and clients against decisions which the professionals believe to be irrational because the outcome may be fatal or at least disadvantageous. In practice, where the consequences are most severe, we all have difficulty in accepting that ordinary people have the right to choose.[27] Some evaluation of the probable outcome of a decision is difficult to avoid when capacity is under discussion. There could therefore be advantages in recognising this. Most of us, however, consider it important to preserve the ordinary person's right to control his own life, however wrong the professionals think him to be. The problem is therefore to distinguish the ordinary from the extraordinary.

3. An "understanding" or "function" test is the approach most frequently applied by the present law. This was also the preferred approach of most respondents. It is usually expressed in terms of whether or not the person can understand the "nature and effect" of the decision in question. We now think that it is better expressed in terms of whether the person concerned can understand the *information* which is relevant to making that decision. The approach has its difficulties. It has to be applied to each decision, each time it has to be made, whereas a status test can continue for some time. It has to

distinguish between the patient who refuses treatment because he does not understand the relevant information and the patient who refuses because he has a different value system or does not care about the consequences or simply disagrees with what the doctors think best. It is still necessary, and difficult, to define the minimum level of understanding. How much relevant information should the patient be expected to be able to understand? And does this differ according to the complexity of that information or the seriousness of the decision? And if the latter, is seriousness to be judged subjectively or objectively, in moral or outcome terms? And are there any people who should be included, however good their understanding, because for some reason they still reach the "wrong" conclusions? But if so, what reasons for being wrong should be included? Should these be limited to the consequences of a recognisable mental disorder or should other factors including family pressures or influences, values or belief systems be included?

Although we are quite clear that the function or "understanding" test has to be a basic component of any test, we are beginning to wonder whether it is asking too much to rely on it alone. It might be wise to combine it with a status test based on mental disorder, so that the person would have to be *both* mentally disordered *and* lacking in the required level of understanding. This would have the advantage of excluding those who reached the "wrong" decisions for reasons which clearly had nothing to do with mental disorder. It might have the disadvantage of tending to include anyone who was mentally disordered, whether or not he did indeed have the required understanding. It also assumes the validity of the definition and diagnosis of mental disorder.[28]

The "function" test will be discussed in more detail in another chapter. Of course, there is the further problem of whether any formal procedures are required in order to decide whether or not the patient is incapacitated. Often the answer may be obvious. But at present we have no appropriate machinery, other than an application to the High Court for a declaration, for overcoming the patient's own opposition or for resolving disputes between professionals, carers, family and others.

Who decides?

But supposing we can agree on an appropriate definition of capacity, and on an appropriate way of deciding it in a disputed case, who should then take the decision on the incapable patient's behalf? At the moment it is the responsible medical practitioner. Should the consent of relatives be required? It is often sensible to obtain this, but the Scottish Law Commission have rejected this as a legal requirement.[29] They considered that it might be impractical and that relatives would not always be appropriate. A "nearest relative" approach need not be particularly complicated but it might still be undesirable. Who is to say what, if any, member of his family an incapacitated person would want to make such intimate decisions on his behalf? It is clearly going to vary from case to case. An alternative approach, which mirrors current practice, would be to require doctors to consult relatives and other people close to the patient, without requiring them to obtain consent.

In some cases it might be possible to rely on decision-makers appointed by the patient himself. The Scottish Law Commission have also considered this. The problem is whether such a person's decision could ever be binding on the doctors. The Scottish paper includes what seems an astonishing argument that: "binding decisions by the patient or his or her attorney downgrades the status of doctors and other health care providers. Their professional judgments and contributions are ignored and they become mere technicians carrying out the directions of the attorney."[30]

Even binding decisions by the patient are said to do this. Yet a capable patient cannot compel the doctor to provide treatment which is contrary to the doctor's professional judgment and similarly the doctor cannot compel the patient to accept treatment. Neither can therefore bind the other and neither is thereby downgraded. So why should the position be any different when the patient is incapacitated and the proxy stands in his shoes? Is there, perhaps, a distinction between allowing the proxy to consent on the patient's behalf to treatment which the doctors advise and allowing the proxy to refuse such treatment?[31]

Usually, however, there would be no attorney, either because the patient never had the capacity or the opportunity to appoint one, or because he did not foresee the need, or chose not to do so. There is reason to believe that a great many financial enduring powers of attorney have been executed but are not, and probably will never be, registered, because the need for them will not arise. But would people do this in relation to matters of personal and particularly medical care if they had the chance? And would it be right to recognise proxies appointed many years ago when the patient's circumstances may have been very different? It is one thing to ask the professionals to consult a proxy and another to expect them always to respect the proxy's views, particularly if this is to decline treatment.

What standard to apply?

One reason for involving relatives or other proxy decision-makers who know the patient well is that they are more likely to be able to apply the "substituted judgment" test, standing in the patient's shoes and trying to make the decision which he would have made had he been capable. This is usually contrasted with the "best interests" criterion, although the distinction may not be straightforward. Substituted judgment is the test which the judge tries to apply when making a will for a person who is incapable of doing so.[32] A person who once had capacity may have had known sympathies and views which the court can at least try to apply to his dispositions. Even with a person who has severe learning disabilities, it may be possible to imagine how he might feel about his situation and those around him and what he might therefore want to do. Nevertheless, there is an air of unreality about trying to decide what a severely disabled woman aged 75, who had lived in a public hospital since the age of 10, might have wanted to do with the £1 600 000 she had inherited.[33] Assumptions had necessarily to be made that she would have been a normal decent person with a sense of obligation, not only to the community in the shape of the people who looked after her but also to the family, who as people knew nothing of her but from which as an entity her fortune derived.

Some have argued, however, that the substituted judgment test is wrong in principle. A will, of course, is very different from a decision which will operate during the patient's lifetime and may have serious consequences for him. There may be circumstances in which it is right to give away or spend some of a person's fortune while he is alive, but it would perhaps be wrong for a proxy decision-maker to give it all away even if there is good reason to believe that this is what the incapacitated person would have wanted to do. It is even more questionable to throw away the person's life or health in such circumstances. For example, a person with severe learning disabilities may require certain medical interventions which are contrary to the religious faith of the family in which he was born and brought up. Should this faith be respected for that person? Applying a substituted judgment test, we can be reasonably certain what he would have wanted had he been capable. But of course the same applies to the children brought up in such families and we do not apply the pure substituted judgment test to them. Also, there may be certain things, such as donating his organs or gametes or participating in medical research, which the proxy may have very good and altruistic reasons for wanting the person to do but which are not in his own best interests. Of course, the definition of "best interests" can be broader than simply medical factors. Medically, it is better to have two kidneys than one. But socially and psychologically, the happiness of the whole family may be crucial to the happiness of its incapacitated member; or he may benefit directly from having a sibling who is alive because of the donation.

Some of our respondents therefore supported an approach which was very similar to that of the courts in cases concerning children. The test would be what was in that person's best interests, but in assessing this a checklist of factors would be taken into account, including the views which he may have had when he was capable and any feelings and preferences which he may have now.[34]

With children, of course, their welfare is the paramount consideration, and it is difficult to say how far, if at all, the interests, wishes and feelings of other people are relevant in their own right as opposed to their bearing (which is often very great) upon the child's welfare. To what extent should the interests of carers of family members be taken into account in making decisions for incapable adults? As there is undoubtedly a risk that their interests will loom large in any decision-making in practice, perhaps the extent to which they should be considered at all ought to be spelt out.

Conclusion

I hope that this is enough to indicate the range and complexity of the issues we have to consider, even if we leave on one side such obviously contentious issues as sterilisation or withdrawal of life-sustaining measures. During 1993, we are publishing consultation papers canvassing provisional proposals for reform in each of the three areas identified earlier[35] and hoping to arrive at some conclusions about the most practical ways forward.

Notes and references

1. I am most grateful to Phil Bates, a Research Assistant at the Commission, for the help he has given me with this paper.
2. Law Commissions Act 1965. The Scottish Law Commission has the same function in relation to Scots law.
3. (1989), Law Com No. 185, Fourth Programme of Law Reform, Item 9.
4. The paper was delivered in April 1992 but revised for publication in December 1992. I have therefore included later developments wherever possible.
5. For example, a small child could not make a will at all; an older child obviously could do so but the law deems him incapable.
6. Perhaps surprisingly in a body set up to promote the modernisation of "lawyers' law" — the law which only lawyers were interested in — our most successful area has been family law.
7. Consultation Paper No. 119 (1991, HMSO).
8. See Consultation Papers No. 128, *Mentally Incapacitated Adults and Decision-Making: A new Jurisdiction*; No. 129, *Mentally Incapacitated Adults and Decision-Making: Medical Treatment and Research*; No. 130, *Mentally Incapacitated and Other Vulnerable Adults: Public Law Protection* (1993, HMSO).
9. The Mental Health Practitioners' Committee of the Law Society published a valuable discussion paper in January 1989 and held an interdisciplinary conference in May 1989 which endorsed its call for reform.
10. *Re F (mental patient: sterilisation)* [1990] 2 AC 1.
11. A review of the experience abroad is contained in our Consultation Paper No. 119, Part V.
12. Scottish Law Commission Discussion Paper No. 94 (1991, HMSO).
13. Consultation Paper No. 119, paras 4.11–4.13.
14. Law Commissions Act 1965, s 3(1).
15. Consultation Paper No. 119, para 4.27.
16. Mental Health Act 1983, Part VII.
17. *Re F (mental patient: sterilisation)* [1990] 2 AC 1; see Consultation Paper No. 119, paras 3.35–3.36.
18. See Consultation Paper No. 128, note 8 above.
19. National Assistance Act 1948, s 47 and National Assistance (Amendment) Act 1951.
20. Mental Health Act 1983, s 135 (1).
21. See Consultation Paper No. 119, paras 3.20–3.23; see also Consultation Paper No. 130, note 8 above, Part III.
22. Mental Health Act 1983, ss 7–10; see Consultation Paper No. 119, paras 3.24–3.34; Consultation Paper No. 130, Part IV.
23. Perhaps by adapting any new private law machinery for taking decisions on their behalf; see Consultation Paper No. 130, Part V.

24. The Secretary of State has just announced a review of the law in this area, following a recent recommendation for community supervision orders made by the Royal College of Psychiatrists: see *Hansard*, Written Answers, vol 216 col 731, 13 January 1993.
25. See *Airedale NHS Trust* v. *Bland* [1993] 1 All ER 821 at 886 per Lord Mustill.
26. Consultation Paper No. 119, paras 2.43–2.44.
27. Witness the difficulties experienced in accepting the decision of the patient to refuse a blood transfusion in the case of *Re T (adult: refusal of treatment)* [1992] 3 WLR 782.
28. See Consultation Papers No. 128, Part III, No. 129, Part II.
29. Discussion Paper No. 94, para 3.14.
30. *Ibid*, para 5.114.
31. Imagine, for example, that the patient in *Re T (adult: refusal of treatment)* [1992] 3 WLR 782 had appointed her Jehovah's Witness mother as her proxy some time before a blood transfusion was urgently required.
32. See *Re D (J)* [1982] Ch 237; *Re C (a patient)* [1991] 3 All ER 866.
33. *Re C (a patient)* [1991] 3 All ER 866.
34. Children Act 1989, s 1(1) and (3).

An ethical framework for surrogate decision-making*

Dan W. Brock

My aim is to sketch an ethical framework for surrogate decision-making about medical treatment for incompetent adults and for thinking about the ethical issues that arise in that decision-making.[1] Surrogate decision-making should seek to extend the ideals of health care decision-making for competent adults, with suitable changes required by and reflecting the patient's incompetence. In the medical ethics literature a substantial, though not universal consensus has developed that health care decision-making should be shared decision-making between the physician and competent patient. Oversimplifying, the physician brings his or her knowledge, training and experience to the diagnosis of the patient's condition and the prognoses, if different treatment alternatives are followed, including the alternative of no treatment. The patient brings his or her own subjective aims and values to the decision-making process for the evaluation of the alternatives, with their particular mixes of benefits and risks, as spelled out by the physician.[2]

What values underlie a commitment to shared decision-making, and what ends are we seeking to promote with it? I believe there are two central values underlying shared decision-making. The first, and most obvious, is the promotion and protection of the patient's well-

* An earlier version of this paper appeared as "Surrogate Decision-Making for Incompetent Adults: An Ethical Framework", in (1991) 58 *The Mount Sinai Journal of Medicine* 388.

Decision-Making and Problems of Incompetence. Edited by A. Grubb.

being. Shared decision-making rests in part on the presumption that competent patients who have been suitably informed by their physicians about the treatment choice they face are generally, though of course not always, the best judges of what treatment will most promote their overall well-being.[3] The other value is respecting the patient's self-determination. I mean by self-determination the interest of ordinary persons in making significant decisions about their own lives themselves and according to their own values. It is by exercising self-determination that we have significant control over our lives and take responsibility for our lives and the kind of persons we become. These then are the values that guide shared decision-making. For incompetent patients we still want shared decision-making, but then the patient lacks the capacity to participate and a surrogate must take the patient's place. Before considering who should be a surrogate and how the surrogate should decide, the prior question is which patients should have a surrogate to decide for them.

The determination of incompetence

In health care this is ultimately a matter of the patient's competence to decide for him- or herself. If the patient is competent, the patient is entitled to decide and to give or refuse informed consent to treatment. If incompetent, a surrogate must be selected to decide for the patient. The concept, standards and determination of competence are complex and there is space here to emphasise only a few important points about competence and incompetence.[4] Adults are presumed to be competent unless and until found to be incompetent. In questionable or borderline cases competence should be understood for two reasons as decision-relative; that is, a patient may be competent to make one decision but not another. The first reason is that different decisions can vary in the demands they make on a patient; for example, in the complexity of the information relevant to the choice. The other reason is that patients can change over time in the decision-making capacities they bring to the decision-making process from the effects on them of medications, their disease and other factors.

The capacities needed for competence in treatment decision-making are three: the capacity for understanding and communication; the capacity for reasoning and deliberation; and the capacity to have and apply a set of values or conception of one's good. Although these capacities are possessed by people in different degrees, it is important to recognise that the determination of competence is a threshold, not a comparative, determination. This follows from the function that the competence determination plays both in health care and in the law — to sort the patient into either the class of patients who are competent to decide for themselves or into the class of patients who must have a surrogate to decide for them. The crucial question about competence in borderline cases then is how defective or impaired a person's decision-making must be to warrant a determination of incompetence. There are two central values at stake in whether a patient is judged competent or incompetent, and so two kinds of errors to be balanced in that determination. One value is protecting the patient from the harmful consequences of his or her choice when the patient's decision-making is seriously impaired. The other value is respecting the patient's interest in deciding for him- or herself when sufficiently able to do so. The two errors to be balanced are failing adequately to protect the patient from the harmful consequences of a seriously impaired choice against failing to permit the patient to decide for him- or herself when the patient is sufficiently able to do so. There is no unique objectively correct balancing of these two values and errors. Instead the proper balancing is inherently an ethically controversial choice.

The evaluation of a patient's competence should address and evaluate the *process* of the patient's decision-making; the standard should not be an outcome standard that simply looks to the content of the patient's choice and whether it is the "correct" choice according to some standard of correctness. Given the values noted above which are at stake for the patient in the competence determination, it follows that the standard for competence should be a variable standard, varying principally according to the consequences for the patient's well-being of accepting his or her choice. The standard should vary along a continuum from high, when the choice appears to be seriously in conflict with the patient's well-being; to moderate, when the patient's choice appears to be comparable to other alternatives in its effect on the patient's well-being; to low, when the choice will clearly best serve the patient's well-being. One controversial consequence of this account of the competence determination is that a patient might be competent to consent to a particular treatment, but not to refuse it, and vice versa. This follows from two facts. First, the process of reasoning to be evaluated will inevitably be different if it leads to a different choice. Second, the effects on one of the values to be balanced — the patient's well-being — if the patient's choice is accepted can be radically different depending on whether the patient has consented to or refused the recommended treatment. Treatment refusal may reasonably trigger an evaluation of the patient's competence, although it should usually trigger as well a re-evaluation by the physician both of the treatment recommendation and of the communication of that recommendation to the patient.[5] The basic question the competence evaluator should be trying to answer is: does the patient's choice sufficiently accord with the patient's own underlying and enduring aims and values for it to be accepted and honoured, even if others, including the physician, may think it not the best choice and not the choice that they would make?

The selection of a surrogate

Let us now assume that a patient has been found to be incompetent to make a particular treatment choice so that a surrogate must act for the patient. There are now two central questions: who should serve as surrogate for the patient? What standard should guide the surrogate's decision? I will first take up selection of a surrogate. If we are to respect the incompetent patient's wishes as best we can, then the surrogate should be the person that the patient would have wanted to act as surrogate for him or her. In a number of American states, it is possible for a person, while competent, to designate legally a surrogate who will make health care decisions for him or her in the case of later incompetence by executing a durable power of attorney for health care (DPOA). This document also allows, but does not require, a person to give instructions to the surrogate about one's wishes concerning treatment. Ethically, even if not legally, an oral designation by a person of a surrogate should have nearly the same weight as a formal DPOA. Patients should be encouraged while competent to designate who will decide for them in the case of later incompetence, and physicians have a responsibility to seek out this information from their patients early in their patients' treatment and while patients are still competent, especially if a period of later incompetence is relatively predictable.

In most cases at present, an incompetent patient will not have explicitly designated who is to serve as his or her surrogate. It is then reasonable to act on a presumption that a close family member of the patient, when available, is the appropriate surrogate.[6] This is also the common practice in health care. There is space here to mention only the most important considerations that support this presumption for a family member acting as surrogate. First, usually a family member will be the person the patient would have wanted to act as surrogate for him or her. Second, usually a family member will be able to arrive at the best decision for the patient because the family member will know the patient best and will be most concerned for the patient's welfare. It is important to underline that the claim is only that the practice of using a close family member as surrogate will result over-all in better decisions for patients than any feasible alternative practice, such as appointing an attorney to act as the patient's guardian. Third, the family is a central social and moral unit in our society to which important responsibilities are assigned and within which important values are realised. The family has important responsibilities to care for its dependent members. While dependent children are the most obvious example, dependent adults are another important instance of this responsibility. The family is also the main place in which most persons in our society are able to pursue and realise the values of intimacy and privacy. Both to fulfil these responsibilities and to realise these values the family must be accorded significant, although not unlimited, freedom from external oversight, intrusion and control.

It is to be emphasised that these and other grounds for the presumption for a close family member to be an incompetent patient's surrogate do not require that the surrogate always makes the best or optimal choice. That would be too high and unrealistic a standard. On the other hand these grounds for the family as surrogate should also make clear that family members' authority as surrogate decision-makers is not unlimited. The presumption for family members as surrogates can be rebutted in particular cases in which these grounds do not hold — for example, there is no close relation between patient and family member, or there is a clear conflict of interest between patient and family member. In such cases, an incompetent patient's physician can have a positive responsibility not to allow the family member to act as surrogate, which can include appeal to the courts to have another appointed as surrogate if that proves necessary.

Sometimes there is no family member available to serve as surrogate. When a close friend is available and willing to serve as surrogate, then most of the reasons that support a family member as surrogate will support using the friend, although if especially controversial or problematic decisions must be made physicians may want to have the friend be formally appointed as guardian by the courts. In other cases there is no family member or friend available to serve as surrogate. Health care institutions vary as to how they handle such cases and flexibility both within and between institutions is desirable because of the wide range of different decisions that must be made. What is important is that institutions have a settled and public policy for such cases so that decision-making does not become paralysed from lack of a natural surrogate. A hospital might have, for example, a policy that for a specified range of decisions to forego life-sustaining treatment or resuscitation, the attending physician's proposed decision would be referred to the Chief of Service, who could review the decision and take any further steps he or she deemed appropriate, such as referral to an ethics committee or to the courts. At least for decisions about life-sustaining treatment, some involvement of one or more others besides the attending physician is desirable when the patient lacks a family member or friend to act as surrogate.

Guidance principles for surrogate decisions

What standards should a surrogate employ in deciding for an incompetent patient? While it is oversimplified in some respects that I will address below, one can think of three ordered guidance principles for surrogates to employ in decision-making: advance directives, substituted judgment, and best interests. These are ordered principles in the sense that the surrogate should employ the first if possible, or if not it, then the second if it is possible, and if neither the first or second can be used, then the third.

The advance directives principle tells the surrogate that if a valid advance directive exists that the patient gave while competent specifying how the decision at hand should be made, there is a strong presumption that it should be followed. Formal advance directives take two principal forms: so-called living wills and DPOAs. Living wills are given legal force in approximately 40 American states, while DPOAs have legal force in far fewer jurisdictions at present.

Living wills have several common features that limit their usefulness, of which I shall mention two. First, they are nearly always formulated in vague terms both as to the patient conditions in which they apply, such as "terminally ill", and as to the treatments they cover, such as "extraordinary measures" or "aggressive treatment". This is to some extent inevitable when they are executed well in advance of the decision to be made and means that there is commonly significant interpretation that others must undertake as to how they should now apply. Second, and probably in response to worries about potential abuses, enabling statutes in some states place two kinds of limitations on living wills: on the conditions in which they can be executed, for example, the person must already have been diagnosed as terminally ill with death imminent; and limitations in the circumstances in which they apply, for example, the decision cannot cover nutrition and hydration. When persons follow these restrictions and limitations in the hope of giving living wills legal enforceability, there will be many circumstances in which they fail to apply. Since living wills are relatively rarely brought into court for enforcement, but more often function as a means of informing others about the patient's wishes, restrictive formulations may be inadvisable.

DPOAs are the most desirable form of advance directive for most persons. First, they commonly allow a person to give more detailed instructions to the surrogate about his or her wishes regarding treatment, although it is important to avoid letting greater detail narrow the application of the instructions. Second, they respond to the importance of the task of later interpreting the patient's instructions by allowing the patient to designate who will do that for him or her. DPOAs will not be the preferable form of advance directive, of course, for persons who have no one to name to act as surrogate for them.

I noted above that there is a strong presumption that a valid advance directive should be followed, but did not claim it should be absolutely binding. This is because there are reasons why advance directives should not have ethically the same degree of binding force as the contemporaneous decision of a competent patient. In the case of a competent patient, the decision can be made attending to the full and detailed context, whereas advance directives must inevitably be formulated before the precise context of future decisions is known. This means that occasionally a treatment decision will arise in circumstances radically different from those assumed likely by the patient when executing the advance directive; in such cases, following the letter of the directive may be contrary to following its spirit or the intentions of the patient. Moreover, the worry about advance directives that the patient might have changed his or her mind about treatment when the time came actually to decide does not arise for a competent patient able to decide. Finally, a decision by a competent patient that appears significantly contrary to the interests of that patient commonly will be opposed by others who care for the patient, thereby testing the understanding and resolve of the patient to an extent not possible with advance directives. Despite these limitations, there are good reasons in practice to accord a strong presumption to any patient's advance directive about care.

At the present time, and probably for the foreseeable future, most patients do not have advance directives and then the substituted judgment guidance principle should be followed. This principle tells the surrogate to attempt to decide as the patient would have decided, if competent, in the circumstances that now obtain. In effect, the principle directs the surrogate to use his or her knowledge of the patient and of the patient's aims and values to infer what the patient's choice would have been.

Physicians have an important responsibility in helping surrogates to understand their role in applying substituted judgment. The physician's approach should not be of the form "What do you now want us to do for your mother?" but, instead, along the following lines: "You of course knew your mother better than I did, so help us decide together what she would have wanted done for her now." This substituted judgment approach helps get decisions more in accordance with the patient's wishes, thereby better fulfilling the values underlying shared decision-making.[7] It also has the practical advantage of leaving the responsibility for the choice made as much as possible with the patient, thereby often making the psychological and emotional burdens of surrogates easier to carry and facilitating their effective participation in decision-making. The answer when life-sustaining treatment is in question of "Do everything" is nearly always unhelpful and to be avoided. Surrogates should always be assured that all appropriate care will always be given, including all care needed to maintain the patient's comfort and dignity. But what care is appropriate will often change with changes in the patient's condition and prognosis, and surrogates must be helped to understand that all possible care is not automatically appropriate care.

Two features of substituted judgment decision-making should be explicitly noted. First, it will let surrogates take account of how the interests of others besides the patient will be affected by the decision to be made, although only to the extent that there is evidence the patient would have given that weight to those interests. Second, it will let surrogates making decisions weigh considerations about the quality of life of the patient, both at present and as it will be affected by treatment decisions, although only quality-of-life for that patient and according to the patient's own values. When foregoing life-sustaining treatment is in question only a very limited quality-of-life judgment is relevant, viz. is the best quality of life possible for the patient with life-sustaining treatment sufficiently poor that the patient would have judged it to be worse than no further life at all? No judgments about social worth or the social value of the patient are warranted under substituted judgment.

When there is no information available about what this particular patient would have wanted in the decision at hand, the best interests principle directs the surrogate to select the alternative that best furthers the patient's interests. This in effect amounts to asking how most reasonable persons would decide in these circumstances, which is justified by the absence of any information about how this patient differs from others. Treatment choices based on best interests can be especially difficult in the common circumstances in which choice is from a range of alternatives about which reasonable persons can and do disagree. Because of this difficulty, it is important where possible to avoid having to appeal to best interests by engaging in advance planning with patients when they are still competent to determine their wishes about future treatment options.

I noted above that a strict ordering of these guidance principles was an oversimplification and we are in a position now to see one reason why that is so. Evidence bearing on the patient's wishes concerning the decision at hand, whether from an advance directive or from the surrogate's knowledge of the patient, is neither fully determinate and decisive on the one hand, or completely absent on the other. Instead, such evidence ranges along a broad continuum in how strongly it supports a particular choice. In all cases, physicians and surrogates should seek confidence that the choice made is reasonably in accord with the patient's wishes or interests. The better the evidence about what this particular patient would have wanted, the more one can rely on it. The less the information and evidence about what this patient would have wanted, the more others must reason in terms of what most persons would want.

What constitutes adequate evidence for surrogates to have about the patient's wishes has been an issue in several recent court cases, most notably in the *O'Connor* case in New York[8] and in the *Cruzan* case in Missouri, which was upheld by the US Supreme Court.[9] In the New York case, where the standard was spelled out more, the court imposed an extremely high standard of evidence for foregoing life-sustaining treatment by a surrogate, requiring clear and convincing proof that the patient had made a settled commitment while competent to reject the particular form of treatment under circumstances such as those now obtaining. Where there is any significant doubt, the court reasoned, the decision must be on the side of preserving life. This decision set a very difficult standard in New York for patients and their surrogates to satisfy, and thereby establishes a very strong presumption in favour of extending the lives of incompetent patients with life-sustaining treatment. The US Supreme Court in *Cruzan* upheld the right of the state of Missouri to impose this same very strong presumption, although without endorsing the wisdom of doing so.

Such a presumption underweights patients' interest in self-determination, and fails as well to recognise adequately the extent to which patients' well-being is determined by patients' own aims and values. But is it not reasonable, the court might ask, always to err on the side of preserving life when there is any doubt about the patient's wishes? At a time several decades ago when medicine only rarely had the capacity to extend life in circumstances where doing so would have been unwanted by, and not a benefit to, patients, such a policy would have been reasonable. It is a commonplace, however, that medicine has gained vastly enlarged capacities to extend life in recent decades. Patients' lives can now often be extended when they would not want this done, and as a result New York's and Missouri's very strong presumption in favour of extending life when there is any significant doubt about the patient's wishes can no longer be justified. Although the US Supreme Court found no constitutional bar to the clear and convincing evidence standard, there remains good reasons for other states not to adopt it.

Conclusion

Having briefly sketched an ethical framework for surrogate decision-making for incompetent patients, I want to conclude with a plea for "preventive ethics" aimed at reducing as much as possible the necessity to resort to surrogate decision-making when the patient's wishes are unknown or significantly uncertain. This can only be done by persons, while still competent, talking with their physicians and families about their treatment wishes should they become seriously ill. This is especially appropriate in the case of persons with chronic, progressive diseases in which both a possible period of incompetence and the nature of later treatment decision likely to arise are relatively predictable. Physicians have an important role in making this prior planning occur substantially more often than it now does by encouraging their patients to reflect about their wishes and to make those wishes known to others likely to be involved in treatment decisions for them.

The need for surrogate decision-making in health care will never be eliminated, nor can all difficult decisions be avoided, but it should be possible greatly to reduce the number of cases in which physicians and surrogates must decide about an incompetent patient's care lacking knowledge about the patient's wishes that could have been obtained earlier, had it been sought.

Notes and references

1. I draw freely here on prior published work I have done on this topic, some of it collaborative work with Allen Buchanan. See especially Allen E. Buchanan and Dan W. Brock, *Deciding for Others: The Ethics of Surrogate Decision-Making* (Cambridge: Cambridge University Press, 1989).

2. Some respects in which this division of labour is oversimplified are explored in my paper, "Facts and Values in the Physician/Patient Relationship", in *Ethics, Trust and the Professions*, (eds) R. Veatch, T. Langen, E. Pellegrino (Washington, DC: Georgetown University Press, 1991).

3. For a discussion of different kinds of cases in which competent patients make irrational choices, and the responsibilities of their physicians in such circumstances, see Dan W. Brock and Steven A. Wartmen, "When Competent Patients Make Irrational Choices" (1990) 322 *New England Journal of Medicine* 1595.

4. See especially Buchanan and Brock, *op cit*, Ch 1.

5. Some studies have shown that the most common cause of treatment refusals is failure of the communication process between physician and patient, and that most refusals are consequently withdrawn when the recommendation is better explained so that the patient understands it adequately. Cf P. S. Applebaum and L. S. Roth, "Treatment Refusal in the Medical Hospital", in *President's Commission for the Study of Ethical Problems in Medicine and Biomedical and Behavioral Research, Making Health Care Decisions: The Ethical and Legal Implications of Informed Consent in the Patient–Practitioner Relationship: Vol. 2 Appendices* (Washington, DC: US Government Printing Office, 1982).

6. In most jurisdictions, a close family member lacks explicit legal authority to act as the patient's surrogate until formally appointed by a court as the patient's guardian. States should consider adopting legislation like the recently enacted Health Care Decisions Act in the District of Columbia which formally authorises a family member to act as surrogate for an incompetent patient without recourse to guardianship proceedings.

7. Confirmation that asking the right question matters in the choices surrogates make can be found in Tom Tomlinson *et al*, "An Empirical Study of Proxy Consent for Elderly Persons" (1990) 30(1) *The*

Gerontologist 54.

8. *In re Westchester County Medial Center (O'Connor)* (1988) 513 NE 2d 607 (NYCA).

9. *Cruzan* v. *Director, Missouri Dept. of Health* (1990) 110 S Ct 2841 (US Sup Ct).

Determining incompetence: problems with the function test

Jennifer Jackson

Good medical practice necessitates that doctors have the ability to recognise whether or not a given patient who refuses to consent to a recommended treatment is or is not competent to make that decision. Relegating the patient to the correct category is of crucial importance since a doctor's obligation in regard to competent patients is to respect their refusals, and in regard to incompetent patients to override them. Since most of us who are destined to reach old age can expect either to become incompetent or at any rate to come to be considered to be so by those on whom we will depend, we all have a keen interest in doctors acquiring this particular ability to tell the competents from the incompetents. We neither want to be nannied so long as we continue to be competent nor to be abandoned if and when we become incompetent. The trouble is, of course, with the considerable number and variety of borderline cases of marginal or problematic competence.

The Law Commission's Consultation Paper *Mentally Incapacitated Adults and Decision-Making: An Overview*[1] enquires into the possibility of giving clearer guidelines to doctors for determining capacity for decision-making where a patient's competence is in doubt. The Consultation Paper favours what it calls a "function" approach to determining capacity and it reviews a number of function tests which have recently been advocated.

I will argue that while the Consultation Paper rightly rejects the

Decision-Making and Problems of Incompetence. Edited by A. Grubb.
© 1994 John Wiley & Sons Ltd.

so-called "status" and "outcome" approach alternatives to the function approach — they are indeed useless for discriminating competence in respect of the borderline cases — none of the function tests which the Consultation Paper reviews is satisfactory either. Moreover, I will suggest, there is no way of mending or refining such tests to make them fulfil the role wanted of them, namely to enable doctors to relegate to the category of incompetence all vulnerable patients towards whom they (and perhaps we) feel paternalist intervention is justified, if not obligatory.

The awkward truth is that some of the patients whom we (may) feel need to be protected against themselves are undeniably competent. If therefore we want still to defend paternalist intervention in *their* case, we need to look elsewhere than to tests of competency for a justification. I will, finally, comment briefly on two possible lines of defence for extending paternalist intervention to some competent patients.

The duty of care that doctors owe their patients is morally and legally constrained by the requirement that patients give genuine consent to treatment. Only two exceptions allow doctors to proceed to treat without their patients' consent: (1) that in an emergency a patient's consent may be presumed; (2) that genuine consent cannot, and therefore, need not, be sought from a patient who is incapable of giving it.

John Stuart Mill allows just these two exceptions to his general injunction against paternalist interference: you may be justified, he says, in forcibly preventing someone from straying unwittingly onto an unsafe bridge. But if the wayfarer upon being informed persisted in wanting to venture onto the bridge, your continued forcible intervention would be justified only if the person were in one way or another incompetent — as if he were "a child, or delirious, or in some state of excitement or absorption incompatible with the full use of the reflective faculty".[2]

Consider the implications of Mill's strictures on forcible paternalist intervention for the moral permissibility of overriding patients' refusals of treatment. The emergency defence would be inapplicable: a patient who refuses *has* had the opportunity to consent. The only remaining defence for paternalist intervention is that the patient is not competent. In borderline cases it may be the patients' very refusals that trigger doctors' doubts about their competence.

Mill does not himself discuss how an individual's competence is to be assessed in borderline cases. People may, surely, have less than "full use of the reflective faculty" and still properly be deemed to be sufficiently competent to be entitled to make their own decisions: after all, we allow people to consent to marriage even though they are "madly" in love. But how much use of the "reflective faculty" suffices to qualify a person as competent to decide and how might doctors be guided in assessing the competence in borderline cases; for example, of patients who are mildly demented or whose short-term memory comes and goes; of young adolescents whose experience of life is limited but not negligible; of people whose suicide attempts may have been foiled and who are liable to make further attempts unless kept under surveillance?

As the Law Commission's Consultation Paper points out, the law does not provide clear guidance to doctors on how to assess the marginal cases. On the one hand, the law firmly supports a patient's right to refuse treatment, however unwisely — "in principle, legal capacity depends upon understanding rather than wisdom: the quality of the decision is irrelevant as long as the person understands what he is doing".[3] On the other hand, practice does not always follow principle: the law allows for "adaptations" of the "basic test". Statutes are introduced "ad hoc to meet specific situations".[4] Thus, for example, doctors can compulsorily admit to hospital patients who would qualify as competent by the basic test provided only that those so detained are suffering from a mental disorder and are a risk to themselves or to others.[5]

This ambivalence in the law reflects the difficulty to which the borderline cases give rise. If the law requires practice to keep to principle, designating everyone competent who passes the basic test requiring understanding not wisdom, doctors are thereby debarred from acting to protect vulnerable people whom it would seem callous to leave unprotected. If the law modifies principle to bring it in line with practice, by adopting for various contexts a stricter test of capacity, requiring (a modicum of) wisdom besides understanding, doctors are thereby entitled to compel their patients to follow sensible advice: in other words, patients are deprived of their prerogative to be irrational.

The Consultation Paper invites views as to whether "there is scope for simplifying and rationalising the various legal tests of capacity in operation at present".[6] Any attempt to set forth new guidelines for testing the capacity of patients whose competence is marginal would need to find some way of accommodating both the duty of care and the duty to respect autonomy. Is it possible to set forth guidelines that are sufficiently strict so as to enable doctors to act paternally to protect vulnerable "incompetent" patients from self-harm but not so strict as to allow doctors to erode "competent" patients' precious right to reject sensible advice?

The Law Commission Consultation Paper reviews the three main approaches to determine capacity to be found in "the literature": the "outcome", the "status" and the "function" approaches.[7] Of these the Consultation Paper favours the last which, as it says, has received "by far the greatest informed support"[8] and which "also happens to be the approach most frequently adopted in theory by English law".[9]

The outcome approach determines a person's capacity to decide in the light of the choice a person makes: a crazy choice betokens a crazy person, crudely speaking. But of course, such a test is too blunt a measure for the borderline difficult cases. There are, after all, degrees of craziness and we competents are naturally anxious to protect our right to make somewhat crazy choices and in any case are not always in agreement with others as to how crazy the choices we make are. To allow doctors to judge our capacity on the basis of *their* application of the outcome test, when we would refuse the treatment they recommend, would be far too dangerous. All the same, the outcome approach is not irrelevant to the assessment of capacity. If a patient appears to be making a crazy choice, a doctor has good grounds for questioning the patient's capacity. In borderline cases, though, the outcome test is not by itself *sufficient* to establish capacity.

The status approach determines our incapacity simply by reference to the categories into which we fall. Anyone who falls within a relevant category, for example a child, a schizophrenic, a victim of Korsakov's disease, is presumed to be incompetent. This test, like the outcome one, is unhelpful in respect of borderline cases. A child aged 3 is not competent to decide whether to submit to medication. But what of a child of 12? Mildly demented elderly patients may or may not be competent to decide against a recommended treatment or they may be competent intermittently. That a person falls within a certain category may be reason for questioning the person's capacity but, characteristically, with the borderline cases it is not on its own decisive for determining the individual's capacity *vis-à-vis* a specific decision.

Whereas both the outcome and the status approaches rely on indirect evidence to determine capacity, the function approach attempts to determine capacity by direct examination of a person's understanding and powers of reasoning. If it is possible to appraise a person's understanding directly this is surely a much more reliable way of determining capacity. In applying the outcome test we have to assume that the patient's understanding is defective from the evidence that the wrong conclusion is reached. But that is a precarious assumption not only because there are other possible explanations why a patient might reach the wrong conclusion, for example our inadequacies in communicating information to the patient, but also because we may ourselves be assuming without adequate grounds that a different conclusion from that which *we* think the patient should reach has to be wrong. In applying the status approach to borderline cases we must make another precarious assumption that simply because a person falls within a category in which capacity is likely to be impaired or absent, this patient lacks capacity in respect of a particular decision on a given occasion. By contrast, the function approach allows us to address our attention to an individual's own capacity on a given occasion in respect of a particular decision.

Yet the function approach is beset with difficulties of its own. Both the outcome and the status approaches provide a single fixed benchmark for determining capacity — either the outcome of your choice is wrong or it is not; either you fall within a given category or you do not. But if we are measuring understandings we have to decide how much understanding is good enough. And then, we may want to shift the bench-mark from one kind of case to another depending on the kind of decision at stake, the complexity of the relevant considerations and the gravity of the consequences.

Were we happy to settle for the basic test in applying the function approach requiring of a person merely that "he understand the general nature and likely consequences of what he is deciding" and can "communicate his decision",[10] the bench-mark would be relatively clear and fixed. But while such a minimal requirement of competence safeguards people's right to autonomy, we may worry that it fails to safeguard vulnerable people who are entitled to our protection from themselves even though they would pass this basic test of capacity. Thus we may want to complicate our account of the function test, requiring more stringent tests of capacity in relation to certain types of decision, for example relating to people's capacity to handle their own financial affairs.

Is it possible to provide a function test which can be applied across the board, which is neither too lax (failing to protect vulnerable people in our care) nor too stringent (failing to protect competent people's autonomy)? The Consultation paper reviews a number of recent tests applying the function approach that have been proposed. I will argue that none of these is satisfactory — they are either too lax or too strict or they are so vague as to give no clear guidance to doctors for deciding the borderline cases.

Tepper and Elwork[11]

Tepper and Elwork's test for patients' capacity to consent to or refuse treatment requires that a patient is able to (i) *understand* the relevant information necessary to reach a decision, (ii) *deliberate* about the information needing to be considered in reaching a decision, and (iii) *decide* to accept or reject a proposed plan of treatment.[12]

This test has the merit that the general guidelines it specifies allow us to adjust the bench-mark of competence from one context of choice to another. It allows us to judge a particular patient to be competent to make some relatively simple choices but not to make other relatively complex ones, or to judge a patient competent to make choices at one time and not at another.

Yet many patients would pass this test whom we may feel are entitled to our interventionist protection nevertheless. If we fail to persuade a frail but articulate person to abandon her cardboard box and accept sheltered accommodation during a severe winter, ought not we to insist that she be removed to shelter for her own protection? A young man who has taken an overdose to punish the woman who has left him for someone else may understand the consequences of his action if his stomach is not pumped. He may be perfectly articulate about his intentions and his predicament, and yet we may consider that we have an obligation to intervene against his wishes. On the Tepper and Elwork test he would probably have to be deemed competent and hence we would have no right to intervene.

With such cases, doctors may be tempted to fall back on the necessity plea for intervention without consent — but disingenuously. The necessity plea applies where there is not an opportunity to seek consent — as if an accident victim is unconscious and bleeding profusely and therefore cannot be *asked* if he wishes to be given a blood transfusion. Someone who has taken an overdose and who has been brought to hospital against his will and who is still fully conscious is not so urgently in need of treatment that the Tepper and Elwork test (or some other) cannot be applied.

Another excuse which we might be tempted to use in such a case for overriding the person's refusal might be that the person's present will does not (for all we know) reflect his true will. In other words, we plead that a person may, owing to agitation or distress of one kind or another, be making a choice which is out of character. Whatever the merits of this excuse it would not bear on the issue of capacity, if we were to stick strictly to the Tepper and Elwork criteria.

Consider another type of case where we may feel intervention is justified. Suppose a 14-year-old boy with cancer needs to have his leg amputated: it is gangrenous. He might well pass the Tepper and Elwork test of capacity yet refuse his consent to the surgery. No doubt his refusal would be overridden on the grounds that he lacked sufficient maturity, had not sufficient experience of life. But by the Tepper and Elwork test he could well qualify as competent. The test does, to be sure, require understanding and perhaps it might be said that a 14-year-old does not yet understand adequately what death is. But do we really have grounds for assuming that a 14-year-old has less understanding of what death is than a 41-year-old? In any case, the law requires only that one understands "in a broad sense" the nature and consequences of one's choice. A normal 14-year-old does surely understand in a broad sense what death is.

Whereas the Tepper and Elwork test protects self-determination but does not enable doctors to protect certain of their vulnerable patients whom it would qualify as competent, other tests described in the Consultation Paper err in the other direction, protecting the vulnerable but enabling doctors to encroach on the right of self-determination of certain patients whom these tests would not qualify as competent. Two such tests are discussed: that which is advocated by the President's Commission in the United States in its *Making Health Care Decisions*[13] and that which is advocated by Appelbaum and Grisso.[14]

The President's Commission (1982)

According to the President's Commission, capacity depends on: "(i) possession of a set of values and goals to provide a stable framework for comparing options, (ii) the ability to communicate and understand information, including linguistic and conceptual skills, plus sufficient life experience to appreciate the meaning of potential alternatives, and (iii) the ability to reason and deliberate about one's choices in a way which enables comparison of the probable impact of alternative outcomes on personal goals and lifestyles".[15]

With the second and third conditions that this tests specifies I have no quarrel. But does not the first condition embody an unwarranted assumption, indeed a number of unwarranted assumptions, namely that rational agents have a "set" of values, that when making choices among various options they make references to their set of values which provides them with a "stable framework" within which options can be compared? It is not clear to me that rational agents do have any such general *set* of values; still less, that rational agents make conscious reference to it when deliberating among options. Quite typically, we make choices among various competing values and goals which are incommensurable and which therefore do not fit in any one framework — which is one of the reasons why the notion of a hedonic calculus for rational choice is a non-starter. It is therefore unreasonable to subject patients whose competence is in doubt to this test: to require that they should be able to demonstrate how their chosen option outweighs other options in the "stable framework" of their values within which their choice can be seen to be better or as good.

Arguably, I have been reading too much into this first condition. Allen Buchanan and Dan Brock in defending a similarly worded condition, namely that a competent decision-maker must have "a set of values or conception of the good"[16] hasten to add that competency does not require "a fully consistent set of goals, much less a detailed 'life-plan' to cover all contingencies".[17] On their minimalist explication of this condition, decision-makers pass it provided at least they can state and adhere to a choice "over the course of its discussion, initiation and implementation."[18] If no more than this modest requirement should be read into the President's Commission's first condition, then I withdraw my charge that the test allows doctors to encroach on the right of self-determination of competent patients. Rather, the President's Commission test would be subject then to the same doubts as I have raised in respect of Tepper and Elwork's — does it allow doctors to exercise their duty to protect certain of their vulnerable patients?

Appelbaum and Grisso

The Appelbaum and Grisso test of capacity requires that a patient reaches a certain standard in each of the following four categories:[19]

(i) communicating choices and maintaining a stable choice long enough for it to be implemented. The ability to express choices is tested by asking a patient who has been informed about a proposed procedure to respond to what he has heard. The stability of the choice is tested by repeating the question several minutes later;

(ii) understanding relevant information which requires a memory for words, phrases, ideas and sequences, intelligence and a reasonable attention span. The patient's ability to remember may be tested by asking him to repeat information, and his ability to understand, by asking him to paraphrase it;

(iii) appreciating the situation and grasping what it signifies for him. Attributes include acknowledging illness when it is shown to be present, evaluating its effect and the treatment prospects and recognising the general probabilities of risks and benefits;

(iv) manipulating information rationally by reaching conclusions which are logically consistent with the starting premises. The patient's chain of reasoning can be examined by asking him to indicate the major factors in his decision, and the importance assigned to them, then assessing whether the outcome generally reflects these factors.

Here, it is just the final condition which seems to me to be unduly taxing. To be sure, simply making sense of choice involves relating it to something wanted by an agent and we might reasonably expect therefore that competent decision-makers could connect their choices to *a* starting premise. But those whose competence is marginal would easily pass this test, requiring only that their choices were intelligible in relation to *something* that they cared about. We understand the motivation of the jilted lover who is intent on suicide as an act of revenge. We understand the 14-year-old boy's revulsion for living the life of an invalid and the elderly person's unwillingness to move into a nursing home. A choice can make sense (be understandable) and yet be unreasonable.

On the other hand, if competent choice must be "logically consistent" not just with a starting premise but with "starting premises" that suggests a much more stringent and complicated test of competence — maybe one which most of us fail in many of our day-to-day choices. At any rate, if competent choice has to pass this test, then any choice which is unwise, for example any acratic choice, demonstrates lack of capacity. On this test we would lose our prerogative to be irrational and doctors would be entitled to force us to diet, to quit smoking and to take regular exercise.

If, as I have argued, none of the versions of the function test that are

reviewed in the Consultation Paper yield clear and satisfactory guidelines for discriminating competence in respect of borderline cases,
should we still persevere in seeking better criteria, or should we
abandon the search as futile?

It seems to me that the search is futile; it is attempting the impossible. Basically, our problem is that the two dominant concerns which
we have been trying to safeguard in our search for criteria require incompatible standards of competency: to protect autonomy we need
lax criteria; to protect vulnerable people we need strict criteria. Any
test of competency which is sufficiently strict to ensure that the vulnerable to whom (I am assuming) we owe a protective duty fail it, is
also too strict for our ordinary acratic selves to pass for competent and
to retain our autonomy — and, therewith, our right to be unwise.

If it is hopeless, then, to rely wholly on criteria of competence to divide those whose refusals should be honoured from those whose refusals should be overriden, might the criteria of competence we
adopt be supplemented in some way that would enable us to justify
paternalism towards the vulnerable but not also towards everyone
who, unrestrained, would make foolish choices? Two candidates
spring to mind: first, we might introduce the notion of retrospective
consent to justify overriding certain refusals; or, secondly we might
argue that respecting people's autonomy does not necessarily mean
complying with their wishes (present or future) and can even neces-
sitate overriding them.

Either of these approaches would allow us to settle for lax criteria
of competency in line with what English law endorses in principle
and both approaches provide a defence for overriding the refusals of
some who would pass the competency test. Both approaches warrant
closer examination than I shall attempt here. I shall merely explain
why I am not sanguine that either approach would really ease the difficulty doctors face with the marginal cases in reconciling their duty to
respect autonomy with their duty to protect the vulnerable.

Retrospective consent

. The appeal to retrospective consent relies on the assumption, surely
reasonable, that on some occasions you are entitled to *presume* that
you have consent for what you are doing. When?

You are sometimes entitled to presume consent when it was formerly given and has not since been withdrawn. There will, of course,
be doubtful cases: you have proposed retiring to bed to make love;

your partner consents but then you are delayed; you linger to watch a late night film or to have a long chat on the telephone with a friend. When eventually you join your partner are you entitled to presume that the consent still holds?

You are sometimes entitled to presume that you have tacit consent although it is neither explicitly given nor sought. Consider, for example, what liberties you consider yourself entitled to take when staying as a guest in a friend's house. There are all sorts of things which you are obviously entitled to do without asking — but again, some doubtful cases: you may help yourself to a drink of water but, of wine? You do not need permission to use the toilet but, the telephone?

As we have already noted, you are entitled to presume consent in an emergency when it is obvious that it would have been forthcoming — as if you break into your neighbour's flat to rescue their cat from a flood. In this case we might say you can justify your presumption on the ground that you know consent *will* be forthcoming, in retrospect — so to speak.

But now, to come to the kind of predicament which concerns us, suppose that the reason why consent cannot be got at the time a decision is taken is not that the people whose consent you presume *can* not then give it but that they *will* not then give it. Can you here too appeal to the notion of retrospective consent on the ground that you know later they would give it and would be grateful for your intervention? Why after all should respecting people's wishes necessarily mean respecting their present over their future (contrary) wishes? The present wish may be a passing (and dangerous) whim.

This justification for paternalist intervention even if legitimate in principle is of limited practical use and no use at all for the kind of cases we are concerned with here. The appeal to retrospective consent only works where you know that consent will be forthcoming later. With cases of marginal competency that is just what you are not in a position to know. And quite apart from the difficulty of predicting patients' later preferences you are not anyway always able to regard later preferences as more authoritative — not, for example, of someone whose mental powers are evidently deteriorating.

Autonomy and consent "in principle"

It may be said that you do not infringe people's autonomy although you act without their actual consent and without realistic prospects of retrospective consent provided only that you act in a manner to which they could consent "in principle", i.e. without deception or coercion.[20] But if we were to allow doctors to override their patients' refusals provided merely they could consent in principle although they did not consent in fact, we would deny our acratic selves any defence against our doctors' reasonable but unwelcome exhortations.

Your doctor, let us suppose, advises you to have a lump investigated — there is a risk of malignancy. But you have a horror of hospitals and surgery — unreasonable, though, maybe, given your past experiences, understandable. Anyway, you point-blank refuse. You *could*, of course, consent without deception or coercion. The point is that in the absence of deception or coercion you do not consent and you are within your rights; no matter that the advice your doctor is giving you is exactly the advice that any responsible doctors would give.

In short, if we were to supplement a lax criterion of competency with reliance on this excuse for intervention we would be protecting the vulnerable to whom protection is owed, at the expense of our acratic selves who have the right to choose unwisely.

Conclusion

Maybe further study of what respect for autonomy entails might yield a better test which doctors could apply to the marginal cases. Meanwhile, I submit that mere refinements of the function test will not serve to protect the vulnerable while safeguarding the rights of the non-vulnerable foolish. Nor is it obvious how function tests might be supplemented to help doctors in handling these difficult cases.

References

1. No. 119 (London: HMSO, 1991). [Editor's note: see now, Law Commission's Consultation Papers, *Mentally Incapacitated Adults and Decision-Making: A New Jurisdiction* (No. 128) and *Mentally Incapacitated Adults and Decision-Making: Medical Treatment and Research* (No.129) — adopting a 'functional' or 'cognitive' test of competence.]
2. On Liberty, In John Stuart Mill, *Utilitarianism, Liberty and Representative Government* (London and Toronto: Dent, 1910) at 152.
3. *Op cit*, para 2.10 at 20.
4. *Op cit*, para 2.10 at 20.
5. *Ibid*.
6. *Op cit*, para 7.4 at 181.

7. *Op cit*, para 2.43 at 50.
8. *Op cit*, para 2.44 at 52.
9. *Ibid.*
10. *Ibid.*
11. A. M. Tepper and A. Elwork, "Competence to Consent to Treatment as a Psychological Construct" (1984) 8 *Law and Human Behavior* 205.
12. See *Law Commission Consultation Paper* No. 119, para 2.40 at 49.
13. See *U.S.A. President's Commission for the Study of Ethical Problems in Medicine and Biomedical and Behavioural Research, Making Health Care Decisions — A Report on the Ethical and Legal Implications of Informed Consent in the Patient–Practitioner Relationship,* Vol 1, (1982).
14. See P. S. Appelbaum and T. Grisso, "Assessing Patients' Capacities to Consent to Treatment (1988) 319 *New England Journal of Medicine* 1635.
15. Cited in *Law Commission Consultation Paper* No. 119, para 2.41 at 49–50.
16. Allen E. Buchanan and Dan W. Brock, *Deciding For Others* (Cambridge: Cambridge University Press, 1989) at 23.
17. *Op cit*, at 25.
18. *Ibid.*
19. Cited in *Law Commission Consultation Paper* No. 119 at 47–48.
20. For an account of respect for persons as requiring only that we treat others in ways to which they could consent in principle see Onora O'Neill "A Simplified Account of Kant's Ethics" in Tom Regan, (ed) *Matters of Life and Death* (New York: McGraw Hill, 1986).

The sterilisation of the mentally disabled: competence, the right to reproduce and discrimination

Will Cartwright

In recent years there have been a number of important cases in which the courts have had to consider applications to sterilise mentally incompetent women and girls. The applicants have typically claimed that the sterilisation would be in the woman's best interests because she could not cope with, perhaps would even barely understand, the processes of pregnancy and child-rearing. Furthermore the immunity from these things conferred by sterilisation would permit her a degree of social freedom that it would not otherwise be prudent for her to have because of the risks of pregnancy. The courts have often allowed such applications and these decisions have generated moral controversy. I shall explore some of the moral and philosophical issues raised by these cases.[1]

Competence

Sterilisation involves a considerable bodily intrusion and the loss of an important capacity, but if a competent woman chooses to undergo the procedure most people would now regard this as morally acceptable in appropriate circumstances. It is of course central to the contro-

Decision-Making and Problems of Incompetence. Edited by A. Grubb.

versial legal cases that the women lacked the competence to make an autonomous choice to accept or refuse the procedure. I shall therefore begin with some remarks of a quite general kind about this topic before relating them to sterilisation.[2]

Competence is an all-or-nothing matter; one is either competent to take a decision or one is not. To call it an all-or-nothing matter does not mean that one must be held either competent to take all decisions or competent to take none. This is just one possible view of competence. On another view, however, one can be competent to take some decisions but incompetent to take others. But even on this latter, decision-specific account competence is an all-or-nothing matter: one is either competent or incompetent to take a specific decision.

However, this feature of competence may engender puzzlement. For competence seems to involve, indeed just to be, the possession of certain capacities, such as being able to understand relevant information, to assess probabilities, to reason and deliberate in the light of one's values. These capacities are matters of degree, in that one can possess them to a greater or lesser extent, whereas by contrast competence is an all-or-nothing matter. But how can a state which is all-or-nothing consist of a number of elements which are matters of degree? Is there not an intellectual incoherence here? In the light of this mismatch one might be tempted to wonder whether competence is some further and distinct fact over and above the possession of the capacities in question. But this would be a mistake, or it would be if we were to think of competence as some further natural fact about the person, such that after establishing the level of his capacities further investigation of him was required to establish if he were competent.[3]

The way out of these difficulties is to understand that the notion of competence embodies a socially determined standard. Society has to determine who is to be classified as competent and who as incompetent. These are matters for decision rather than discovery. It is true that the capacities relevant to competence are matters of degree, but there is no incoherence in society stipulating that a person will only be regarded as competent if his capacities match or exceed a certain socially determined threshold. The distinction between competence and incompetence does not mark a natural break in the upward curve of the capacities in question, but is rather a conventional line drawn through the natural continuities of these capacities. These thoughts further enable us to see why it would be a mistake to regard competence as some further natural fact over and above the capacities in question. If competence is a fact at all, it is a social fact, to be determined in the light of a social standard. What this standard should be is initially a matter for decision. Once it is set we can talk about someone's competence being a matter of fact in the sense that he manifestly meets the standard, but the fact is a social rather than a natural one.

The purpose of determinations of competence and incompetence is to distinguish between those people whose decisions will be respected and those whose decisions will not be. Moreover those in the first group are assigned power to take decisions on behalf of those in the second group. These facts invite certain questions. Even if the threshold conception of competence, the all-or-nothing view described above, accurately captures how the notion functions in our social life, does competence have to be conceived like this? Could we not have a notion of competence that admits of degrees? After all, as we have seen, the capacities that constitute competence are themselves matters of degree. On this view people would not just be competent or incompetent, but they would be more or less competent. The exceptionally able would be regarded as more competent than the average, whereas at the moment they are all classified indiscriminately as competent. And if under the current arrangements the competent are empowered to take decisions on behalf of the incompetent, then perhaps under the new dispensation the very able should be empowered to take decisions on behalf of the average, at least in complex matters. The case for the former kind of paternalism seems equally to be a case for the latter kind. Such a system therefore might seem to be fairer as well as more likely to lead to good decisions.[4]

But this reconception of competence is open to a fatal objection. It is hard to see how a competence of degrees could be coherently embodied in social practice. We may be misled by a certain confusion into thinking that it is fairly clear what a system based upon such a conception of competence would look like. We may suppose that in outline the presently incompetent would continue to have decisions taken on their behalf by others whereas, unlike now, the average would have some of the more complex decisions taken on their behalf by the exceptional. But it is crucial to see that this would not be a system of competence by degrees. It would still be a threshold system in which people are adjudged either competent or incompetent to take particular decisions. The thresholds would exhibit more variety than they do now, so that the patterns of competence and incompetence would be more complex, but a threshold system it would remain. But what then would a genuine system of competence by degrees look like? Let us consider a particular type of decision. Then we can discriminate various degrees of competence with respect to it, ranging from low to high. Those of low competence would have decisions of this type taken on their behalf by those above them in the scale, including the average. But then the average would presumably have their decisions taken on their behalf by those further up the scale. But then why were the average included in the decision-making on behalf of those with low competence? One might think that the way out of these difficulties would be to put all decisions of this type into the hands of the highly competent. But then, of course, one has converted the system into a threshold system, with those of high competence being judged competent and everyone else incompetent. The practical need to establish a coherent system for determining who takes what decisions seems to lead unavoidably to a threshold system. These difficulties in envisaging a system of competence by degrees suggest that there is an incoherence in the idea. The notion of competence gains its sense from its role in social life and that role constrains the interpretations that we can put upon it. It seems to exclude an interpretation in terms of degrees and to require a threshold conception. In a similar way the notion of responsibility in virtue of its role in social life is a threshold concept and cannot admit an interpretation of it in terms of degrees. This is, I think, part of the reason why the notion of diminished responsibility in section 2 of the Homicide Act 1957 has struck some as very odd.

But even if a threshold conception of competence is unavoidable, there remain questions to ask. Have we fixed the threshold in the right place? One might think that one could answer this question by reflecting upon the skills required to take the central and common decisions of our social life and judging whether the current threshold ensures an adequate level of these in people who meet it. But it is not as simple as this. This view presupposes that there is some naturally appropriate level at which to fix the threshold, which we have to discover. But, as we have seen, where to fix the threshold requires a decision — a decision that involves balancing certain values against each other. We may fix it at various points, higher or lower, depending upon how we weight the competing values. The higher we place the threshold the better the decisions might seem likely to be, though since an increasing number of the decisions will therefore be taken on behalf of others, this is likely to constrain the rise in the quality of the decisions. How good decisions are is a function, not only of the skill of the decision-maker, but also of the level of his concern. The former would be enhanced, but the latter diminished, by raising the threshold of competence and increasing the number of decisions taken by some on behalf of others. Even if the quality of decisions would be improved on balance by raising the threshold, such an enhancement would be purchased at the price of excluding a larger number of people from control over key aspects of their lives. To lower the threshold, by contrast, would diminish the level of exclusion at the cost of impairing the quality of decisions. A way out of this dilemma might seem to be to rearrange the common tasks of social life to make them less complex and risky. This way the threshold of competence could be lowered, enlarging the class of decision-makers, while at the same time the diminished quality of decisions would not matter since it would be adequate to the new arrangements. But this solution to the one dilemma would merely create another. For making central social activities less complex and risky would lead to an etiolation of social life, an unwelcome thinning of its texture for the competent. The rewards of activities are frequently related to the challenge of their complexity, and the taking of risks has an important place in life. What we have here appears to be an issue of distributive justice: what diminution of the richness of life should the competent be called on to bear in order to enfranchise the incompetent?[5]

It may be prudent here to re-emphasise a point made earlier. I have endorsed a threshold conception of competence, but have raised the question as to whether the current threshold is appropriate. This may foster the impression that competence is a global matter: one is either competent to take all decisions or competent to take none. But this global conception of competence is not entailed by the threshold conception. The latter is quite compatible with the view that the threshold ought to vary with different decisions. But a system of varying thresholds may seem vulnerable to the charge of being excessively complex. This need not be true, however, for even though the thresholds vary, it may still be the case that most people will surpass all these thresholds and thus be globally competent. And equally there will be some people who will fail to reach any of the thresholds and thus be globally incompetent. It is only the group in the middle that will display a complex pattern of competence and incompetence, for the individuals in this group will surpass the thresholds for some decisions but not for others.

I said earlier that where the threshold(s) of competence should be pitched is a matter for decision, a decision that will involve the weighing of fundamental values, but that whether or not someone surpasses that threshold is a matter of fact. However, to say it is a matter of fact puts it too baldly. Though appropriate for those who evidently surpass the threshold and for those who no less evidently do not, it does not do justice to those in the middle who cluster around the threshold and for whom the answer is unclear. Some might hope that science can produce tests of competence which will yield accurate and precise answers. But I think this hope embodies an error. The question of whether or not someone meets the criterion of competence is not a scientific question, but a question of common sense and understanding, and its resolution calls for the exercise of a necessarily imprecise judgment. No doubt scientific tests of such things as cognitive impairment can be vitally helpful, but such tests must be regarded only as aids to judgment rather than as substitutes for it. In this respect determinations of competence are like determinations of responsibility in law. Psychiatric evidence may be crucial in judging someone's responsibility, but ultimately that judgment is one of common sense and understanding, for the concept of responsibility, like that of competence, is not a scientific one, but an informal notion of everyday life. And that is why disagreements about competence and responsibility, which there will inevitably be given the inherent imprecision of these notions, are aptly settled in the end by lawyers and juries rather than by scientists. Competence cannot be determined by scientific tests, therefore, and, more generally, whatever the framework of rules and guidelines with which we surround such determinations, considerable resources of human insight and understanding will be required to make a judgment in the difficult cases. Assessments of competence are thus resistant to routinisation. This is an awkward fact, not just because of the natural tendency of a large medical bureaucracy, like any bureaucracy, to routinise procedures, but also because some will fear that the imprecision of judgments of competence will enable traditional paternalistic attitudes to continue to flourish. But the attempt to curb those attitudes by surrounding competence determinations with an overly precise and directive set of rules will achieve that aim, if it does so, only at the cost of a damaging insensitivity to the nuances of particular patients.

A further factor that adds complexity to judgments of competence in borderline cases is that some patients can be helped to make competent choices. By imaginatively searching for a suitable form in which to convey the relevant information to the patient, by gently helping him to understand and explore the implications of the various options and by displaying a sensitivity to his fears and anxieties, a doctor may help a patient to make a decision that can be regarded as competent when, in the absence of such resourceful assistance, the decision could not reasonably have been so regarded.

When someone is judged to be incompetent to take a particular decision, someone else must decide on his behalf and the issue then arises as to what the basis should be for this surrogate decision. If a patient while competent has made an advance directive as to what should be done if he becomes incompetent, then there is a powerful moral case for respecting such a directive. In the absence of this there are the standards of best interests and substituted judgment as possible bases for the decision. These require that the surrogate decision-maker decide in the best interests of the patient or decide as the patient would have decided had he been competent. In order for this latter standard to get a purchase on the situation there must be some evidence about the patient's values and preferences from which to infer what his decision would have been. But this condition may not be fulfilled, either because the patient was never competent and therefore never formed the necessary values and preferences or because, though he did once have such things, there is now insufficient evidence as to what they were. In circumstances like these the "best interests" test seems the appropriate ground for the surrogate decision.

In the cases of an advance directive and the substituted judgment test attention is paid to the patient's decision, past in the former case, hypothetical in the latter. But even in applying the "best interests" test account can and should be taken of any rudimentary decision and preference of the patient. Such decision and preference may be too uncomprehending and unconsidered to found any judgment as to what he would have decided if competent, but nevertheless be factors to be taken into account, along with others, in determining the patient's best interests. For example, an incompetent patient's refusal of a recommended treatment is plausibly to be assigned more weight than his acceptance of it. To treat despite such a refusal is a more serious matter than not to treat despite an acceptance of the treatment. In many cases such a refusal may be decisive. This is not to abandon the "best interests" test and to allow that the patient is competent to refuse, if not to accept, the recommended treatment. As long as the refusal is just one element in determining the patient's best interests, albeit sometimes a decisive one, and is not in principle determinative of the issue, the "best interests" test continues to be applied.

Let me now draw these remarks on competence together. As we have seen competence is an all-or-nothing matter that rests upon the possession of capacities to take decisions which can vary in degree. To possess these capacities is to possess autonomy, which also therefore varies in degree. Philosophers have thought a good deal about the nature of autonomy, but they have been principally interested in articulating the elements of full autonomy and the implications of the moral requirement to respect it. They have reflected much less on the nature of partial autonomy and on what it would be to respect that. The incompetent include not only those who more or less completely lack autonomy, but also those with seriously diminished autonomy. Some of the principal points that I have made about competence may thus be thought of as elements in an adequate account of what it is to respect the partially autonomous and I summarise them accordingly.

First, the threshold of competence must be fixed in a place that is consistent with justice. A threshold that is pitched too high will constitute an injustice to the partially autonomous. Secondly, when a threshold has been fixed, sensitivity and judgment are required to determine whether a partially autonomous person meets this threshold, or perhaps could be helped to meet it. To fail to display these qualities is a failure of respect. And thirdly, once it has been determined that a partially autonomous person is not competent, the requirement to respect them nevertheless means that some account must be taken of their decisions and preferences in assessing their best interests, if this is the appropriate test. Whether or not the partially autonomous persons who have been the subject of the sterilisation decisions have had their partial autonomy adequately respected is an arguable matter. It has been suggested that the application of the label "mentally handicapped" has led the courts rather too quickly to assume that the subjects lacked competence, and not to think sufficiently about the possibility that with imaginative handling they might have been enabled to decide competently for themselves.[6] This, if true, would constitute a failure to comply with the second of the points mentioned above. If this point is not being observed in the cases that come to court, it would be very surprising if the same was not true in the many cases that do not.[7] And even if the subjects of the legal cases were properly judged to be incompetent, some account should have been taken, in assessing their best interests, of any rudimentary preferences concerning the sterilisation that they may have had.

The right to reproduce and discrimination

The courts decided the sterilisation cases on the basis of the best interests of the incompetents; others have argued that they should have been decided in terms of the patients' rights.[8] I shall explore a right that has been mentioned both in the cases and in discussions of them — the right to reproduce.

If there is a right to reproduce, its scope is contentious. Since reproduction no longer occurs only by sexual intercourse, should the right cover the use of non-coital techniques between a couple such as *in vitro* fertilisation and artificial insemination? Should it extend to enlisting the assistance of a third party donor or surrogate to provide the gametes or uterine function necessary for the couple to acquire a child genetically related to one of them? Whatever the answer to these questions, something that is rather clearer is that the right to reproduce cannot be thought of just as a right to beget or bear children. For this would mean that a couple who have a child and then put it up for adoption have exercised their right to reproduce. But rights are meant to protect important human interests and whatever interests are satisfied by this bare sort of reproduction, surely other and deeper interests are normally thought to underlie the right to reproduce. The interests in question are surely the ones satisfied by parenthood, for it is very widely supposed that becoming a parent is a central and deeply fulfilling human experience. The right to reproduce is best understood then, not simply as the right to beget or bear children, but as the right to beget or bear and rear children.

An objection that has been made against a right to reproduce is that reproduction requires the cooperation of another person who is under no obligation to provide it.[9] If we stick to the uncontentious case of reproduction by sexual intercourse, the right to reproduce does not entail that I can insist that someone cooperate with me for reproductive purposes. But that does not mean that there can be no right to reproduce. The right will be a right to reproduce with a willing partner. The fact that the act-type which specifies the content of the right is not just reproducing, but the more complex reproducing-with-a-willing-partner, does nothing to undermine its status as a right. This just shows that it is a liberty-right rather than a claim-right.

If there is a right to reproduce, however, there are two constraints on it which mean that many of those who are the subject of sterilisation decisions will lack it. The first constraint is that one cannot have a right to act in a certain way if through a fundamental lack of understanding one is incapable of acting in that way or, at least, of choosing to do so. To act is not just to move one's body; it is also to have a certain understanding of what one is about in so doing. To act therefore requires not just an ability to move the body, but also certain conceptual resources. Thus a monkey is incapable of casting a vote even though it might go through the appropriate bodily motions of marking a ballot paper in the correct manner. The reason is that it lacks the resources of understanding needed to see itself as casting a vote; in particular, it lacks the concept of voting and, more generally, the complex conceptual setting in which that notion is embedded. Since it cannot understand itself as voting, it cannot vote and therefore can have no right to vote. Now let us consider a parallel argument in the case of reproduction. Imagine a woman who does not understand the nature of sexual intercourse and its causal connection with conception, what it is to be pregnant and to give birth, and the nature of parenthood. Despite this lack of understanding we would have to allow, I think, that the woman can perform the action of reproducing herself, in the sense that she can get pregnant, bear the child and even perhaps act in a minimal way as a parent to it. This case is not then parallel to the monkey example. But although she can reproduce, the woman's lack of understanding prevents her from reproducing intentionally or out of choice. To choose to act in a certain way does require one to understand, minimally, what bodily movements would count as performing the action. This incapacity to choose the act in question is just as fatal to the right to do it as the incapacity to perform the act at all. For the function of liberty rights, of which the right to reproduce is arguably an example, is to secure to people the freedom to choose to engage in certain activities.

It would be a mistake, however, to infer from this that all liberty rights are designed to protect just one value, that of choice, because underlying such rights is also a sense of the fundamental value of the various activities which liberty rights give one a choice to engage in. What liberty rights protect is not just choice in and of itself, nor performing certain actions, but, compositely, performing those actions out of choice. Thus the right to reproduce protects not just the activity of reproduction, but engaging in it out of choice. A woman who can reproduce uncomprehendingly, but who through lack of understanding is incapable of doing so out of choice, thus lacks the right to reproduce, and this will no doubt apply to some of the women who are the subject of sterilisation decisions.

This is perhaps the point, or at any rate one of them, underlying

Lord Hailsham's remarks in *Re B (a minor) (wardship: sterilisation)*: "To talk of the 'basic right' to reproduce of an individual who is not capable of knowing the causal connection between intercourse and childbirth, the nature of pregnancy, what is involved in delivery, unable to form maternal instincts or to care for a child appears to me wholly to part company with reality."[10] Elsewhere in his judgment he puts the point more explicitly: "But this right [of a woman to reproduce] is only such when reproduction is the result of informed choice of which this ward is incapable."[11] And Lord Oliver made a similar remark in the same case: "But the right to reproduce is of value only if accompanied by the ability to make a choice and in the instant case there is no question of the minor ever being able to make such a choice or indeed to appreciate the need to make one."[12] These remarks have led some commentators to conclude that there is no right to reproduce in English law, but only a right to choose to do so.[13] This conclusion does not, I think, follow and is a potentially misleading way of capturing the good point discussed above. That point is that one cannot have the right to reproduce unless one has sufficient conceptual grasp to enable one to choose to reproduce, but it does not follow that the right to reproduce is a right only to choose to do so. If the right in question was only the right to choose to reproduce, this would mean that if I chose to reproduce and someone then prevented me from actually reproducing, my right would not have been violated. But we would surely think that it had been, and this suggests that the right in question is actually to reproduce, not simply to choose to do so. It is true that the action protected by this right is an action that is chosen, but it misstates this fact to say that the right in question is simply a right to choose to do this action. The objects of our liberty rights are actions, not choices, although the actions in question issue from choices.

One of the constraints on the right to reproduce is then the possession of a certain minimal conceptual competence. But, as I said earlier, there is a second constraint relevant to the sterilisation cases. Those who choose to procreate incur obligations towards their offspring. What those obligations are exactly is a matter for debate, but we might say in general terms that parents have an obligation to do whatever is minimally required to equip their children to lead independent adult lives in the society in question.[14] This obligation may be thought to constrain the right to reproduce and thus those who are unable or unwilling to comply with the obligation will lack the right. This is perhaps the other point underlying the remarks cited earlier of

Lord Hailsham in *Re B*. As I have suggested, some of his observations there are best explained as pointing to a certain level of understanding as a precondition of a right to reproduce. But he also talks of inability "to form maternal instincts or to care for a child" and suggests that to assign a right to reproduce to someone with these inabilities (and the others) is "wholly to part company with reality".[15] However, these inabilities are rather different from the conceptual limitations referred to, although they may be thought to be just as fatal to a right to reproduce as those limitations. But the reason that they are fatal to that right is that they infringe the second constraint on the right, not the first. People with these inabilities will be unable to meet the minimal requirement of parenthood, which is to equip a child to lead an independent adult life. Once again those who are the subject of sterilisation decisions may lack a right to reproduce for this reason too.[16]

However, this claim is open to two objections. One way of stating the point made in the last paragraph is that parents who are unable to bring up their children in a minimally adequate manner wrong them by giving them life. As John Stuart Mill remarked in *On Liberty*:

> The fact itself, of causing the existence of a human being, is one of the most responsible actions in the range of human life. To undertake this responsibility — to bestow a life which may be either a curse or a blessing — unless the being on whom it is to be bestowed will have at least the ordinary chances of a desirable existence, is a crime against that being.[17]

Some argue, however, that this is a philosophically incoherent view, because one can neither harm someone nor indeed benefit him by conferring life upon him. If therefore the argument made in the last paragraph is that parents, unable to bring up children adequately, lack the right to reproduce because by doing so they would harm their offspring, then the argument fails. This is the first of the two objections.

In assessing this objection let us consider a case in which the parents have conferred a life that is not worth living on their offspring. This is perhaps more likely to arise from the inheritance of a major disability than from the incompetence of the parent to raise the child. In this case it would seem clear that the child has been harmed by being given a life that he would be better off without. However, this has been contested. It has been said that to make such a judgment requires a comparison between the child's present life and non-existence and that such a comparison makes no sense. Non-existence is not a state whose merits can be compared with the disadvantages of life.[18] This is unpersuasive. At the other end of life those contemplating suicide or euthanasia make similar comparisons. They sometimes conclude that being dead would be preferable to continuing with life. I think that these judgments are in order and, if they are, then the judgment that not being conceived would have been preferable to being given this life seems likewise to be in order. But how can such judgments be shown to be coherent? There are perhaps various ways in which this might be done, of which the following is one possibility. We can certainly compare being alive and conscious with being indefinitely unconscious, and in some circumstances we may prefer the latter to the former, if, say, our lives involve unrelieved acute suffering. But from a subjective point of view, from the inside as it were, being indefinitely unconscious is indistinguishable from being dead or never existing, because, precisely, these various states involve the lack of a subjective point of view, an inside. Thus if we can compare being alive with being indefinitely unconscious, it would seem to follow that we can compare being alive with being dead or with never existing.

However, a further difficulty has been alleged. To say that the child has been harmed by being given a life not worth living is to say that it has been made worse off and that it would have been better off if it had not been conceived. But, even assuming the problem of comparison can be overcome, this has been said still to be incoherent. How could the child be better off if it had not been conceived, since if it had not been conceived it would not be around to be better off? The problem is now not one of comparison but of attribution.[19] This problem separates out the case of death from the case of not being conceived. If one concludes that someone would be better off dead, this benefit when realised would be attributable to someone, namely the person who is then dead. This does not commit one to supposing that dead persons remain mysteriously present, but rather to the proposition that past persons can be benefited, or indeed harmed. That this proposition is plausible is attested to by such familiar thoughts as that dead persons can be injured by not having their wills executed. By contrast if someone supposedly would have been better off had they not been conceived, there would have been no subject of that benefit, neither a present nor a past one. A different solution to the attribution problem is thus called for in the case of non-conception from the one applicable in the case of death. It has to do with the logic of harm judgments. It is true that harm is a comparative notion in the sense that to harm someone is to make him worse off than he otherwise would have been. So to say that someone has been harmed by being given a life not worth living seems to entail that he is worse off than if he had not existed and thus that he would have been better off not existing. These entailments indeed do not make sense because of the attribution problem, but the conclusion to draw, I think, is not that the judgment of being harmed by life cannot therefore be made, but that in this sort of case judgments of harm do not have these entailments. In most cases judgments of harm are comparative, but this is no ordinary case of harm. Life is the precondition of most harms, but in this case life itself is the harm. In this special case judgments of harm might be expected to behave differently, and they do so by not being comparative. If someone has been given a life not worth living, he has been harmed, but it does not follow that he has been made worse off or that he would have been better off if not conceived. A judgment that someone has been harmed by being given such a life can coherently be made therefore.[20]

Having considered the case where the life conferred on the child is not worth living, let us now consider the case where the life is worth living but involves considerable disadvantages. Let us suppose that a woman of moderate disability produces a child whom she is incapable of bringing up adequately. Has she harmed the child by giving it this life? It looks as though this must be so if we are to sustain the claim that she has no right to reproduce in these circumstances. But here we run into further difficulties. Since the life is worth living and preferable to non-existence, there is to this extent no harm in being given it. Perhaps the harm resides in the fact that the life conferred is less desirable than one without the disadvantages of an incompetent parent. But the parent could only be accused of harming the child in this way if she had been able to confer that more desirable life, and in the nature of the case she lacked that ability. For the child, then, the only available life was the one he has got with the disadvantages of an incompetent parent. It was either that life or nothing, and since the life he has got is worth living, it does not seem that he was harmed by being given that life.[21] This means that if we wish to retain the judgment that children should not be born in these circumstances and that people have no right to reproduce so as to give birth to them, then rather surprisingly it cannot be based upon a concern for the children, who are not harmed by having life conferred on them in such circumstances. At this point we may be tempted to abandon a rather plausible moral principle: that if something is bad, it must be bad for someone. Perhaps things can be bad in a more impersonal way. It may be bad in this sense that parents produce children whom they are incapable of rearing adequately, even though it is not bad for the children. This judgment may be enough to sustain the claim that people have no right to reproduce in these circumstances. It may be thought, however, that if people are denied a right to reproduce in these circumstances at the behest of these impersonal values, then not only will their wishes be contravened, if they want to have children, but the children they would have will be denied worthwhile, though disadvantaged, lives. One might then wonder whether these impersonal values are being assigned too much weight. But there is a confusion in this. The children are not being denied worthwhile lives because they do not exist and so cannot be deprived of anything. No one is harmed by being denied existence, although one can be harmed by being given it.

This concludes the discussion of the first objection to the claim that those who are incapable of bringing up their children in a minimally adequate way have no right to reproduce. If the lives they confer on their children are not worth living, they harm them. If the lives are worth living, but otherwise disadvantaged through their incompetence, they do not harm the children, but there are more impersonal considerations for objecting to what they do. Either way they have no right to reproduce.

Let us turn to the second objection. If a capacity to rear children in a minimally adequate way is a requirement of the right to reproduce, what is the standard of adequacy here? And whatever it is, our arrangements for enforcing that standard have struck some as erratic. Thus those who wish to adopt or foster children are subjected to a stringent prior screening process to ensure that they are suitable, as are infertile people who seek assistance with conception from infertility clinics.[22] By contrast, no such preliminary vetting process is applied to those who have children in the normal way, although they may lose their children, once they have them, for inadequate parenting. John Harris has argued that these arrangements are both inconsistent and discriminatory.[23] The structures for advance assessment of prospective parents in the areas of adoption, fostering and infertility suggest a degree of concern for the quality of parenting which is hardly apparent in the more relaxed regime of retrospective assessment of natural parents. Moreover these arrangements discriminate unfairly against the infertile and those who wish to adopt and foster because they make becoming a parent unwarrantably more difficult for them than it is for other people. Harris argues that consistency and justice require that we should either scrutinise all prospective parents in advance, allowing only those who pass the test to become parents, or we should scrutinise none in advance, allowing anyone to become a parent and removing children from them only if they prove manifestly inadequate to the task. Harris favours the latter option; others have argued for the former option in the shape of a licensing system.[24]

In assessing Harris's view it is worth observing a distinction that he himself does not draw clearly. It is one thing that in some areas of parenting we deploy advance assessment whereas for the rest the assessment is retrospective; it is a further thing that, as appears to be the case, the standards applied in advance assessment are more stringent than those applied in retrospective assessment. In addition to the cases of adoption, fostering and infertility Harris refers to an example of a disabled person being held to standards for parenting that are higher than normal, and this brings me to what I have called above the second objection.[25] If mentally disabled people are to be denied a right to reproduce on the ground of incapacity to meet the standard of minimally adequate parenting, then we need an account of what that standard is and we must be vigilant to ensure that the standard applied in their case is no more demanding than that applied in the case of ordinary parents. To tighten the standard surreptitiously, as some might think we sometimes do, would be a form of discrimination against the handicapped.

I shall say nothing about what the minimal standard is or ought to be, but will only address the discrimination point, and I shall do so through a consideration of the wider issues that Harris raises. The differential arrangements that he criticises are more defensible than he allows. The cases of adoption and fostering have two features which the situation of ordinary parenting lacks. First, there is a choice of parents and in the light of this it would seem at least permissible, and maybe even obligatory, to apply higher standards to the prospective parents. Secondly, there is a child in existence to be fostered or adopted and to place it with parents who are only minimally adequate rather than with good parents will be to harm it, or at least to fail to benefit it, in a significant way. By contrast, in the case of normal parenting a child born to minimally adequate parents has not been harmed thereby because that was the only life available to it. It was either born to those parents or it was not born at all. In the case of the child placed with only minimally adequate foster or adoptive parents a better alternative was available to it, namely placement with good foster or adoptive parents, and so it can coherently be said to have been harmed, or at least not benefited, by the placement. This is a recurrence of an issue discussed under the first objection above. These two features of the adoption and fostering cases may be thought to warrant the more demanding regime that applies to them, a regime of advance rather than retrospective assessment and one moreover that employs higher standards.[26]

Neither of these features applies in the case of infertile people seeking assistance with conception. Are there other grounds that warrant the more demanding regime applied to them? One line of argument might be as follows. The infertile need the assistance of others in order to procreate, but arguably they have no right to that assistance. If there is a right to procreate, it is not a welfare right, a right that others assist one in procreating. Rather it is a liberty right, a right to procreate with willing others. As the infertile have no right to assistance in reproducing, others are under no obligation to supply it. They are free to render such assistance if they wish, and in the exercise of this discretion they may properly decide to help some rather than others, to help those who will be good parents and not those who will be only minimally adequate. On this view a community might properly limit infertility treatment to those judged likely to be good parents. Some will think this an adequate justification for a system of advance rather than retrospective assessment, that employs more than ordinarily demanding standards.

Let us return to the case of the mentally disabled. In deciding whether or not to sterilise such individuals consideration must be given to the question of whether they could be minimally adequate parents. In so far as the disability raises a doubt about the capacity of the person to be a parent, an assessment that is prospective rather than retrospective is justified, but is there any case for applying standards of assessment that are more stringent than usual? None of the features that justified this in the case of adoption, fostering and infertility is present here. We are clearly not dealing with a case where the children already exist nor do the disabled normally require assistance with procreation. So it would seem that there is no ground for raising the standards in the case of the disabled, and that to do so would be a form of discrimination against them. Nonetheless there may be a tendency for the standards unwittingly to be raised in such cases, because the professionals involved may be unwilling to acknowledge, or reluctant to remember, just how minimal the standards are that apply to other people. An interesting example of this is the case of Mary, which concerned abortion rather than sterilisation.[27] Mary was a 17-year-old mentally disabled girl with an IQ of 45, who was found to be pregnant. Her case was discussed at the weekly meeting of the general practice where she was a patient. Her situation was described by a trainee general practitioner who was present at the meeting as follows:

> Here was an unsupported, mentally handicapped girl, who had become pregnant unwittingly, staying with an elderly couple in appalling housing conditions. Under those circumstances it seemed impossible that Mary would be able to look after her baby and it was likely that it would be taken into care. The feeling of the meeting was that the trauma of having a termination was likely to be less painful and damaging to Mary than the seemingly inevitable separation from her child after it had been born.[28]

Accordingly it was decided that an abortion would be the appropriate solution. It is a striking feature of the case that the precise extent of Mary's disability was not really known nor, so far as one can see, seriously investigated. It was just clear that she was of low intelligence. But as John Harris comments:

> If appalling housing conditions, low intelligence and lack of support were established as general criteria for disqualifying parents the world would soon become depopulated.[29]

The suggestion is clearly that Mary was being disqualified from parenthood on grounds that do not debar other would-be parents and that she was thus being held to a higher standard than normal. Perhaps the normal standard should be higher than it is, but as long as it remains what it is we treat the disabled unjustly if we demand more of them.

If the standard should be raised, it should be raised for all and not just for the disabled. But perhaps the standard should be lowered. When discussing competence to take decisions, I pointed out that where to fix the threshold of competence requires a decision balancing certain values. Lowering the threshold would enlarge the number of people who control their own lives. Similarly where to fix the threshold of parental competence involves a weighing of competing values. To lower it would have the advantage of admitting a larger number of people to this central human activity, but at a cost of lowering the quality of parenting. A more attractive suggestion, which would secure the advantage without incurring the cost, would be to leave the threshold where it is, but to help the mentally disabled reach it, if they need help to reach it, by providing them with assistance in parenting. Thus if a disabled parent has a supportive family prepared to help in rearing the child, then the normal minimum standard of parenting could be met. This sharing of parental tasks would be nothing new. Many parents have historically delegated or transferred some or all of their tasks to nurses, governesses, boarding schools and au pair girls, to mention just a few of the possibilities. Although the right to reproduce requires compliance with some minimal standard of parenting, it does not require that the rearing be done solely, or even perhaps at all, by the natural parent. What it does require, however, is that those parents unwilling to rear the child, wholly or even in part, should make arrangements for it to be reared adequately by others.[30] Similarly for those unable to rear a child on their own, such as the mentally disabled, the requirements of the right to reproduce can nevertheless be satisfied if adequate arrangements exist for others to help with the rearing. But suppose the mentally disabled person has no family or others willing and able to help with the rearing of a child; should society provide that assistance through its social agencies? It can be argued that it should. A widely shared principle of justice is that of equality of opportunity. As applied to the mentally disabled, the principle would seem to imply that, if through assistance we can bring within their grasp opportunities that others take for granted, then in justice we should do this. This would seem to be the principle rather naturally underlying the current efforts to secure a sexual life to disabled persons, and in a similar way it would seem to require supportive efforts to bring parenting within their grasp. However, this conclusion does not sit well with the proposition considered earlier that society has no obligation to help the infertile become parents. If the principle of equality of opportunity requires assistance in the one case, why not in the other?

Conclusion

The sterilisation cases which have come before the courts have focused attention on two distinct types of competence; namely, to take decisions and to be a parent. One critic of the legal decisions has suggested that the courts have tended to assume rather than to establish an incompetence to take decisions,[31] and the case of Mary suggests that health care professionals sometimes have a like tendency to assume rather than to establish an incompetence to be a parent.[32] Such tendencies — to assume vital things about the mentally disabled — are one way of failing to respect them. Such respect requires us to think more openly and imaginatively than perhaps we do about how we might help some of them to achieve both kinds of competence.

Notes and references

1. For an account of the cases see J. K. Mason and R. A. McCall-Smith, *Law and Medical Ethics*, 3rd edn (London: Butterworths, 1991), at 85–95. For more detail see I. Kennedy and A. Grubb, *Medical Law: Text and Materials* (London: Butterworths, 1989), at 312–330, 595–606A.

2. For a helpful recent study of this topic, to which I am indebted, see A. Buchanan and D. Brock, *Deciding for Others: The Ethics of Surrogate Decision Making*, (Cambridge: Cambridge University Press, 1989).

3. These problems about competence resemble to some degree the well-known philosophical issue of personal identity. If you want to hold me responsible for something that I did twenty years ago, what are the grounds for holding that I am the same person as the agent who did the act then, altered no doubt in certain respects but nevertheless the same person? A favoured suggestion is that there are psychological continuities between me now and the agent who performed the act — continuities of memory, character and conviction. But we now run into difficulties. Personal identity is an all-or-nothing thing — either I am the same person or I am not — whereas psychological continuities are matters of degree, so how could the latter be criteria of the former? If, in order to avoid these difficulties, we suggest that personal identity is some further and distinct fact over and above these continuities, then it looks a suspiciously mysterious one. See D. Parfit, "Personal Identity" (1971) 80 *Philosophical Review* 3.

4. D. Wikler, "Paternalism and the Mildly Retarded" (1978–9) 8 *Philosophy and Public Affairs* 377.

5. *Ibid.*

6. M. Brazier, "Sterilisation: Down the Slippery Slope?" (1990) 6 *Professional Negligence* 25.

7. J. K. Mason and R. A. McCall-Smith, *op cit*, at 93, reference should be made to evidence from C. Dyer ((1987) 294 *British Medical Journal* 1219) to the effect that some dozens of mentally disabled minors are sterilised each year in England and Wales by parent–physician decision.

8. I. Kennedy *Treat Me Right* (Oxford: Clarendon Press, 1990), ch 20.

9. J. K. Mason and R. A. McCall-Smith, *op cit*, at 89.

10. [1987] 2 All ER 206 at 213.

11. *Ibid*, at 212. The case involved an application to make the 17-year-old girl, who was the subject of the sterilisation issue, a ward of court.
12. *Ibid*, at 219.
13. A. Grubb and D. Pearl, "Sterilisation and the Courts" [1987] CLJ 439 at 448; J. K. Mason and R. A. McCall-Smith, *op cit*, at 90.
14. O. O'Neill, "Begetting, Bearing and Rearing" in *Having Children* (ed O. O'Neill and W. Ruddick) (New York: Oxford University Press, 1979) at 25.
15. *Supra*, at 213.
16. Perhaps people also lose the right to reproduce if they run a significant risk of passing a serious genetic defect on to any children. Such a risk was sometimes alluded to in the sterilisation cases.
17. Penguin Books, 1984, at 179.
18. D. Heyd, *Genethics* (Berkeley: University of California Press, 1992), ch 1.
19. *Ibid*.
20. D. Parfit, *Reasons and Persons* (Oxford: Clarendon Press, 1984), Appendix G.
21. D. Parfit, *ibid*, ch 16; M. Bayles, "Harm to the Unconceived" (1975–6) 5 *Philosophy and Public Affairs* 292; G. Kavka, "The Paradox of Future Individuals" (1982) 11 *Philosophy and Public Affairs* 93.
22. See the Human Fertilisation and Embryology Act 1990 s. 13(5) and the Code of Practice published by the Human Fertilisation and Embryology Authority, paras 3.10–3.27.
23. J. Harris, *The Value of Life* (London: Routledge and Kegan Paul, 1985), at 50–5.
24. H. Lafollette, "Licensing Parents" (1979–80) 9 *Philosophy and Public Affairs* 182.
25. J. Harris, *op cit*, at 153–4; "Case Conference. Making up her mind: consent, pregnancy and mental handicap" (1983) 9 *Journal of Medical Ethics* 219. See Commentary 2 by J. Harris at 222.
26. An example of these higher standards is reported in the press even as I write. The British Agencies for Adoption and Fostering (BAAF) are recommending that children under the age of 2 should not be placed for adoption or fostering in households with smokers because they are at particular risk from passive smoking. See *The Independent*, 25 March 1993, p. 5. By contrast, people who have children in the ordinary way are evidently not in danger of losing their children because someone in the household smokes. In justifying the recommendation the director of BAAF referred to the fact that the placement agencies have a choice: "there are four to five couples for every baby and for every suitable couple who smokes there will be a suitable couple who are non-smokers". As I have suggested, such a choice is part of the justification for imposing higher standards on adoptive than on normal parents, although it is a further question what those standards should be and whether they should include a provision about smoking. The BAAF recommendation was criticised by Tim Yeo,

Under-Secretary of State for Health, for introducing "dogma or ideology" into adoption, and it was the subject of a satirical editorial in the edition of *The Independent* referred to, p 27.

27. See "Case Conference" cited at note 25.
28. *Ibid*, p. 219.
29. *The Value of Life*, at 153–4.
30. O'Neill, *op cit*, at 27–8.
31. See note 6.
32. See note 27.

Decision-making and the sterilisation of incompetent children

Mylène Beaupré

Introduction

For centuries, philosophers have argued the necessary relationship between man and his freedom. John Stuart Mill in *On Liberty*[1] states that the only freedom which deserves the name is that of pursuing our own good in our own way. The concept of freedom may indeed be understood as having independent control over the course of our own lives. One basic means a person uses to exercise her freedom is to determine what is going to be done to her body. Such is the essence of a right to bodily integrity.

Medical procedures are invasive of one's bodily integrity. The right to bodily integrity is protected in law by the tort of battery. English medical law recognises a patient's right to bodily integrity through the doctor's duty to obtain his patient's consent to treatment.[2] Incompetent children, however, are deemed incapable in law to enter a valid consent to medical treatment.

This chapter examines the current legal justification for the sterilisation of incompetent children in England and Wales. It seeks to assess whether this justification serves to protect the well-being of incompetent children, through a comparison with the Canadian situation.[3]

Decision-Making and Problems of Incompetence. Edited by A. Grubb.
© 1994 John Wiley & Sons Ltd.

Decision-making, medical procedures and incompetent children

Under English law, if a doctor holds the opinion that a sterilisation procedure[4] is in an incompetent child[5] patient's best interests, he may proceed with the operation, provided he receives permission from the child's parents[6] or, if the child is a ward of court, from the High Court. It is through the need to obtain this permission that the incompetent child's right to bodily integrity is protected.

Three agents may therefore be involved in the decision-making process whether to sterilise an incompetent child: the doctor, the child's parents and, possibly, the High Court. Initially, it is necessary to raise three questions regarding general medical procedures and incompetent children.

What legal criteria limit a doctor in the exercise of his authority to determine whether a particular medical procedure is appropriate for his incompetent child patient?

Doctors owe their patients a duty of care. They are required to act in their patient's best interests. The "Bolam test"[7] was adopted by the House of Lords[8] as determinative of the doctor's duty of care in the tort of negligence. The "Bolam test" defines the doctor's duty in terms of the reasonable doctor: he exercises his professional authority in law if he holds the opinion that it is in his patient's best interests to undergo a particular medical procedure, and such an opinion would also be held by a body of medical doctors placed in similar circumstances.[9]

The House of Lords has handed over to the medical profession the legal determination of the scope of the doctor's duty of care in the tort of negligence.[10] It is the medical profession's opinion that limits a doctor's authority to determine the best interests of his incompetent child patient.

What legal criteria guide parents in the exercise of their authority to determine whether to authorise a particular medical procedure upon their incompetent child?

Parents also owe a duty of care towards their incompetent child. Their power to authorise medical treatment on their incompetent child's behalf derives from this duty.[11] They must evaluate whether the proposed treatment is in their incompetent child's best interests. They are expected to weigh the dire consequences of a doctor overriding the incompetent child's right to bodily integrity against the beneficial results of his receiving treatment. What is promotive of their incompetent child's welfare is the parents' guide to the application of the "best interests" test.[12]

What legal criteria guide the High Court in the exercise of its authority to determine whether to authorise a particular medical procedure upon a ward of court or under its inherent jurisdiction?

The High Court is involved in the decision-making process of whether to authorise a medical procedure upon an incompetent child when he is made a ward of court or its inherent jurisdiction is invoked. In practice, this may occur, for example:

1. When a dispute arises between parents and the medical profession regarding the treatment of the incompetent child patient.
2. When it is brought to the attention of a local authority that parents and doctors intend to impose upon an incompetent child a medical treatment with which it disagrees.
3. When the medical treatment sought has so serious implications that it is found necessary for either parents or doctors to seek assistance from the court.[13]

When a child is made a ward of court, no important decision may be taken in his life without consulting the High Court.[14] It follows that any invasive procedure such as a sterilisation ought always to be authorised by the High Court before it is performed upon a ward. In the exercise of its wardship jurisdiction, the High Court seeks to protect the welfare of the child. It acts in what it considers to be the child's best interests, as would an affectionate and wise parent.[15]

The High Court has the last word over the judgment of the ward's parents. It may even supersede the parents' rights and authorise a medical procedure against the parents' wishes. This may occur even if it is the court's opinion that the parents' position is a responsible one.[16] The background to this "distinct" authority could be found within the court's protective jurisdiction over incompetent wards. It is this jurisdiction that enables the court to decide for the child what the parents cannot.[17]

Summary

The "best interests" criterion arises when doctors are involved in the decision-making process whether to recommend a medical procedure be performed upon an incompetent child. Doctors are protected from liability in the tort of negligence if they act in the incompetent child's best interests, as defined by the medical profession.

The "best interests" criterion also arises when permission is sought by doctors, from parents or the High Court, to perform a medical procedure upon an incompetent child. The child's best interests are defined by what promotes his welfare. Although both parents and the High Court are expected to apply the same criteria in their decision-making process, the High Court's authority over the incompetent ward is "distinct" from that of its parents.

In England and Wales, when medical procedures such as sterilisation of incompetent children are considered, it is through the examination of the court's "ultimate" authority in wardship that one measures the level of protection of incompetent children's welfare.

Re Eve[18] and *Re B*:[19] raising the issues

Two cases dealing with the sterilisation of incompetent women were brought to the attention of the courts in the important cases of *Re Eve* and *Re B*. It is relevant to consider both cases together, even if the former concerns an adult and the latter a child. The *parens patriae* jurisdiction under which the Supreme Court of Canada acted in *Re Eve* is comparable with the wardship jurisdiction under which the House of Lords acted in *Re B*.[20]

Re Eve

Eve was a mentally disabled adult. There was concern over the possibility that she might become pregnant. Sterilisation was sought in order to deprive her of the capacity to bear a child.

It was argued that sterilisation would be in Eve's best interests: it would save her from the trauma of giving birth. Also, she would be protected against the resultant obligations regarding her fitness as a parent and her ability to cope with the financial burdens associated with being a parent. Another argument in favour of Eve's sterilisation was to relieve Mrs E (Eve's mother) from the anxiety that Eve might become pregnant and give birth to a child, the responsibility for whom would most probably fall upon Mrs E.

First, the court had no evidence that the effect of giving birth for Eve would be any different from that of any other woman. This reality trumped the "trauma of birth" argument.

Secondly, the court found the purpose for sterilising Eve was non-therapeutic: it was not intended to treat any existing or predictable medical condition. It was the court's opinion that this purpose was a social one that fell outside the court's *parens patriae* jurisdiction.

Finally, it was established that an intervention carried out for the benefit of someone other than the protected person also fell outside the court's *parens patriae* jurisdiction. Hence, Mrs E's anxieties were judged irrelevant to the court's determination of Eve's best interests. The court concluded that there was no danger to Eve's health in not authorising her sterilisation.

In terms of human rights, the court recognised that sterilisation was invasive of an individual's right to bodily integrity. This, of course, is true of any medical procedure. Nonetheless, the court found sterilisation to be a social procedure: except in rare cases, it is not ordinarily performed for the purpose of medical treatment.[21] It is major surgery with related harmful consequences. It is irreversible in that it permanently incapacitates an individual's ability to bear a child.

The court held that the non-therapeutic purpose for a sterilisation, taken with its irreversible and invasive features, could never justify the overriding of an incompetent person's right to bodily integrity.[22]

Re B

B was a mentally disabled child, aged 17. She apparently did not understand and could not learn the causal connection between sexual intercourse, pregnancy and the birth of children. There was a risk that she might become pregnant since she had shown herself vulnerable to sexual approaches. Sterilisation was also sought to prevent her from becoming pregnant. It was argued that sterilisation was in her best interests: first, she was incapable of raising or caring for a child; secondly, she was unable to cope with normal labour, which would render her "distressed, terrified and extremely violent"; and thirdly, a Caesarean section would not be a suitable solution, as having a high pain threshold, she would be likely to pick at the operation wound and tear it open.

The House of Lords rejected the Supreme Court of Canada's distinction in *Re Eve* between a therapeutic and non-therapeutic sterilisation because it was irrelevant and unhelpful to the determination of what would promote a ward's best interests.

In contrast to *Re Eve*, evidence was brought to the attention of the court in *Re B* that normal labour would be more difficult for B than for other women. This evidence, taken together with the fact that B would be unable to care for a child, convinced the Law Lords that sterilisation would be in her best interests.

The House of Lords emphasised that no other consideration than B's best interests were taken into account in their decision-making process. The judges specifically excluded any reference to questions of eugenic theory and sterilisation for social purposes. As in *Re Eve*, the Lords recognised that its powers in wardship were limited to the consideration of what was beneficial to the ward, not to others. Parents' anxieties about their child becoming pregnant could not be taken into account.

In terms of human rights, the House of Lords considered whether B had a right to reproduce. It established that such a right could only be held by an individual capable of choosing whether to exercise it, which was not B's case, since she was permanently incompetent.[23]

Taking the issues further

Sterilisation: a distinct procedure

Sterilisation is not usually performed to treat medical conditions, but rather for contraceptive purposes. It is major surgery with harmful consequences. It is an irreversible procedure in that it permanently incapacitates an individual's ability to bear a child.

With regard to mentally or physically handicapped individuals, or to those who are members of an ethnic minority, sterilisation may still carry with it the emotional overtones linked to the events of recent history, when sterilisation was sometimes performed in the name of eugenics or.for purposes of population control by the state.[24]

Sterilisation is indeed a distinct medical procedure which commands careful consideration, particularly if sought for an incompetent individual.

Therapeutic versus non-therapeutic: a relevant distinction

Various reasons for sterilising incompetent women were considered in both *Re Eve* and *Re B*. They touched on issues of the trauma of birth, fitness to be a parent, ability to cope with the financial burden of caring for a child and parents' anxieties over the thought of having to take responsibility for a future grandchild. In both cases it was made clear that the parents' anxieties fell outside the courts' jurisdiction over the incompetent individual. In LaForest J's opinion, an incompetent individual's best interests were served solely if sterilisation was carried out for therapeutic purposes. He defined therapeutic as that which is necessary for the mental or physical health of the person. He accepted that this included not only injury that has occurred but also injury that is apprehended.[25] In other words: "that which is necessary to preserve life, physical or mental health of the incompetent minor . . . thereby clearly includes anticipated disease, illness, disability or disorder [which] can be demonstrated".[26]

In addition to LaForest J's opinion that issues of fitness to be a parent and financial ability to cope with caring for a child qualified as non-therapeutic, thereby falling outside the courts' *parens patriae* jurisdiction, he emphasised that those questions were value-laden and related to social problems rather than to the issue of benefiting the incompetent person. He insisted that if sterilisation of the mentally incompetent was to be adopted as desirable for general social purposes, the legislature, not the courts, would be the appropriate body to decide.[27]

Curiously, the House of Lords rejected the value of LaForest J's distinction between a therapeutic and a non-therapeutic sterilisation, on the basis that it is meaningless and irrelevant to the correct application of the "best interests" test. It is suggested that the House of Lords misunderstood the meaning intended to be given to therapeutic, interpreting it as solely concerned with an existing malfunction or disease[28] rather than including anticipated health problems.

It is suggested that if LaForest J had been a judge in *Re B*, like the House of Lords, he might have concluded that it was in B's best interests to be sterilised. The evidence that B would be traumatised by normal labour and would be unable to undergo a Caesarean section may have convinced him that sterilisation in her case was therapeutic, and therefore in her best interests.

Ironically, by explicitly rejecting issues of eugenics, social purposes and parental anxieties, the House of Lords did in fact apply the distinction between therapeutic and non-therapeutic to determine B's best interests. By doing so, it was left to consider one sole argument in favour of B's sterilisation: that she would be distressed by normal labour and unable to undergo a Caesarean section. Performing a sterilisation for this purpose undoubtedly qualifies as therapeutic.

It is not sufficient that the House of Lords in practice applied the distinction between therapeutic and non-therapeutic sterilisation. The House of Lords must explicitly recognise it as a general guiding principle in the determination of an incompetent child's best interests.

Rights

In *Re Eve*, LaForest J weighed the dire consequences of overriding Eve's right to bodily integrity against the benefits of treatment. He concluded that because one's right to bodily integrity ranked so high in our scale of values, it was never justified to proceed on non-therapeutic grounds when a sterilisation was contemplated.[29]

In *Re B*, the Lords referred to a right to reproduce rather than to a right to bodily integrity.[30] The Lords rejected the idea that an incompetent individual could have a right to reproduce, which in their opinion was necessarily linked to an ability to choose whether to exercise it.

Whether any individual has a right to reproduce is a contentious matter commanding careful consideration. A right to reproduce could impose not only negative duties upon others not to interfere with the person holding it, but also positive duties. For example, how far can an infertile woman go in claiming her right to reproduce? Must her doctor always act upon her requests for medication, artificial insemination or *in vitro* fertilisation? For how long must he provide such treatments? At what cost?

It is suggested that the sterilisation of incompetent children should be approached in terms of a basic right to bodily integrity rather than in those of a right to reproduce. Every human being, whether competent or not, has a right not to be interfered with unless there is valid justification.[31]

In the case of sterilisation, the invasion of one's bodily integrity is all the more serious in that it is a distinct procedure: it is not usually sought for medical treatment. For some people, it may carry emotional overtones. It is harmful and irreversible. In the exercise of its wardship jurisdiction it is the principle of the court not to risk incurring damage to children which it cannot repair. Rather it seeks to prevent damage being done.[32] This is why the sterilisation of incompetent children ought only to be performed for therapeutic purposes.

Finally, when weighing the dire consequences of overriding an in-

competent child's right to bodily integrity against the benefits of sterilisation, it is suggested that a distinction should be made between
permanently incapacitated and temporarily incapacitated children.
The motives for sterilisation ought to be all the more therapeutic (possibly limited to that which is necessary to save her life) in the circumstances of a child who will eventually become competent. The
damage done to an individual who is unjustifiably denied the preservation of her autonomy is indeed irreparable.

Conclusion

Courts must explicitly recognise the distinction between therapeutic
and non-therapeutic sterilisation as the ultimate means for identifying
an incompetent child's best interests. That a sterilisation procedure
must qualify as therapeutic constitutes the sole guarantee against it
being performed upon an incompetent child for the interest of others
rather than her own.[33] The distinction defines the limit to the court's
jurisdiction over the incompetent ward as acting in its "best interests".

As discussed above, at present if a body of medical doctors supports the value of sterilisation on non-therapeutic grounds, no re-
proach can be made to whoever performs the operation, for he will
be protected in negligence because of the existence of the body of
professional opinion. Neither can parents be criticised for consenting
to the non-therapeutic sterilisation of their incompetent child. Indeed, parents are expected to act as would a court in the exercise of
its wardship jurisdiction, and vice versa.

When sterilisation is sought upon an incompetent child for non-
therapeutic purposes, it is wrong that the decision rest solely within
the clinical judgment of doctors and the good will of parents. Both
parties are ill equipped to deal with issues of how society should care
for those unable to care for themselves. Courts in wardship are no
better at dealing with this matter.[34]

As suggested by LaForest J, if non- therapeutic sterilisation of incompetent children is to be adopted as desirable for general social
purposes, the legislature is the appropriate body to do so. It is society's responsibility to let its members choose when social interests
ought to override those of an individual. When basic human rights are
at stake, not only is this a responsibility but it is also an obligation.

Finally, sterilisation is not the sole means for preventing a permanently incompetent child from becoming pregnant. Less drastic alternatives, such as oral contraceptives, appear too quickly ruled out.

Surely in some cases it must be possible to consider controlling the "future father" rather than focusing solely on the "future mother". Of course to think carefully through alternatives to non-therapeutic sterilisation is time consuming. The exercise demands creativity, imagination and commitment from the part of decision-makers. Is the preservation of an incompetent child's right to bodily integrity not worth this extra effort?

Notes and references

1. J. Berlin, "Two Concepts of Liberty" in *Four Essays on Liberty*, (1969, OUP) 127.
2. *Chatterton* v. *Gerson* [1981] QB 432.
3. This excludes the Province of Québec, whose civil law system is distinct from that of the rest of Canada.
4. For the purposes of this chapter, the sterilisation procedures concerned are those of hysterectomy or tubal ligation.
5. The Family Law Reform Act 1969 section 8(1) establishes a presumption of competence for children aged 16–18 years. The criteria defined by the House of Lords for establishing whether a child under 16 is competent is that he or she be capable of understanding what is proposed and of expressing his/her own wishes (*Gillick* v. *West Norfolk and Wisbech Area Health Authority* [1985] 3 All ER 402 (HL) per Lord Fraser at 409). Even children under 16 may be capable of entering valid consent to treatment. For the purposes of this paper, it is presumed that the child's status of incompetence is not contentious.
6. Or those acting *in loco parentis* such as a local authority. This ought to be taken into consideration whenever parents are discussed in this paper.
7. *Bolam* v. *Friern Hospital Management Committee* [1957] 1 WLR 582.
8. *Re F (a mental patient: sterilisation)* [1990] 2 AC 1.
9. Disagreement within the medical profession about a particular procedure will not affect the legality of the treatment proposed. See A. Grubb and D. Pearl, "Sterilisation — Courts as Decision-Makers" [1989] CLJ 381.
10. *Sidaway* v. *Governors of Bethlam Royal Hospital* [1985] AC 871 at 881 per Lord Scarman.
11. Blackstone's Commentaries 1 B1 Com (17th edn, 1830) at 452.
12. *Gillick* v. *West Norfolk and Wisbech Area Health Authority* [1985] 3 All ER 402 (HL) per Lord Scarman. I. Kennedy and A. Grubb, *Medical Law: Text and Materials* (London: Butterworths, 1989) at 332: "Finally, in making any decision, the criteria the court uses are those which the law expects a parent to use, namely 'best interests' and all this implies."

13. In practice, unless a local authority is already involved with the child's family, it is rarely informed about decisions concerning the child made in private by parents and doctors. Presumably, parents and doctors will usually agree about an incompetent child's best interests. In reality, the opportunities for a court to take part in such decisions are rare.

14. *Re D (a minor) (wardship: sterilisation)* [1976] 1 All ER 326 at 335: "It is quite clear that once a child is made a ward of court, no important decision can be taken in the life of that child without the consent of the Court" (per Heilbron J).

15. *Re B (a minor) (wardship: sterilisation)* [1987] 2 All ER 206 at 212 (HL): "There is no doubt that, in the exercise of its wardship jurisdiction, the first and paramount consideration is the well-being, welfare or interests (each expression occasionally used, but each, for this purpose, synonymous) of the human being concerned, that is the ward himself or herself" (per Lord Hailsham of St Marylebone LC). *Re D* [1976] 1 All ER 326 at 333: "It is of course beyond dispute that the welfare of the child is the paramount consideration, and the court must act in her best interests" (per Heilbron J).

16. *Re B (a minor)* [1981] 1 WLR 1421. The High Court authorised doctors to operate on a Down's syndrome baby, thereby acting against its parents' wishes.

17. See *Re R (a minor) (wardship: medical treatment)* [1991] 4 All ER 177 for an illustration of the extent of the powers of the court in wardship.

18. *Re Eve* (1987) 31 DLR (4th) 1 (Can Sup Ct).

19. *Re B (a minor) (wardship: sterilisation)* [1987] 2 All ER 206 (HL).

20. In *Re Eve* (1987) 31 DLR (4th) 1 at 13–22, LaForest J argues that the origin of the Canadian courts' *parens partriae* jurisdiction over incompetent adults is found within the principles of the English wardship jurisdiction.

21. The Law Reform Commission of Canada, *Sterilization* (1974) Working Paper No. 24. See note 18 at 30 (per LaForest J).

22. See note 18 at 32: "The grave intrusion on a person's rights and the certain physical damage that ensues from non-therapeutic sterilization without consent, when compared to the highly questionable advantages that can result from it, have persuaded me that it can never safely be determined that such a procedure is for the benefit of that person. Accordingly, the procedure should never be authorized for non-therapeutic purposes under the parens patriae jurisdiction" (per LaForest J).

23. See H. L. A. Hart, "Are there any natural rights" in J. Waldron (ed), *Theories of Rights* (Oxford: Oxford University Press, 1990), at 77. Hart attributes a natural right to freedom to all men who are capable of exercising a choice. Under his account of liberty, the justification for one person overriding another's right to freedom is found in the latter's choice to let the former do so.

24. See *supra*, note 18 at 29: "To begin with, the decision involves values in an area where our social history clouds our vision and encourages many to perceive the mentally handicapped as something less than human. This attitude has been aided and abetted by now discredited eugenic theories whose influence was felt in this country as well as in the United States. Two provinces, Alberta and British Columbia, once had statutes providing for the sterilisation of the mentally defectives". See also, *Re B* [1987] 2 All ER 206 (HL) at 215 per Lord Oliver of Aylmerton. S. Trombley, *The Right to Reproduce, a History of Coercive Sterilisation* (London: Weidenfield and Nicholson, 1988).

25. See *supra*, note 18 at 28–9: "a court may act not only on the ground that injury to the person or property has occurred but also on the ground that such injury is apprehended … I have no doubt that the jurisdiction may be used to authorize the performance of a surgical operation that is necessary to the health of the person … and by health I mean mental as well as physical health."

26. A. Grubb and D. Pearl, "Sterilisation and the Courts" [1987] CLJ 439 at 443–4.

27. See *supra*, note 18 at 32–3: "Judges are generally ill-informed about many of the factors relevant to a wise decision in this difficult area. They generally know little of mental illness, of techniques of contraception or their efficacy. And however well presented a case may be, it can only partially inform. If sterilisation of the mentally incompetent is to be adopted as desirable for general social purposes, the legislature is the appropriate body to do so. It is in a position to inform itself and it is attuned to the feelings of the public in making public policy in this sensitive area. The actions of the legislature will then, of course, be subject to the scrutiny of the courts under the Canadian Charter of Human Rights and Freedoms and otherwise."

28. See *supra*, note 19 at 219: "If in that conclusion the expression "non-therapeutic" was intended to exclude measures taken for the necessary protection from future harm of the person over whom the jurisdiction is exercisable, then I respectfully dissent from it for it seems to me to contradict what is the sole and paramount criterion for the exercise of the jurisdiction, viz. the welfare and benefit of the ward" (per Lord Oliver of Aylmerton).

29. See *supra*, note 18 at 34.

30. They were influenced by Heilbron J's judgment in *Re D* [1976] 1 All ER 326. There was evidence that D might have been suffering from a temporary condition and that, eventually, she might have become competent and have wished to exercise her right to reproduce. B, however, was thought to be permanently incompetent, and therefore never able to exercise her right to reproduce.

31. See note 2. John Stuart Mill in *On Liberty* argues that an individual should be left free to determine the course of his life, so long as he is

not harming anyone in the process. Harming others is the justification for overriding his right not to be interfered with.

32. *Wellesley* v. *Duke of Beaufort* (1827) 2 Russ. 1, 38 ER 236 at 242 per Lord Eldon.

33. See I. Kennedy and A. Grubb, *Medical Law: Text and Materials* (London: Butterworths, 1989) at 596 for a discussion of the narrow and broad approaches to determining "best interests".

34. See *supra*, note 27.

Paternalism, care and mental illness*

Eric Matthews

In modern medical practice it is increasingly taken for granted, at least in relation to purely bodily illness, that adult patients normally have a right to make their own decisions about their treatment, and especially about non-treatment. It is the standard view, at least amongst ethicists and lawyers, if not always amongst medical practitioners, that there is a duty to respect the patient's autonomy. Conversely, medical paternalism, in the sense of the imposition of treatment upon a patient against the patient's will, because the *doctor* regards it as in that patient's best interests, is regarded by the same ethicists and lawyers as a grave moral fault. However good the doctor's intentions may be in so doing, the imposition of treatment upon a patient without the patient's informed consent is regarded as an insult to the patient's human dignity.

In cases of mental illness, however, that opinion is far less common. The very nature of mental illness, it is often thought, may make a degree of medical paternalism justifiable, or at least excusable. All patients are vulnerable; but those suffering from mental illness, just because it is *mental*, are seen as particularly vulnerable. If someone's thoughts and feelings are disordered, then their power to form their own conceptions of what is in their best interests and to make de-

---

* This chapter has been radically revised as a result of the helpful criticisms and other comments made by the audience at the presentation of the first draft at the King's College conference. I am most grateful for these comments. The changes are, however, only in presentation, not in the substance of the ideas expressed.

Decision-Making and Problems of Incompetence. Edited by A. Grubb.
© 1994 John Wiley & Sons Ltd.

cisions in the light of them is reduced. Patients in this position, it is argued, thus lose their capacity for autonomous decision-making and so forfeit their right to respect for their autonomy. The doctor's overriding obligation to care for his or her patients must thus create a moral necessity for the doctor to make decisions on the patient's behalf, even if the patient's expressed wishes about treatment at the time in question may be contrary to the doctor's decision. This line of thinking presumably provides the ethical justification for the insertion of provisions allowing for such paternalistic decision-making into mental health legislation in many jurisdictions: such provisions are, for instance, a feature of both the (English) Mental Health Act of 1983 and the Mental Health (Scotland) Act of 1984.[1]

My main aim in this chapter is to explore the whole concept of autonomous decision-making and paternalism, especially in relation to mental illness and the peculiar problems which that creates, but also more generally. The reason for this exploration is to try to see whether there is any philosophically acceptable basis for making a distinction between mental and bodily illness in this respect, and if so what it is and what implications it has for clinical practice, ethics and law.

For the purposes of this chapter, at least, I take it for granted that there is such a thing as mental illness, which has objective causes just as bodily illness does — although it is an empirical rather than a philosophical matter to decide what the nature of those causes is. Many, of course, deny that there is such a thing: by which they presumably mean, not that people do not suffer as a result of their behaviour, thoughts, feelings or desires, but that such suffering is different in kind from any resulting from an *illness* and so needs help of a different, non-medical, sort. Those who reject the medical model of mental disorder will not be faced with the problems which I seek to deal with in this chapter. What interests me here is whether these problems can be resolved for those (the majority of people in modern society) who do accept the medical model, even if (like me) they think that the scope of application of that model to mental disorders is narrower than psychiatrists themselves usually think.

An essential preliminary to any such discussion, however, is some attempt to state clearly what is meant by key terms like "autonomy", "paternalism" and "care". The literature of medical ethics is, of course, full of discussions of these concepts and their meaning: it may nevertheless be helpful to be clear at the outset what meaning I shall attach to them in this chapter. At least then readers who wish to dispute my claims can decide whether they disagree with my definitions of concepts or accept my definitions and disagree with my views on how those concepts can be applied in this context.

"Autonomy" means, uncontroversially, "self-determination". Ethicists regard respect for patient autonomy as morally required because it is the patient's life and well-being which is at stake in medical treatment, and respect for human dignity entails that the person himself should ultimately determine what his well-being consists of and so what should or should not be done to the patient in order to achieve it. This conception of autonomy clearly implies that the patient has a "self" which is capable of determining what should or should not happen: that is, a set of values, in the sense of concepts of what is or is not in the person's interests, which can be said to be the patient's "own" values. To be the patient's own values, I want to suggest, means those values which result from the patient's own experience of life and his or her own reflections on that experience. This is why very small children and perhaps those adults who are severely mentally disabled have little or no capacity for autonomous decision-making. In the case of small children, they have neither had sufficient experience as yet to formulate values of their own nor have they as yet developed their powers of reflection sufficiently to do so. In the case of people with severe mental disabilities, the experience may be there, but the capacity for the right kind of reflection on experience is probably lacking. Since the theme of this chapter is neither children nor mentally disabled adults, however, I mention these cases only to help to clarify what I said earlier: nothing in my present argument rests on the claims just made.

"Paternalism", as I am here using that term, means making decisions on treatment or non-treatment on the grounds of the views of the doctor or other carer about what is in the patient's best interests, rather than on the basis of the patient's own values. Paternalism in this sense is most clearly evident when the doctor's view of what is in the patient's interests is contrary to the patient's expressed view: but it is also exercised when the doctor simply fails to take account of the fact that the patient may have different values — fails to consult the patient, for instance, about treatment decisions. On a charitable interpretation, medical paternalism is simply the result of a mistaken view of what is required by the doctor's duty of care: to care for a patient is to do what is best for that person. The paternalist mistakenly takes that to mean "to do what the doctor thinks is best for the patient". What is best for a patient can only mean what is best *in terms of the patient's own values.*

There are two main sources of confusion in discussions of paternalism and autonomy, especially in relation to mental illness. The first is this. Mental health legislation normally makes provision for the involuntary hospitalisation and treatment in some cases of mentally ill people for the protection of others. For instance, section 62 (1) (d) of the Mental Health Act 1983 states that the patient's consent is not required for any treatment "which (not being irreversible or hazardous) is immediately necessary and represents the minimum interference necessary to prevent the patient from behaving violently or being a danger to himself or to others".[2] Again, section 17 (1) (b) of the Mental Health (Scotland) Act 1984 states that a person may be admitted to a hospital and there detained on the grounds that he needs treatment for a mental disorder and "it is necessary for the health or safety of that person or *for the protection of other persons* that he should receive such treatment ... " (my emphasis).[3]

These are certainly provisions for involuntary treatment of persons with a mental disorder: but they are not in any real sense paternalistic. Medical paternalism, as defined above, is the practice of making decisions for patients without the patient's consent but for what is considered to be the patient's own good. Hospitalisation and treatment are imposed on patients in the cases mentioned, not only for their own good, but for the good of others. It is no more paternalistic to treat mentally ill persons in this way than it is to imprison criminals for the protection of society at large or to detain those suffering from highly contagious and lethal diseases in isolation hospitals. It may be paternalistic to do such things in relation to those who are thereby protected from harm: but it is not paternalistic in relation to the patient himself.

In such cases of detention for the protection of others, there may of course be other limits on the kinds of treatment which may be imposed. Such treatment is morally unacceptable if the possible harm caused to others by forgoing the treatment is less than, or even no greater than, the harm caused to the patient by the treatment. The legislation quoted above acknowledges this: it speaks of "the minimum interference necessary" and rules out "hazardous or irreversible" treatment. Respect for the patient's human dignity does not require us to allow that patient to do harm to others: but it does entail that we should not cause the patient greater harm than we are preventing. It may, for instance, be justifiable to confine someone in a secure mental hospital if his mental disorder leads him to make sexual attacks on women or children: but it is almost certainly not justifiable, for instance, to ill-treat the man while in hospital, to deny him the opportunity to develop his life in other ways, or chemically to castrate him.

A second potent source of confusion is that doctors may sometimes be justified in overriding a patient's wishes, especially in cases of mental illness, in order to protect themselves: either to protect their own physical well-being (as when a patient seems likely to attack them) or to protect their own moral integrity (as when a patient wishes them to connive in his desire to end his own life, either by their actions or, more likely, by their failure to act in certain ways). When a doctor overrides a patient's wishes on such grounds, it is not medical paternalism: the doctor is acting, not from his own conception of what is in the patient's best interests, but from a concern for his own well-being. Here again, there may be constraints on how far doctors may go in overriding a patient's wishes in this way: the harm done to the doctor must be at least as great as the harm done to the patient by acting against the patient's wishes, for instance. But these constraints are independent of any considerations of paternalism or autonomy.

Involuntary treatment on such grounds, then, is not paternalism in the sense of this chapter. We are here concerned with the argument that a doctor's duty of care creates a moral requirement to choose treatment for mentally ill patients which the doctor regards as in their best interests, even if they themselves vehemently reject such treatment. Why is it so readily assumed that there is such a requirement in the case of mental illness? One common basis for this assumption is the belief that mental illness, by its very nature, is a disturbance of human rationality, and that the possession of an undisturbed capacity for the exercise of rational thought is a precondition of having the right to autonomous decision-making. This association between autonomy and rationality goes back, of course, to Kant, although it is significant that Kant was concerned with autonomy in the context of a general theory of the objectivity of moral duties, rather than in that of an individual's competence to make decisions about his well-being. For Kant, therefore, rationality was an inseparable characteristic of all human beings, and choices of moral maxims were autonomous when motivated by reason rather than by personal emotions.

When those who are suffering from mental illness are described as "irrational", however, it is not usually because they are motivated by emotions more than mentally able people. It is rather that the emotions which motivate them are different from those which motivate "normal" people, and such as "normal" people find difficult, if not impossible, to comprehend. Someone who is suicidally depressed, for instance, is not more motivated by emotion than someone who simply "instinctively" wants to go on living: neither person is more "rational" in Kant's sense (although the belief that it is morally acceptable to kill oneself is, for Kant, not universalisable and so not rationally justifiable). The sense in which a mentally ill person's desires or feelings or moods may be "irrational" is simply that they deviate from what is regarded as normal in a particular society; and it is hard to see why abnormality in that sense should on its own justify any lack of respect for one's autonomy. That someone's notions of what is good for them, or of what constitutes reasonable behaviour, differ from what is generally held in their society is not, in other contexts, thought to diminish that person's right to live their life by their own standards, as long as they do no harm thereby to others. Indeed, if the point of emphasising the right to autonomy is to respect the right of human beings to live their own lives as they please, then the non-conformist is as much entitled to that right as anyone else.

A further point is relevant here. The apparent "irrationality" (even in the sense of the last paragraph) of someone diagnosed as mentally ill may often turn out to be merely superficial. An attempt at suicide may be perfectly intelligible, to the most "normal" of persons, when it is seen in the context of the would-be suicide's life in general: in some circumstances, as we may all recognise, a human being might well feel that life was not, or no longer, worth living. We might still feel that we ourselves would want in such circumstances to struggle on, but that is not the same as to say that we could not see a certain rationality in the desire to end it all. It is factors such as this which lead to an uncertainty over the whole concept of "mental illness", which then infects the consideration of the right to autonomous decision-making in such cases and of the point at which proper "care" shades over into unacceptable "paternalism".

Nevertheless, it does not follow from the fact that it is difficult to draw a precise boundary around the concept of mental illness that the concept has no legitimate application. It seems beyond doubt, indeed, that some mental problems may properly be described as "illness", at least in the sense that they cause distress to those who suffer from them, that they have causes which are "objective" in the sense of not being removable simply by the sufferer's taking thought and that they therefore need the skilled care of trained professionals. Some of these disorders may involve "irrationality" in a sense in which that is not simply equivalent to "unconventionality". For example, sufferers from some mental disorders may hold irrational beliefs — that is, beliefs which are not grounded in rationally adequate evidence and which are not affected by rational criticism. In some cases, these beliefs may have a bearing on a person's capacity to make rational decisions about their treatment. For example, suppose a schizophrenic sees his psychiatrist as part of a malign conspiracy to harm him: then the drugs which the doctor innocently offers as part of treatment may be seen as poisons intended to kill the patient. The patient will therefore reject such treatment, not because he does not want treatment, but because he does not see it *as* treatment.

Surely in a case like this, it might be felt, the doctor's duty of care overrides any duty to respect the patient's non-treatment decision. Perhaps: but we should first consider such a case more closely. It is, after all, a somewhat contrived example. However common irrational beliefs in this sense may be in cases of mental illness, beliefs such as this which have such a direct bearing on the rationality of treatment decisions are relatively rare. It is only because this particular schizophrenic includes the doctor in his malign conspiracy that the problem arises. Such an example, therefore, tells us nothing about the many other cases of paranoid beliefs in which the treatment offered is not seen as intended to do harm — still less about the cases of mental illness which do not involve irrational beliefs at all. In short, such examples cannot provide a basis for a distinction between mentally ill patients as such and other people in respect of their right of autonomy. Secondly, it is not only those who are diagnosed as mentally ill, after all, who hold irrational beliefs — beliefs not based on adequate evidence and not yielding to rational criticism — or whose irrational beliefs may affect their decisions about treatment. To a liberal agnostic like myself, for instance, the beliefs of Jehovah's Witnesses about blood transfusions seem as irrational as those of our imaginary schizophrenic. No doubt, many of my beliefs would seem equally irrational to a Jehovah's Witness. Witnesses and liberal agnostics simply accept different standards of rational justification for beliefs of this kind. The Witness's beliefs clearly have a bearing on some kinds of decisions about medical treatment: a consistently believing Jehovah's Witness could not agree to accept a blood transfusion, however necessary it might be to save one's life, since at the spiritual level, in the Witness's belief, a transfusion would endanger something far more important than mere physical survival. But then, our imaginary schizophrenic, if he were consistent, could not accept the psychiatrist's proffered treatment, since its intention and its effect, in his belief system, would be to kill him. Any reason we have for respecting the Jehovah's Witness's non-treatment decision, despite our disagreement with it, would apply equally to the schizophrenic's decision.

At this point, another line of thought may suggest itself. It might be argued that, if we follow up certain hints contained in the earlier account of autonomy, we may see a significant difference between the "irrationality" (if such it is) of the Jehovah's Witness and that of the schizophrenic or other mentally ill person. The suggested distinction would be as follows. However "irrational", in the sense of "unconventional", the Jehovah's Witness's belief may be, it may nevertheless be the Witness's *own* belief in a sense in which the schizophrenic's is not. By this I mean that Witnesses come by their beliefs as part of the normal process of reflection on one's own life and experience which all of us engage in to a greater or lesser extent. To speak of a process of reflection here need not imply anything very profound or intellectual. The suggestion is not that Witnesses (or holders of any other religious or non-religious belief) engage in meditation and come to a conclusion about the nature of human life as a result. All that is implied is that a person's coming to hold a particular religious or similar belief can be seen to "fit in" to the normal process of development of a human life. Even a sudden conversion may be seen in retrospect as intelligible in the context of one's other experiences.

Such beliefs may not be "rational" in the sense of being justifiable by something like philosophical argument: but they are intelligible in the context of the believer's other experiences. This does not seem to be true in the case of the schizophrenic's beliefs. If there is such a thing as genuine schizophrenia, then it is a disorder, not so much of rationality as of personal identity. The beliefs of someone suffering from schizophrenia affect competency, not because they are out of line with standardly held beliefs in the community, but because they are not the outcome of the believer's normal development and reflection on his own experiences. Rather, they are the result of whatever it is which has caused the schizophrenia — whether it be a brain disorder or the lingering effect of childhood traumas or whatever. Our concern here is not with the fundamentally empirical question of what factors cause schizophrenia. It is with a philosophical analysis of what is meant by calling schizophrenia, or any other condition, a "mental illness'. I have discussed this question more thoroughly elsewhere,[4] but for the present purposes I want simply to assert dogmatically, but as a suggestion worth considering, that at any rate some mental illnesses may be so called because they result from causes which disturb the normal processes of human development in which later stages are intelligible in the light of earlier. If this analysis is accepted, even provisionally, as applying to our imaginary schizophrenic, then it would follow that he was not in a certain sense making a non-treatment *decision* at all: what looks like a refusal of treatment was not something which came from within him as his own decision, linked to his own conceptions of what he wants from life, but was simply an expression of that cause external to his own development which was responsible for his schizophrenia.

The same analysis, *mutatis mutandis*, can be applied to moods, motives, desires, etc. as well as to beliefs. If there is such a thing as clinical depression, for instance, then the "rationality" of any suicidal feelings associated with it would be neither here nor there from this point of view. What would matter would be how intelligibly they fitted into the person's natural development. Could they be seen as an intelligible response to the objective wretchedness of the person's life, such that even those who think it irrational or immoral to take one's own life could understand how someone in such a situation might come to the decision to end it all? Or is the suicidal mood rather out of joint with the rest of the life of the person concerned, such that it seems not merely irrational, but unintelligible in terms of the person's own values?

One virtue of this argument is that it seems to make some sense of the view that mental illness has a bearing on the patient's right to make his own treatment decisions. If to have the capacity for autonomous decision-making is to be able to make decisions which are "one's own", decisions which flow from one's own values, conceptions of what is good or bad for one; and if mental illness may undermine one's personal identity, in the sense of causing one to act on the basis of values other than those formed in the course of normal development; then it becomes clearer why mental illness may affect one's competence. If one then adds the further premise that only those competent to make their own decisions have a right to respect for their autonomy, it becomes easy to see why paternalistic conclusions might be thought to follow. For then it might be thought to be part of the doctor's duty of care that he should take decisions on one's behalf which more truly reflect one's own best interests than the decisions one appears to take oneself. But before we are too readily carried away by the thought that this justifies medical paternalism in such cases, we need to call to mind some cautionary points.

First, this argument will lead to the paternalistic conclusion only (if at all) in cases where the mental disorder is of such a kind as to disturb normal personal identity, and to disturb it in a way which is relevant to treatment decisions. Nothing said so far implies that all mental disorders are of this kind. The category of conditions called "mental disorder", and falling within the scope of psychiatric treatment, is after all very broad, and the same analysis may not apply to every condition which is so described. Someone who is suffering from anorexia nervosa, for instance, may well not experience any change in his normal values, beliefs or concepts as a result of the illness: indeed, it may be precisely reflection on the conditions of one's life which is one of the factors precipitating such a disorder. Again, someone suffering from agoraphobia may well be describable as experiencing a disturbance in normal identity in some respects, but not necessarily in any respect which is relevant to treatment decisions. In such cases, there would therefore be no loss of normal autonomy in any relevant respect, and so no justification for taking paternalistic treatment decisions. (There might, nevertheless, as argued earlier, be non-paternalistic reasons for overriding such a patient's wishes.)

Secondly, even in cases where mental illness creates a relevant disturbance of personal identity, and thus makes the patient's current decisions less than fully autonomous, this does not justify genuine paternalism. In the case of any patient who has previously developed the capacity to make autonomous decisions and has subsequently become incompetent (whether through mental illness, senility, coma or whatever), considerations of human dignity require that autonomy still be respected. Since the capacity to make autonomous decisions is at the relevant time in abeyance, such respect for autonomy must take the form of basing decisions on what the patient *would have* chosen if he had still been fully competent. The practical problem is then to decide what that choice would have been in those hypothetical circumstances. But this problem, although difficult, is not insuperable. In the case of the demented or the comatose, we can discover their probable wishes either on the basis of previous written statements of their own (e.g. "living wills") or by consulting those who know them well enough to be able to determine what those wishes would be. Where such proxy decision-makers have been previously appointed by the patients themselves, of course, then this strengthens their position. There does not seem to be any obvious objection to using similar methods in the case of those who are mentally ill, and so of preserving respect for patient autonomy even in cases where mental illness renders a patient incompetent. Indeed, in an issue in 1992 of the *Hastings Center Report*,[5] there was news that the New York Superior Court had recognised the validity of a psychiatric "living will", enabling a woman to refuse electroconvulsive therapy on that basis. The clear parallels between such psychiatric cases and other cases of decision-making for people who have become incompetent would suggest that this practice should become more widespread.

Previous written statements, or suitable proxies, may not always be available. Even then, however, medical paternalism in the true sense is not justified. If the patient is someone who has already developed values of his own, then it is these values which ought to determine the treatment given. In the absence of any other evidence as to what these values might be, doctors have simply to use their judgment and imagination to guess what they might be. Because of the danger that the doctor, through a failure of imagination, might simply attribute his own values to the patient (and thus end up in effect being paternalistic), great care must be taken to discount the doctor's own views. The final safeguard is that no treatment should be undertaken which would permanently prevent the patient's return to the full exercise of autonomy, except where that is the only way to prevent some even greater harm to the patient. Such forbidden treatments might include radical brain surgery or confinement of a kind likely to make the patient permanently dependent emotionally on the carers. This case, like the others considered in this chapter, indicates the importance of distinguishing between the question of whether a patient's autonomy ought to be respected and that of whether the patient is competent to make treatment decisions at the time when they need to be made. Respecting the autonomy of someone who has developed an autonomous self, and who has at least the possibility of returning to fully autonomous existence, must at the very least entail safeguarding that possibility as far as it is possible to do so.

We can summarise the themes of this chapter by saying that the whole question of the justification of paternalism *vis-à-vis* those suffering from mental illness is much more complex than it is sometimes supposed to be. First, it is not justified by the alleged essential irrationality of the mentally ill. Not all mentally ill people are anyway irrational in the relevant respects, and even where mental illness does involve irrationality of thought, belief or behaviour, this would not in itself justify overriding treatment decisions made by mentally ill people. Respect for human dignity implies respect even for the irrational decisions of human beings. What might justify overriding decisions made by people while they are mentally ill is that in some cases these decisions may not be, in a certain sense, truly "their own". If some forms of mental illness can be described as a disturbance of personal identity, so that patients are, as we say, "not themselves" because of their illness, then the decisions made by them during their illness will not represent their own deepest values, convictions and feelings about life. Even in these cases, however, there is no justification for paternalism in the true sense. The patient's decisions should be overridden, not in the name of the *doctor's* values, but in that of the patient's own values, as reflected where possible in previously written statements or the decisions of proxies who know the patient well. At the very least, as argued just above, nothing should be done to prevent the patient's return to full autonomy, except in order to avoid an even greater harm.

Nor is paternalism justified by the doctor's obligations of care. To care for a patient is to promote, as far as one can, that patient's good. What counts as a patient's good is what is determined as such by the patient's own reflections on his experience: above all, it is the patient's interest to preserve or, where necessary, restore that autonomy which expresses the capacity to reflect on one's own experience and formulate values on that basis. In short, the duty of care entails respect for patient autonomy.

References

1. See *The Mental Health Act 1983* (with annotations by R. M. Jones; London: Sweet and Maxwell, 1983); and the Mental Health (Scotland) Act 1984.
2. *Ibid*, at 97.
3. *Ibid*, at 13.
4. See my paper "How to treat the mentally ill", initially given at the joint conference of the European Society for Philosophy of Medicine and Health Care and the Royal College of Psychiatrists Philosophy Group, St Catherine's College, Oxford, July 1991, in K. W. M. Fulford and B. I. B. Lindahl (eds), *Nature and Narrative: Themes in the Philosophy of Mental Health* (Kluwer) (forthcoming).
5. (1992) 22 *Hastings Center Report* 48.

Mental disorder and decision-making: respecting autonomy in substitute judgments

Christopher Heginbotham

Introduction

Mental disorder covers a wide range of conditions, including mental illnesses and mental handicaps (learning disabilities). Many people who have a form of mental disorder are subject to compulsory interventions in their own interests and in the interests of other people. In the UK, compulsory admission to mental health facilities and compulsory treatment (separate but linked concepts) are based on a two-pronged test: essentially a *best interests test* and a *dangerousness test*. In the UK patients may be detained for significant periods of time on the sanction of two recognised doctors, without immediate recourse to a court or similar body.

Recent concern has focused on the needs of people with learning disabilities, particularly adults who are unable to give valid consent to non-life-saving interventions which some deem necessary. An example might be the non-therapeutic sterilisation of mentally handicapped women.[1] Recent developments in public policy have emphasised the importance of informed consent and assisting people with mental disorders to live the most autonomous and fulfilled lives possible subject to continuing disability. New ways have been proposed to derive an improved balance between the paternalism inherent in compulsory interventions and respecting the autonomy of the

Decision-Making and Problems of Incompetence. Edited by A. Grubb.
© 1994 John Wiley & Sons Ltd.

individual.

This chapter will suggest a unifying framework into which a variety of methods for improving decision-making can be fitted. A distinction will be drawn between "strong" and "weak" paternalism; and between "substitute judgments" and "best interests". Substitute judgment will be characterised in two ways: "authentic" judgment, usually made by a legally nominated attorney operating within guidelines drawn up by the donor or power of attorney; and those substitute judgments which might be considered "free", which will sometimes be an amalgam of best interests, patient preferences and administrative requirement.

Four approaches to decision-making will be considered briefly and "mapped" within the framework proposed. From this process it will be evident that a clear separation can be drawn between legally sanctioned substitute judgments and professionally dominated decisions made ostensibly in the patient's best interests. If a clash occurs (say because a health professional wishes to use statute to override an advance directive) arbitration should be effected by judicial review.

Capacity

The difficulties inherent in decision-making for and, with people with mental disorders turn on the individual's ability to understand and consent to invasive and life-changing interventions.[1] Patients are sometimes said to lack the capacity to make decisions or in other cases to be incompetent. The terms capacity and incompetence are *not* the same. Lacking capacity implies that an individual has a fundamental cognitive (or perhaps volitional) defect such that the person cannot understand the nature, cause and effect of some proposed course of action.

Capacity is thus a necessary but not sufficient condition for competence. Competence suggests both a minimal capacity to understand basic information about an issue in hand, sufficient education to make use of that information and a context in which the patient can act upon that information. An individual may be capable of learning and understanding about a range of subjects, but, if he has not undergone specific training for a particular discipline, he will not be competent to undertake work within that discipline. Competence thus requires support, training, education and a context in which the individual can demonstrate capacity.

A person does not, however, have to lack capacity to be detained compulsorily for treatment. The Mental Health Act 1983 (England and

Wales) or Mental Health (Scotland) Act 1984 allows mental health practitioners to detain individuals involuntarily and to effect various treatments subject to certain consent provisions.[3] By and large such detention and treatment are undertaken on people whose capacity is impaired to some degree, but may not be fully impaired, and indeed may fluctuate. The more a person lacks capacity to make decisions for themselves the more likely it is that a court or other similar body will be asked to step in and make a judgment about appropriate treatment for that individual.

Strong versus weak paternalism

The example of Mental Health Act detentions by professional staff under civil procedures without recourse to a court or similar body is a form of strong paternalism. The Mental Health Act 1983 allows a person with a mental illness to be detained "on the grounds of his safety or the health and safety of other people". Sections 57 and 58 of the Mental Health Act 1983 are extensively paternalistic in that a patient requiring, say, psychosurgery must not only consent personally but that consent must be validated by the Mental Health Act Commission, *and* the treating doctor's decision must be supported by a second opinion.

Weak paternalism is usually described as that which only sanctions interventions when a person is significantly dangerous to himself or other people. In practical terms this means allowing individuals to make decisions for themselves unless there is some overriding reason why an intervention is required. Two types of personal decision may be suggested. The first is where a person *has* some capacity to make decisions for himself. Such weak paternalism therefore allows advocacy or guardianship arrangements and only intervenes in the most serious circumstances. The second is where the person "more or less" *lacks* capacity but has established some form of continuing power of attorney or advance directive. Weak paternalism provides that the attorney or directive is followed other than in the most serious of circumstances.

Framework for decision-making

The preceding discussion of capacity and paternalism provides the basis for a simple two-dimensional map (Figure 1). One axis is a continuum from full capacity (but not necessarily full competence) to incapacity (and thus incompetence); the other axis is a continuum from

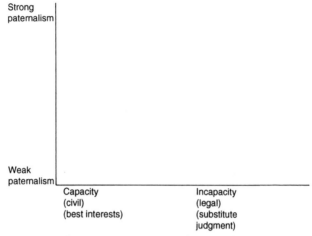

Figure 1. Capacity and paternalism.

weak paternalism to strong paternalism.

The capacity axis can profitably be described in a number of alternative ways. Full capacity is linked to decisions made by professional staff under civil procedures and is associated with "building autonomy". The left-hand side is a *tendency* towards decisions made in what the health professional considers are the "best interests" of the patient.

Incapacity can be allied with formal legal sanctions and with "respecting autonomy". To the right-hand side is a *tendency* towards substitute judgments which may or may not include a standard "best interests" test.

Figure 2 offers some suggestions as to where a number of approaches to decision-making may sit within this framework. Four of these will be considered in further detail. These are: compulsory treatment in the community; guardianship; compulsory intervention panels; and powers of attorney.

Four proposals

Compulsory treatment in the community

The last few years have seen proposals for a "community treatment order" (a form of legislated "section") which might be activated by appropriate professional staff. The order would allow some form of

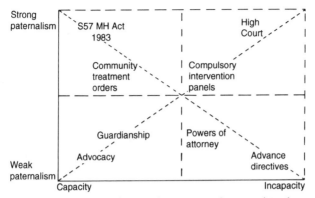

Figure 2. Approaches to decision-making within the capacity/paternalism framework.

treatment to be provided compulsorily in community settings. The arguments in favour of such an order are that it enables treatment to be given in a home setting to patients with low treatment compliance, and thus enables patients to leave hospitals but with an incentive to continue treatment.

The arguments against are that:

- The availability of such an order might obviate the need to improve community care resources.
- Such an order is only valuable if it can generate compliance and is enforceable. As Richards[2] has pointed out, a community order is designed "not only to persuade the persuadable but compel the unpersuadable". He goes on to say that the paradox appears to be that "a community order only 'works' if the patient consents. If the patient does not comply then the order becomes a hospital detention." In other words the only enforcement of such an order is to fall back on compulsory admission under the existing mental health legislation.
- A community order may deter potential voluntary patients from accepting help, if they fear they are likely to become the subject of long-term compulsory treatment. This is a more subtle objection as voiced by Richards. As he puts it: "it will not take long for most patients to realise that the best way of getting out of hospital is to cooperate with the medical and nursing staff. Equally it will not take them long to realise that if they cooperate with a community order there is no reason for it ever to end."[3]

Compulsory treatment in the community also suffers from a "rights" problem — should a patient who is ostensibly well on discharge from hospital be subject to a continuing compulsory order? This turns on the notion of wellness and the treating physician's view of likely compliance with continuing treatment following discharge if some order is not available.

A compulsory community treatment order is a form of strong paternalism. Its proponents would enable such an order to be effected through civil procedures under amended mental health legislation. The brief discussion here demonstrates the problem of highly paternalistic professional interventions. Such an order may easily conflict with the patient's desires articulated before or after the event or at a time of sufficient capacity to comment on treatment.

Guardianship

Improving guardianship may be a way forward in effecting compulsory interventions with patients. At present guardians have relatively limited powers under the Mental Health Act 1983 and cannot require patients to accept a particular treatment. The advantage of guardianship is in the trust that can be established between guardian and patient where a court has ruled on the extent of the guardian's powers. The disadvantages of guardianship, however, include the need to find a guardian acceptable to the courts, the mental health service and the patient; the likelihood of conflict arising between guardian and patient, especially if the guardian is a relative (which may exacerbate any intra-familial problems); and the powers of the guardian will always be limited unless they are vested in a professionally qualified person.

"True" guardianship is concerned with building autonomy and is weakly paternalistic in linking a "best interests" judgment by the guardian with an ability for the patient to influence decisions. Guardianship offers the advantage of a "sliding scale" relevant to the degree of constraint. This meets the objective of the "least restrictive alternative" canvassed by, among others, Gostin.[4]

Compulsory intervention panels

A significant problem with existing procedures is that patients are unable to test detention swiftly and speedily following an initial admission. Partly this is because people with mental illnesses (in particular) are dealt with under specific legislation by a specialist group of staff, and partly because UK legislation allows remarkably long periods of detention by professional staff without the necessity of recourse to a court or similar body (i.e. up to six months in the first instance under S3 of the 1983 Act). In order to deal with this the idea of a compulsory intervention panel was proposed[5] concerned prospectively with treatment. Such a panel would receive a report from a responsible medical officer or other professional staff as well as a patient's advocate. Using a Scottish children's panel non-adversarial model, such a panel would come to a view on appropriate treatment and the length of that treatment. The patient or patient's advocate would be fully involved in decisions on appropriate treatment.

The advantage of such a panel would be to improve trust and reduce conflict. The autonomy of the patient is enhanced (or at least respected), the control element is reduced and the care element increased. Paternalism is moderated by debate in front of the panel, although such a panel falls towards strong paternalism as it allows interventions with people deemed to require help.

The disadvantages of such a system are that it requires substantial change to current procedures and a major amendment to legislation. In particular, to be truly effective such a system requires generic health legislation where any person showing a lack of capacity to provide for himself or herself could be the subject of a compulsory intervention order. Compulsory panels are not dissimilar to Mental Health Review Tribunals (Sheriff Court in Scotland) and the final arbiter of the two would, in any event, be the High Court. The idea of such panels is, however, concerned mainly to provide for those who lack capacity and thus could offer a substitute judgment based largely on best interests for the patient whilst taking into account other relevant circumstances.

Enduring powers of attorney

Under British legislation it is now possible for a person to nominate an attorney to continue administrating that person's properties and affairs beyond some point when he (the principal) becomes mentally incapacitated. The Enduring Powers of Attorney Act 1985 enables a principal (donor) to confer on an attorney (donee) a general or specific authority. If the attorney believes the principal is becoming mentally incapable he must apply to the Court of Protection to register the power and notify the donor and nearest relatives. The Court of Protection may give various directions on the use of power.[6]

There are clearly significant advantages and disadvantages to such a power. The main advantage is that an elderly person can make arrangements for his further care and protection following the point at which he begins to lack capacity to make such determinations for himself. The disadvantages turn on the point at which the attorneyship begins to have an effect. This has been beautifully illustrated by Richard Simon in his cleverly written piece about the application of continuing powers of attorney in the case of King Lear.[7]

Some countries, notably the USA, allow the notion of a "living will". This is a device used to enable a person to say in advance whether they want heroic expensive life-prolonging treatment once terminally ill. In some ways living wills are similar to advance directives, but in the former a third party can decide on the patient's behalf within some broad guidelines, whereas the latter is much more passive. Springing (or contingent) powers of attorney are to some extent a mixture of a continuing power of attorney and a living will. A principal can nominate an attorney who decides (a) when the principal is becoming incapacitated and (b) subject to appropriate registration or other safeguards, can propose and effect relevant health care provision.[7]

Other substitute judgment mechanisms include nomination of substitute decision-taker, to extend minority, expanding the role of the Court of Protection, multidisciplinary tribunals (similar to the compulsory intervention panels suggested above) and use of second-opinion doctors under the Mental Health Act 1983.

Some form of springing or contingent power of attorney could be used for people other than elderly people likely to lose capacity because of old age or some progressive disorder such as Alzheimer's disease. One possibility would be for people with fluctuating severe mental illnesses to nominate a health professional who would act with "continuing power of authority" as and when the principal became disordered once again.

The advantage of a "continuing power of authority" is that the patient during periods of insight and lucidity is able to nominate a person of his choice; this might often be a general practitioner or other person with whom the patient is familiar. The patient can discuss all aspects of his care and set fairly stringent criteria as to the way in which he will be treated if and when illness strikes. Such a proposal has the advantages of genuine substitute judgment rooted in the patient's expressed wishes, maximises the autonomy of the patient, reduces paternalism, enshrines a patient's rights and leads to a fiduciary duty on the practitioner to respect the wishes and requirements of the patient.

The disadvantages of the approach are similar to those of guardianship. The scope of the "continuing power of authority" would have to be agreed by some formal body such as a court or similar institution unless a watertight administrative system could be laid down. Clearly some review and oversight would be required. In use, such a power of authority could be misused or become a "best interests" vehicle. This could lead to a breakdown of trust and the undermining of any treatment or placement. The significant disadvantage, however, is that people who have never had some form of mental illness are unlikely to believe they will ever need to create such a power. It will only be those people who have had significantly disabling illnesses and have sufficiently overcome their effects who will properly be able to consider carefully the advantages of such a power who will take advantage of the opportunity.

Discussion

From these brief descriptions, it can be noted that there are advantages and disadvantages to each of the four methods of decision-making for compulsory detention described here. Two of these proposals (community treatment orders and guardianship) fall to the left-hand side of the framework (towards best interests, building autonomy and civil jurisdiction); two (compulsory intervention panels and continuing power of attorney) fall towards the right-hand side (respecting autonomy, court or similar body decisions).

Although there is a right/left distinction there is also a "diagonal" line separating interventions which do not require a court or similar body to sanction activity (the top left-hand part of Figure 3) and that which requires some form of court action. These might reasonably be distinguished as those interventions based on legislative permission and those which require administrative fiat. This distinction is important. It suggests that administrative actions cannot be overridden by civil action rooted in legislation (or for that matter common law) without effective review.

Advance directives and powers of attorney once established demand of the attorney or donee an "authentic" substitute judgment based on the clear wishes and demands of the donor. The attorney is thus acting as the principal, and as if the principal still had capacity to

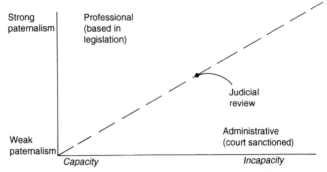

Figure 3. Distinction between legislative and administrative interventions within the capacity/paternalism framework.

make decisions on his or her own behalf. Those decisions might be seen to be incorrect by an observer but this does not entitle a health professional, by using some other legislation, to take a "best interests" view of the patient's needs.[9]

Conclusion

This chapter has sought to distinguish a number of methods of making decisions for patients with varying capacity and competence as a result of mental illness. Capacity and competence are distinct concepts; capacity matters most. Capacity turns on cognitive and volitional attributes of the individual. Tests for capacity must note the functional ability of the person, but any arbitration will require a composite decision which:

1. Respects a person's advance demands.
2. Listens respectfully to any attorney or nominated substitute.
3. Examines carefully the person's immediate context.
4. Considers the person's "best interests" as they appear in the light of (1) to (3) above.

In deciding for persons whose capacity is impaired, it is essential to err on the side of weak paternalism and thus judicial review. Any conflict between civil actions demanded by health professionals, and "authentic" substitute judgments of donee attorneys or advance directions can only be dealt with by court arbitration.

References

1 W. Bingley "Mental Incapacity in Personal Law" (1988) 28 *Med. Sci. Law* 9.

2. H. Richards "Compulsory Detention". Paper to the World Federation for Mental Health Congress, Auckland, NZ (August 1989).

3. *Mental Health Act 1983; Code of Practice*. HMSO, London 1990.

4. L. Gostin, "A Human Condition", Vol 1. (1977) *MIND*, London.

5. See T. Campbell and C. Heginbotham, *Mental Illness: Prejudice, Discrimination and the Law* (Aldershot: Dartmouth, 1991).

6. The Law Commission Discussion Paper No. 119, *Mentally Incapacitated Adults and Decision-Making: An Overview* (London, 1991) at 65 ff.

7. J. T. Farrand, "Enduring Powers of Attorney" in J. Eekelar and D. Pearl (eds), *An Aging World: Dilemmas and Challenges for Law and Social Policy* (Oxford: Clarendon Press, 1989), at 647–8. (A quote from an article by R. Simon in *Law Society Gazette*, Vol 83, p. 2079).

8. R. Higgs, "Living Wills and Treatment Refusal". *Br Med J* 295, No. 6608, 1221–2.

9. For a discussion on this point see Scottish Law Commission Discussion Paper No. 94, *Mentally Disabled Adults* (Edinburgh, 1991).

Recent American developments in the right to die: the *Cruzan* case, living wills, durable powers and family consent statutes

Ronald C. Link

Introduction

This paper examines recent American developments in the right to die: the *Cruzan* case, living wills, durable powers and family consent statutes. My perspective is that of a teacher of wills and trusts law: what documents should be executed and what should they say? I offer these recent American developments not as a ready-made solution but as an illustration of the questions, patent and latent, one nation has encountered in approaching the complex issues surrounding the right to die.[1]

I find these issues difficult to think about, probably because they require me to confront my own mortality. The existential psychotherapists would teach us that the fear of death motivates man.[2] In their view, Freud almost got it right, but it is death and the fear of death, rather than sex and the drive for sex, that compel our behaviour. The difficulty of contemplating one's own mortality is illustrated by the psychotherapist's story of the elderly couple discussing their

Decision-Making and Problems of Incompetence. Edited by A. Grubb.
© 1994 John Wiley & Sons Ltd.

future plans: one spouse said to the other, "If one of us dies first, I think *I'll* move to Paris."[3] Another illustration: a few years ago the American playwright William Saroyan died in California. He telephoned his official last words to the Associated Press: "Everybody has got to die, but I have always believed an exception would be made in my case. Now what?"[4]

On the other hand, as Dr Johnson observed, the prospect of death wonderfully concentrates the mind,[5] so let me turn to my topic.

Over the last decade or so, right-to-die issues have become increasingly prominent in the USA. A new branch of law — generally known as elder law — focuses on the legal problems of the elderly.[6] Estate planners now recommend new kinds of documents — living wills, durable powers of attorney and medical directives — that were unknown twenty years ago.[7] Why this surge of interest?

The explanation lies in the combination of medical advances with the ageing of the American population. Various surgical and non-surgical technologies are now used to manage previously life-threatening conditions. The non-surgical technologies include cardiopulmonary resuscitation (CPR), respiration (mechanical ventilation), renal (kidney) dialysis, tube feeding (artificial nutrition and hydration) and antibiotics.[8]

Coupled with these new technologies is the ageing of the American population. Some illustrative statistics: In 1900, the life expectancy at birth of an American white male was 48 and of a white female was 53. By 1990 those life expectancies had advanced to 73 and 80, respectively.[9] "The segment of our population over the age of 65 is growing twice as fast as the rest of our population; and the '85 and over' group is the fastest growing group of all."[10] When the 76 million "baby boomers" (those born between 1946 and 1964) begin to reach 65 around the year 2010, they will increase the over-65 segment of our population from its present 12% to 20% by 2030.[11] "A high proportion of people over 65 have children over 65. At no point in their lives will today's average working couple have more young children than they will have living parents. A couple is likely to spend more years caring for their parents than they will raising their children."[12]

"While the American population has been getting older, the expected human life span has not been getting longer. It has remained relatively fixed at about 100 to 105 years. Thus, medical advances are permitting more people to reach the limits of their life expectancies."[13] "In the past 50 years, the causes of death in America have shifted from infectious diseases, such as tuberculosis and pneumonia, to chronic degenerative diseases. In the United States today, more than 75% of the deaths of people over the age of 65 result from heart disease, cancer or stroke. Thus death has become a prolonged process, the timing of which can be controlled by modern medical technology. The time of death is often less a matter of fate than of conscious choice."[14]

It might be noted that the so-called greying of the population is not an American phenomenon: the older population of the world is swelling, too.[15] About 495 million people (9.1% of the world's population) are age 60 or over, up from 300 million (8.3%) just two decades ago. In nine countries, all of them European and including Britain, more than one-fifth of the population is age 60 or over. The only two non-European countries in the top 20 of elderly populations are Japan at 19th and the USA at 20th. The 60-plus group is 16.9% of the US population.

This ageing of the population is not confined to developed countries. "Developing countries account for 57% of the world's total of people 60 and over, and this share is projected to reach 69% by 2020."[15a]

Two other factors have contributed to the surge of American interest in right-to-die issues. One is the AIDS epidemic. Typical planning for a person with AIDS includes not only a will and a durable power of attorney for the client's property, but also a durable power of attorney for health care.[16] A principal objective of these documents is to recreate in the person with AIDS a sense of control over his life[17] — hearkening back to the existential psychotherapists.

The other factor is the decline of the family doctor. The avuncular general practitioner who cared for the patient for decades, and knew the patient's and his family's beliefs and attitudes about death, is a relic of a bygone era.[18] The attending physician now may need a document to tell him what he once knew from experience over the patient's lifetime.[19]

Terminology

Was it Mr Churchill who once commented that the British and the Americans are "two peoples divided by a common language"?[20] Let me define a few terms.[21] A *durable power of attorney* is one that remains good notwithstanding the principal's mental incapacity.[22] The usual rule of agency law is that death or incapacity of the principal revokes the authority of the agent; after all, if the principal lacks capacity, how can anyone act on his behalf? A durable power changes this rule; incapacity does not revoke a durable power, hence the term "durable". (Note that death of the principal still revokes even a durable power.)[23] These durable powers are authorised by current American statutes, although it appears that the widespread use of durable powers predated statutory sanction. The first durable powers statute dates to a 1950 Virginia statute,[24] although most states did not adopt statutory durable powers until after the 1969 promulgation of the Uniform Durable Power of Attorney Act.[25] Durable powers are known as "enduring powers" in Britain, and are recognised by The Enduring Powers of Attorney Act 1985.[26]

The classic durable power evolved to provide management of the incapacitated person's property.[27] An even newer application of durable powers is the *durable power of attorney for health care*, also known as a health care power of attorney or a health care proxy. This is similar to the original durable power, and may even be combined with it in a single document,[28] but grants the attorney-in-fact the power to make decisions about the incapacitated principal's health care or person, not about his property.[29] In Britain the usage again is an "enduring power", but the 1985 Act appears not to have been intended to encompass the power to make health care decisions,[30] although some terms in the Act (e.g. "to act . . . in relation to . . . the . . . affairs of the donor",[31] "authority to do on behalf of the donor anything which the donor can lawfully do by an attorney")[32] might be stretched to encompass health care decisions.[33]

Another term is the *"springing" power of attorney*. This is a durable power, but it is drafted so as to become effective not upon execution but upon the principal's subsequent incapacity, if it occurs. Hence the power "springs" into operation when needed — upon the principal's incapacity. This option has proved quite attractive in the USA, avoiding as it does the reluctance of a competent person to grant someone else his power of attorney. The original durable powers statutes in the USA often did not expressly sanction the "springing" power, but estate planners often drafted them anyhow, and legislation eventually caught up to real-world practice. Where statutes did not sanction "springing" powers, another way of accomplishing the same result was to execute a present power, but to manipulate registration or delivery (withhold it from the attorney-in-fact) so as to delay effectiveness until the principal's incapacity. The Enduring Powers Act 1985 makes no provision for springing powers.[34]

The term *"living will"* means the same thing in the USA and Britain.

This is an instrument usually providing that if the person executing it becomes incapacitated due to illness or accident, with no predicted hope for recovery, certain medical treatments are to be withheld or withdrawn. (Of course, the living will may take the opposite view — that medical treatment is to be continued, not terminated.) The first American living will statute was enacted in California in 1976.[35] It is not clear whether these statutes merely sanction an existing common law right (the better view) or whether the right is solely dependent upon statute.[36] Britain has no living will statute.[37] I have always felt that the term "living will" is something of a misnomer, since the usual "living will" says that if the individual has a terminal illness and no chance for recovery, he wants to die, not to live. I suppose the term is accurate in that the individual exercises control over the health care decision while living and competent.[38]

A little-publicised but potentially very significant statute is a *family consent statute*, also known as a surrogate decision-making statute. These statutes provide that if a terminally ill person has not executed a living will or a durable power of attorney for health care, and has no chance for recovery, he may be removed from medical treatment if the attending physician and designated family members concur in the decision to withdraw treatment. The patient may avoid these statutory provisions by a document executed while competent.[39] There is no comparable legislation in Britain.

Another term in the current American vocabulary is the *medical directive* or advance directive. This is simply an instrument in which the individual states in advance his wishes regarding various specific types of medical treatment in several representative situations.[40] The most publicised American form, for example, lists 12 potential treatments (e.g. cardiopulmonary resuscitation, respiration, renal dialysis) and four potential scenarios (e.g. a coma with no known hope of recovery, a coma with a small likelihood of recovery but a larger likelihood of survival with brain damage or death).[41] The individual thus has a dizzying menu of 48 potential choices. The medical directive differs from a living will in that it may cover numerous situations other than the use of extraordinary measures in cases of terminal illness. The medical directive differs from the durable power of attorney for health care in that the individual makes his decision on a set of fixed hypotheticals in advance, rather than delegating his authority to an agent to act as the agent deems best on the facts are they actually arise. There are a few American statutes dealing with medical directives, but more often they are based on assumed common law rights or extrapolated from living will or durable power legislation.[42] Britain has no specific legislation for medical directives.

Please note that the term "medical directive" or "advance directive" is sometimes used in America and Britain in a broader, catch-all sense to encompass any instrument (such as a living will or durable power) making health care decisions in advance. I will use the term in its more restricted sense as an instrument stating in advance the patient's desires about specific kinds of medical treatment.

A final term is the *personal statement*. There is no particular statutory regime in the USA or Britain; the individual simply states his personal desires with respect to one or more aspects of medical treatment.[43]

The foregoing summary is somewhat oversimplified. In fact there is a great deal of variation in relevant statutes from state to state, and many statutes and documents combine more than one concept.[44] For example, about one-quarter of the living will statutes authorise the appointment of health care proxies.[45] In about one-third of the states health care proxies are authorised in a statute separate from any living will legislation and often, although not always, in the form of a durable power of attorney for health care.[46]

The *Cruzan* case

In the welter of American litigation over the right to die, two cases stand out. Both involved young women in a persistent vegetative state. *In re Karen Quinlan*[47] led to enactment of the first generation of living will statutes. The recent case of *Nancy Beth Cruzan* v. *Director, Missouri Department of Health*[48] triggered a second-generation expansion of living will and related statutes. *Cruzan* is my text for this chapter.

The *Cruzan* case was decided in June 1990 by the United States Supreme Court. It was the first right-to-die case to be decided by our Supreme Court and was the most widely noted decision of the court's October Term 1989.

Cruzan is a story for the ages, but more a paradigm than a unique one. In 1983 Nancy Beth Cruzan, from her photographs a bright young woman in her twenties, lost control of her car as she travelled a Missouri road. The car overturned, and Nancy was found face-down in a ditch, with no detectable respiratory or cardiac function. Paramedics were able to restore breathing and heartbeat, but it was estimated that she suffered probable brain contusions and 12–14 minutes of oxygen deprivation or anoxia. Permanent brain damage usually results after 6 minutes of anoxia. Nancy remained in a coma for about 3 weeks, then progressed to an unconscious state in which she was able orally to ingest some nutrition. In order to ease feeding and further her recovery, surgeons implanted a gastrostomy feeding and hydration tube with the consent of her then husband. Subsequent rehabilitative efforts proved unavailing. Some months later Nancy was transferred to a state hospital. For 5 years she lay in a persistent vegetative state — a condition in which a person exhibits motor reflexes but evinces no indications of significant cognitive function.[49] Even the cold court record is tragic: Nancy was oblivious to her environment except for reflexive responses to sound and perhaps to pain; she exhibited her highest cognitive brain function by grimacing in response to pain. She was a spastic quadriplegic, suffering contracture of her four extremities, with irreversible muscle and tendon damage. She had no cognitive or reflex ability to swallow food or water. It was agreed that she would never recover these abilities, but that she might remain — "live" is too positive a word — in this state for as long as 30 years. It was agreed that if the gastrostomy tube were removed, Nancy would die. The Supreme Court later seemed to go out of its way to note that Nancy's mother and father were "loving and caring parents".[50]

After it became apparent that Nancy had no chance of recovery, her parents asked the hospital to terminate the artificial nutrition and hydration. The hospital refused to do so without court approval. Her parents, who had also been appointed her guardians, therefore sought Missouri court approval to terminate tubal nutrition and hydration.

A guardian *ad litem* was appointed, and he and the state of Missouri opposed the parents' request. Apparently the state of Missouri became involved because Nancy lay in a state hospital, but it was later reliably reported[51] that the state's opposition to the parents' action was based on a desire to strengthen the state's right-to-life position in a prominent abortion case, *Webster* v. *Reproductive Health Services.*[52]

Certainly Nancy's parents had reason to believe that their court action would be successful. There is little statutory authority, but generally the court decisions in other states have held that a competent individual has the right to refuse medical treatment.[53] This right has been based variously on the doctrine of informed consent or on the right to privacy. Under the doctrine of informed consent, any touching of the patient's body by the doctor without the patient's consent is a technical battery; hence, the patient has the right to refuse consent.[54] The other basis — the right to privacy — has been found by some courts to be a common law right and by other courts to be a constitutional right; some courts have based the constitutional right on the state constitution, others on the federal constitution.

Although there are prominent exceptions, as a general rule the right to refuse treatment has been extended to incompetent persons. If the patient's wishes are known, they must be respected, even if not in writing. If the patient's specific wishes are not known, but family members or other representatives, because of closeness to the patient and knowledge of his general value system, are reliable spokesmen, state courts have held that the family members may make the decision to withhold or withdraw treatment. This view is usually labelled the "substituted judgment" doctrine. Where evidence of the patient's actual desires is lacking, termination of treatment has even been allowed on a theory of "best interests" of the patient.

The Missouri trial court granted the request of the parents,[55] concluding from evidence of Nancy's "somewhat serious conversation" at age 25 with a housemate that if sick or injured she would not want to continue to live unless she could live at least halfway normally, and from representations by her family, that Nancy would not want continuation of artificial nutrition and hydration. The trial court treated the right to refuse treatment as a fundamental interest embodied in the federal constitutional right to privacy. In the trial court's view Nancy's interest was not outweighed by any state interest in the preservation of life.

On appeal, the Missouri Supreme Court reversed.[56] It expressed doubt that either the state or federal constitution embodied a right to die asserted on behalf of an incompetent patient. Any right to refuse treatment in Nancy's circumstances was outweighed by the state's interest in promoting life generally. The court suggested only two scenarios where the incompetent's desires might be given greater weight: one, where the patient had executed a living will[57] and, two, where the guardian could prove by "clear and convincing evidence" that the patient would have preferred the termination of treatment. In the Missouri Supreme Court's view, Nancy's oral statement to her housemate failed to meet the standard of clear and convincing evidence: it lacked the reliability and deliberation of specificity and reduction to writing.

This, then, was the posture of the case as it came to the United States Supreme Court. The trial court decision was typical of decisions in many other state courts: it treated the right to die as a fundamental constitutional interest. In the American system of jurisprudence, any state infringement on a "fundamental interest" is subject to "strict scrutiny".[58] The Missouri Supreme Court decision, on the other hand, reduced the right to die to something less than a fundamental interest and found it outweighed by an unqualified state interest in the quantity (certainly not the quality!) of life. Then, in contrast to the usual rule that appellate courts defer to trial court findings of fact, the Missouri Supreme Court found that the trial court had used the wrong standard of proof. Instead of the usual civil standard of a "preponderance of the evidence", the court imposed a higher but indeterminate standard — "clear and convincing evidence"[59] — and found that testimony as to Nancy's statement (to her housemate) and likely desires (per her parents) did not rise to that standard.

By the time the case reached the United States Supreme Court, it had attracted wide interest. Significant groups filed briefs as *amici curiae*. Among those favouring the right to die in Nancy's circumstances were the American Medical Association and two organisations advocating choice in dying.[60] Among those opposing Nancy's parents were legal advocacy groups for the handicapped[61] as well as Missouri Citizens for Life, an anti-abortion group.

Right-to-die advocates were hopeful of success in *Cruzan*, in view of the general trend of decisions in the state courts. On the other hand, they were uneasy because of the possible impact on the case of recent United States Supreme Court decisions on abortion. In 1973 the Court held in *Roe* v. *Wade*[62] that a woman's decision to abort was a constitutionally protected "fundamental interest" based on the right to privacy. (The right to privacy, by the way, is not expressly mentioned in the United States Constitution.)[63] *Roe* v. *Wade* became one of the most controversial decisions in American constitutional history. It was almost universally despised by Christian fundamentalists, who furnished a strong pillar of support for President Reagan's election victories in 1980 and 1984. Although the President steadfastedly denied any abortion litmus test for his appointees to the Supreme Court, an almost unbroken line of recent decisions has circumscribed *Roe* v. *Wade*: the constitutionality of various state legislative restraints on the right to an abortion has consistently been upheld. For example, in the 1989 case of *Webster* v. *Reproductive Health Services*[64] the court upheld a *Missouri* law that requires a second physician to attend an abortion as early as the 20th week of gestation. The Webster in the case name was the Attorney General of Missouri — the same official who opposed, in the name of the state, the petition of Nancy

Cruzan's parents.

So, what did the United States Supreme Court decide in *Cruzan?* By a five to four majority,[65] the court affirmed the Missouri Supreme Court decision denying the parents' request.[66] The United States Supreme Court framed the issue very narrowly. The appeal had been based on the Due Process Clause of the Fourteenth Amendment to the United States Constitution. That clause provides that no state shall "deprive any person of life, liberty, or property, without due process of law".[67] In the court's view, then, the issue was whether the Fourteenth Amendment prohibited the state from requiring clear and convincing evidence of the incompetent person's wishes to withdraw life-sustaining treatment. The court assumed that the person had a "liberty interest" (not a "fundamental interest") in refusing treatment,[68] but found that the state could constitutionally seek to preserve human life while providing only narrowly defined protection to Nancy Cruzan's autonomy.

Despite this defeat, there was a peaceful ending to Nancy's ordeal. Drawn forward by publicity of the case, three former co-workers recalled specific conversations in which Nancy had said she would never want to be kept alive in a vegetable-like condition.[69] Armed with this new evidence, her parents again petitioned a probate judge for an order to remove tube feeding. The probate judge found that the new evidence met the "clear and convincing evidence" standard approved by the Supreme Court. By this time, the State of Missouri had withdrawn from the case, feeling that its right-to-life position had been vindicated in the Supreme Court. Nancy's attorney supported the ruling. Euthanasia opponents — including legal advocates for the handicapped — sought to intervene, but state and federal courts held that they lacked standing. Nancy's feeding tubes were removed, and she died 12 days later — 6 months and a day after the United States Supreme Court decision and nearly 8 years after falling into a persistent vegetative state.

Legal significance of the *Cruzan* decision

What is the legal significance of the Supreme Court's decision? Right-to-die advocates were disappointed but sought to put the best light on it, citing it as the first holding that a competent individual has a constitutional right to refuse life-sustaining treatment.[70] That interpretation is suspect, however: although the court's language is equivocal in places, the court seemed merely to assume the existence of

the right for purposes of deciding the case.[71] Moreover, the assumed
right was a "liberty interest" (whatever that means), not a "fundamental interest" deserving enhanced judicial protection. The court's
vague reference to a balancing test (the societal interest in preserving
life) leaves open the existence of a constitutional right to die.[72]

Second, the decision seems to confirm that the definition of medical treatment includes artificial nutrition and hydration. This has
been a much-debated point in the literature,[73] since the simple provision of food in its traditional form scarcely seems to be medical treatment. Nevertheless, the Supreme Court nowhere questioned that
tubal hydration and nutrition are medical treatment. If tube feeding
were *not* regarded as medical care but only as comfort care, it probably would not be removable under any circumstances if it would
cause the patient discomfort.[74] Treating tube feeding as medical care
therefore may bring it within the scope of "medical" decisions that are
within the discretion of physicians and family.

Third, by approving the Missouri requirement of clear and convincing evidence, the court in effect held that a state may place limits on
the right of a surrogate decision-maker (e.g. family or guardian) to refuse treatment on behalf of a previously competent patient.[75]

Fourth, the majority expressly declined to decide whether the
states are constitutionally required to protect the autonomy of even
competent patients, for example, by enacting living will legislation or
family consent statutes.[76] The court did not mandate that a state allow
some weight to be given to the individual's preferences or to some
means of assessing them. The legal counsel to the American Medical
Association subsequently wrote that a logical corollary to the decision was the proposition that a state must permit withdrawal of
treatment where there is clear and convincing evidence that the patient would want treatment withdrawn.[77] Although counsel's reading
of *Cruzan* seems attractive to me, his reasoning appears to be falla-
cious: the proposition that if there is clear and convincing evidence
then treatment must be terminated does not logically follow from the
proposition that if there is not clear and convincing evidence then
treatment may not be terminated.[78]

Indeed, in a concurring opinion Justice Scalia, perhaps the intellectual leader of the Reagan appointees,[79] said that he would have preferred a decision that "the federal courts have no business in this
field".[80] On the other hand, in her concurring opinion, Justice O'Connor endorsed the use of durable powers and living wills: "These procedures for surrogate decisionmaking, which seem to be gaining in

acceptance, may be a valuable additional safeguard of the patient's interest in directing his medical care."[81]

An influential group of bioethicists issued a statement on the *Cruzan* decision.[82] Among the inferences they drew from the case were that other states were not required to adopt Missouri's standard nor was Missouri prohibited from enacting a different standard. They also inferred that the law's ethical standards and clinical practices were not changed by *Cruzan*.[83] It remains to be seen whether their reading was correct.

Was the United States Supreme Court's decision in *Cruzan* a poor one, as many right-to-die advocates believe? I think not. As the issue was framed, a contrary decision would have required the court to hold, in effect, that Nancy's parents had a constitutional Due Process right to terminate her life.[84] What checks and balances, if any, would have been imposed on such a right? I think the court simply did not want to write on a *tabula rasa*. The 1973 abortion decision, *Roe* v. *Wade*,[85] had attempted just such a process. It laid out, as a matter of constitutional interpretation, various rights and restrictions on abortion, according to whether the woman was in the first, second, or third trimester of her pregnancy. These conceptions were soon rendered obsolete by advances in medicine,[86] leaving the court in the embarrassing and hotly controversial position of having found very specific and now outmoded medicolegal tests in the Constitution. As I previously indicated, Justice Scalia frankly indicated his desire to keep the Supreme Court from making the same error on the issue of the right to die.[87] Further, he observed that if there were a constitutional right to die: (1) Would statutes making attempted suicide a crime be constitutional? (2) Would statutes allowing commitment to a mental health facility for attempting suicide be constitutional?[88] Assuming that *Cruzan* is not read as limiting state legislative discretion in the law of death, the decision leaves room for growth in the law as medical conditions and practices change. The court properly did not write the existing state of medical practice into a constitutional strait-jacket.

Effects of *Cruzan*

Let me now describe some effects of *Cruzan*[89] and then conclude with some tentative observations about issues that are latent in the right to die.

The media coverage of the *Cruzan* decision raised public consciousness of right-to-die issues. This consciousness was manifested in many ways. The leading advocacy group for the right to die, Choice in Dying, reported over 400 000 enquiries about living wills in the months following the decision.[90] In the fall of 1991 the lists of the top ten non-fiction best-sellers included a book entitled *Final Exit*, published by the Hemlock Press.[91] The book, written by Derek Humphry, the national executive director of the Hemlock Society,[92] a group advocating euthanasia for the terminally ill, is a manual on how to commit suicide. The dust jacket of the book notes that it is printed in large type for its likely readers (the elderly!). The *Cruzan* case spurred over 200 000 voters to sign Initiative 119,[93] to place on the ballot in Washington state in the November 1991 election the following proposition: "Shall adult patients who are in a medically terminal condition be permitted to request and receive from a physician aid in dying?"[94] The patient was required to be competent and at least two doctors had to determine that the patient had less than 6 months to live.[95] The measure almost passed, finally losing by a margin of 54% to 46%.[96]

Significantly, *Cruzan* has not been read by state courts as requiring states to adhere to a clear and convincing evidence standard for surrogate decisions to terminate treatment. Two particularly notable recent cases involve the right of surrogate decision-makers to terminate tubal nutrition and hydration of patients in a persistent vegetative state. The extraordinary fact in each of these cases was that the patients, aged 42 and 33 respectively, had never been mentally competent. In one, *In re Sue Ann Lawrance*,[97] a September 1991 Indiana Supreme Court decision, the patient had been mentally retarded since childhood. She had been disabled since 1958, when she was diagnosed as having a brain tumour. In 1987 she fell out of a wheelchair and lapsed into a persistent vegetative state. In the other, *Guardianship of Jane Doe*,[98] a January 1992 Massachusetts Supreme Judicial Court decision, the patient had been mentally retarded since infancy. She suffered from a degenerative disease of the brain and displayed no awareness of her surroundings and apparently did not feel pain. Since these patients had never been mentally competent, there was no way they could have formed any opinion as to the continuation or termination of treatment. I suppose this cuts both ways: certainly it is impossible to style the family's decision as merely carrying out the patient's intention; on the other hand, since the patient never had capacity to make a decision, perhaps it is necessary to look to the family as the decision-maker.

In any event, both cases upheld the surrogate decisions to terminate treatment. Indiana, by a four to one majority, said the patient's family had the authority to halt tubal feeding *without court approval*.[99] Massachusetts, by a four to three majority, sustained the decision of the patient's parents, guardian and physicians.[100] These cases may reflect a desire to give families and health care professionals more leeway to make medical decisions without intervention by courts or advocacy groups for the disabled.[101]

Perhaps the most significant effect of *Cruzan* was not in the public consciousness, nor in the courts, but in the legislatures. At the national level, Congress passed, in the fall following the decision, the Patient Self-Determination Act.[102] This Act, a bipartisan creation of Senators Danforth (Republican of Missouri)[103] and Moynihan (Democrat of New York), had been introduced but not passed in the preceding session.[104] Spurred by the *Cruzan* case, the Act was added by overwhelming vote to an omnibus budget bill.[105] The Act mandates, effective 1st December 1991, that all hospital and other health care providers receiving federal aid (Medicare, Medicaid and the like, i.e. most health care institutions) provide written information upon admission of all adult patients on their rights under state law to make decisions about their medical care, including the right to accept or refuse care and the right to formulate an "advance directive", defined as a written instruction such as a living will or durable power of attorney. While the point of hospital admission may not be the ideal time to confront the patient with these issues and decisions,[106] it would seem better than no time at all.

At the state level, *Cruzan* prompted many legislatures to review their statutes. The case of my home state, North Carolina, a fairly conservative, mid-Southern state with a substantial Baptist population, is instructive.[107] A first-generation living will statute had been on the books since 1977, but it spoke in terms of withholding or discontinuing "extraordinary means" of treatment from a patient whose condition is "terminal" and "incurable".[108] The statute seemingly would not apply to a person in Nancy Cruzan's position: she was receiving artificial nutrition and hydration — not extraordinary treatment — and she might live as long as 30 more years — scarcely a terminal illness. The legislature therefore amended the statute to recognise living wills dealing with (a) withdrawal of artificial nutrition and hydration from (b) a person in a persistent vegetative state.[109] Note that other medical technologies (e.g. cardiopulmonary resuscitation, respiration) and other possible conditions (e.g. coma, severe dementia) still are not expressly addressed in the statute.[110]

Significantly, for patients without a living will, the legislature also expanded the family consent statute to permit consent to the withholding or withdrawal of artificial nutrition and hydration if the patient is in a persistent vegetative state.[111] The statute previously dealt only with extraordinary means of treatment for a terminally ill person.

The North Carolina legislature also reviewed its power of attorney statute in light of *Cruzan*. The existing statute, enacted in 1983,[112] dealt principally with property matters. There was a subsection permitting the attorney-in-fact "to provide medical, dental and surgical care, hospitalization and custodial care for the principal".[113] Attorneys' opinions differed as to whether this language merely permitted the attorney-in-fact to make non-treatment decisions, such as whether to place the principal in a nursing home or hospital, or whether it allowed the attorney-in-fact to make treatment decisions such as whether to withhold a respirator.[114] Responding to *Cruzan*, the legislature amended the durable power of attorney statute to allow the principal to give his health care agent the same power as the principal has to make medical decisions, including the power to consent to a doctor giving, withholding or discontinuing any medical treatment, service or diagnostic procedure, including life-sustaining procedures.[115] Thus a durable power for health care could be drafted to authorise removal of artificial nutrition from a persistent vegetative state patient.[116]

Cruzan prompted many other state legislatures to review their living will and health care powers statutes. In general, it seems fair to say that the statutes were expanded to remove any doubt that they would apply to a person in Nancy Cruzan's situation. Before *Cruzan*, about 25 states had durable health care powers statutes. After *Cruzan*, it appears that 40–45 states have durable health care powers statutes, in one form or another.[117] Some states incorporated the *Cruzan* clear and convincing evidence standard into their living will statutes, while others rejected it.[118]

Possible lessons from the American experience

What lessons and issues, then, might be extracted from the American experience? Certainly your perspective will identify several.[119] Let me discuss a few.

First, what (if anything) should be done about the vast majority of persons who never execute living wills or durable powers? In his dissenting opinion in *Cruzan*, Justice Brennan chided the majority for failing to come to grips with this problem.[120] In his view the decision was out of touch with the reality that most people do not compose elaborate documents describing their wishes about the manner of treatment. (Indeed a majority never execute ordinary wills to dispose of their property.) He cited various statistics, including an American Medical Association survey, that no more than 15% of adults sign living wills.[121] He also cited the figures that an estimated 10 000 American patients are maintained in a persistent vegetative state;[122] the cost of their care is estimated at $120 million to $1.2 billion per year.[123] Eighty per cent of patients who die in hospitals are likely to be sedated and betubed.[124] A fifth of all adults reaching age 80 will suffer a progressive dementing disorder prior to death.[125] Eighty per cent of American deaths occur in an institutional setting (i.e. in a hospital or nursing home),[126] and perhaps 70% of those deaths are preceded by a decision to stop some form of care.[127]

Perhaps the Patient Self-Determination Act will increase the use of living wills. Nevertheless, the comparative infrequency of living wills highlights an endemic problem in the American law and practice of wills and trusts: if the individual takes no action to plan his estate, the plan provided by law is a poor one. But if he pays the expense of a lawyer, a better plan is easily available. Why should it be so? Why should not the plan provided by law — the "default position" if you will — be a good one in accord with likely intention? Let me give a few illustrations, drawn from the law of intestate succession and the law of guardianship.

If one dies intestate (without a will) the law should provide a statute of descent and distribution that comports at least roughly with likely intention. Empirical studies show that the typical American owner of a small to medium-sized estate prefers that all of his property pass to the surviving spouse, in preference to his children.[128] Yet the typical intestacy statute — no doubt reflecting ideas as old as common law dower and the Statute of Distribution (1670)[129] — divides the estate one-third to the spouse and two-thirds to the children. This result is especially aggravating if the children are minors and a guardian must be appointed to receive and manage their shares. The law in effect forces one to the time and expense of a will. The default position — the intestacy statute — is unacceptable.

For another example, if one does nothing and becomes incompetent, a guardian must be appointed to manage one's property. The disadvantages of guardianship are legend: the proceedings are public, initial delays are common, the ward loses personal autonomy; the judge lacks jurisdiction beyond state lines; the guardian must secure court approval for almost any act (since he lacks legal title to the ward's property); continuing court supervision via inventories and accountings is cumbersome and expensive; and the ward may lose significant civil rights such as the capacity to marry.[130] As one specialist put it, "In thirty-five years of practice, I have *never* met a client who sought court guardianship."[131] Again the law forces one to the time and expense of some alternative arrangement — typically a revocable *inter vivos* trust or a durable power. The default position — guardianship — is unacceptable.

The current law of living wills is similar. If one does nothing (executes no instrument) the law presumes that he wants all possible means to be used to preserve his life, even if he is terminally ill or in a persistent vegetative state. Yet the studies show that most people would not want to continue to live in such a condition.[132] I do not gainsay that the studies also show that a significant minority strongly favours the use of all possible medical treatments in such cases.[133]

What, then, is the solution? Obviously education and notice, to be considered in a moment, are important, but they will not reach everyone. One is tempted to advocate that the law provide a default position in accord with likely intention. That is, in the event of silence, it might be presumed that the patient would want the same treatment as elected by most people who execute living wills or durable powers. This notion of presumed intention seems radical at first blush, but the point is that the law already makes a decision for the person who fails to execute a living will or health care power: all possible means are to be used to preserve life. Why should not the law make the choice that most people favour, namely to terminate treatment? Of course, it is one thing to honour a living will — a document with the inherent reliability of specificity and written solemnity — and quite another to presume consent to withdrawal of medical treatment from silence. Yet the point remains that even under current law a decision is, in effect, made — namely by the state or its courts in favour of continuation of treatment. Is this decision not better made by the consensus of those individuals who think about the issue?

This new kind of approach is not without problems. Is it constitutional, for example, to presume that a patient would not want his life preserved if he were in a persistent vegetative state with no chance of recovery? What limits, if any, would be placed on a new notion of presumed consent by the requirements of due process of law? Perhaps the law of presumed consent to organ donation would provide some useful guidance on these questions.[134]

It would be vital in any statutory regime to allow the patient to opt out of the statutory scheme by properly executing an appropriate instrument.[135] Perhaps some provision should also be made for overcoming the statutory presumption by non-documentary evidence of the patient's likely desires.

On further reflection, it appears that there already exists a solution to the dissonance between likely patient desires and the law's imposed treatment regime. That solution is the family consent (surrogate decision-making) statute. These statutes are already in effect in about one-third of the states,[136] often as a part of the living will or natural death act.[137] In those states, if the patient has not executed a living will or durable power, the attending physician, with the concurrence of specified family members,[138] is empowered to withhold or withdraw treatment if the patient is terminally ill (or, under some statutes, in a persistent vegetative state).[139] Some of the statutes expressly allow the patient to opt out of the statutory regime;[140] all should do so. These statutes seem not to have engendered any right-to-life controversy, and may be a more flexible and graceful solution than a fixed presumption of presumed consent to termination of treatment.

A second question is related to the first: if most people do not consider living wills or other advance directives, how can they be encouraged to do so? Obviously we prefer individual choice to a statutorily imposed regime. How and when (if at all) should people be encouraged to consider living wills? The Patient Self-Determination Act, mandating that information be given at the time of hospital or nursing home admission, is one approach. It has been suggested that the point of admission to the institution is not the most propitious one,[141] due to its attendant anxieties and myriad other questions clamouring for resolution. Perhaps the better time and place would be in the doctor's office upon a routine visit. Ideally the doctor and patient would fully explore the patient's feelings in a sympathetic atmosphere.[142] But at least our experience suggests the possible efficacy of some provision for notice and advice within the system of health care delivery.

A third question is cost. In my previous discussion I assumed that individual choice was the desired objective. Yet it appears that a significant minority would choose to be kept alive without regard to cost of treatment.[143] It is estimated that 10 000 patients lie in a persistent vegetative state in America, at an estimated annual cost of care between $120 million and 1.2 billion.[144] Whether one's country has a National Health Service or not, society is ultimately bearing that cost of care. At what point, if at all, should cost of care limit individual freedom? Who should decide? How?[145]

A fourth point is suggested by the existing range of alternative devices for expressing or implementing choice. That is, each device seems to approach the treatment decision in a slightly different way. The living will and the medical directive reflect patient choice, but require the patient to anticipate possible medical conditions and treatment alternatives. The durable power of attorney for health care avoids these problems of foresight, by delegating the patient's power of choice to an agent selected by the patient. The family consent statute leaves the decision to the patient's physician and family. The substituted judgment doctrine in theory carries out the patient's intention, perhaps as tempered by the family. The "best interests" standard seems less subjective and more of an objective reasonable person test. The point is that all of these approaches illustrate different ways of making the decision. Perhaps we do not want to choose one to the exclusion of the others, but in approaching, say, the drafting of a statute to apply in the event the patient has executed no document, we need carefully to choose our model or models.[146]

Fifth, the need for foresight in drafting is illustrated by the post-*Cruzan* state legislative activity. Skill in anticipating unlikely eventualities is a hallmark of the good wills and trust drafter: what disposition, for example, does the client want if the intended principal beneficiaries in fact pre-decease the testator or settlor? We tend only to draft for the obvious and to overlook the unlikely. For example, the first generation of living will statutes apparently was drafted in response to the highly publicised case of Karen Quinlan.[147] The statutes focused on the use of heroic measures to maintain the terminally ill. We now realise from the *Cruzan* case that statutes need at least to consider whether to deal with a number of questions:[148]

1. *Possible medical conditions*: terminal illness, persistent vegetative state, coma and severe dementia.[149]
2. *Possible treatments*: cardiopulmonary resuscitation, respiration, renal dialysis, artificial nutrition and hydration,[150] antibiotics, surgery.
3. *Scope of treatment*: life sustaining, ordinary medical care, comfort.[151]
4. *Positive/negative decisions*: authorising treatment, withholding treatment, withdrawing treatment.[152]

Sixth, as I reviewed the living will and durable powers statutes, I realised that they incorporated a number of concepts from the traditional property law of wills and trusts. For example, I noticed that once executed, a living will remains valid unless revoked. Only a few states require the living will to be relatively fresh: in California, for example, the living will must have been executed within 5 years of the patient's illness.[153] The general rule — that the living will is ambulatory and remains good unless revoked — is the time-honoured rule for wills disposing of property.[154] This led me to consider how many of our other property rules may potentially be imported into the law of living wills and durable powers, and I found many.[155]

For example, should certain interested persons such as health care providers or relatives who would profit by inheritance or devise from the patient's death be barred from acting as witnesses or attorneys-in-fact? Should multiple copies of a living will be executed? (The property law rule for duplicate original wills is that each copy is the will. Hence if an executed copy is traced to the testator's possession but cannot be accounted for after death, it is presumed to have been revoked by physical act of destruction, and that revocation extends to all copies of the will.)[156] Is a durable power of attorney for health care naming the spouse as attorney-in-fact revoked by divorce? (The provisions for the spouse in an ordinary will, not the entire will, are revoked by divorce.)[157] Should there be any statutory requirement for a hearing to prove the validity of a living will or durable power? (Typically no hearing is required, in contrast to wills of property.)[158] What is the test for capacity to execute a living will or durable power?[159]

This is not to say that using traditional property concepts is bad. The point is that we need to be careful to consider whether property law concepts — for example, conflict of interest — are appropriate in the context of living wills or durable powers. We should not apply the property concepts blindly without asking whether the underlying policies are similar or different for a given issue.[160]

Seventh, some observations about our middle-class assumptions. The current regime is based on the assumption that the matter is best handled by document. This may be so, but one writer has decried the growing regime of documents for health care decisions.[161] To her, these documents resemble the law for commercial transactions between middle class white males; she finds them intrusive into an intimate personal and family decision. Further, who protects the disenfranchised: the poor, persons with no close or involved relatives, the mentally retarded, minors? I have already advocated an expanded family consent statute, but what if there is no defined "family"? One suggestion that has been made is to provide for a decision, as it were, by a family of peers.[162]

One other assumption we make about ordinary business documents is that, if executed, they should be binding. In this regard, some caution may be advisable for living wills. Researchers at the University of North Carolina recently studied whether living wills were in fact followed by a health care provider.[163] They found that living wills were followed in about three-quarters of the cases but disregarded in about one-quarter of the cases. The cases of disregard fell into two categories: cases where the living will directed termination of treatment but the health care provider thought that aggressive treatment would improve the patient's condition, and cases where the living will directed continuation of treatment but the health care provider thought that treatment would not improve the patient's condition. This study suggests that we may not want to make health care documents completely binding, and most living will legislation allows the doctor to disregard the patient's instructions, without liability.[164] On the other hand, individual autonomy and choice deserve protection, and some means has to be found of honouring the patient's intention while preserving some discretion for the doctor. The North Carolina study also found that health care providers sometimes were not aware that the patient had executed a living will; clearly there are systemic problems in communicating notice to the health care provider. The Patient Self-Determination Act, requiring hospitals to ask entering patients whether they have advance directives and requiring the hospital to include this information in the patient's medical record, may solve this problem.

Conclusion

Finally, a few observations about the organic nature of the law.[165] Two of Mr Justice Oliver Wendell Holmes' most famous aphorisms were: "The life of the law has not been logic, it has been experience"[166] and "Upon this point a page of history is worth a volume of logic."[167] The American experience to date seems to indicate the value of patience. Estate planners seem to have led the law: durable powers for property management, even springing ones, apparently came into wide use before they had comprehensive statutory recognition. Similarly, durable powers for health care seem to have been widely employed before clear statutory sanction. It seems useful for the statutory law not to interfere with the evolution of consensus on good drafting. This drafting experimentation and evolution means that the legislature will have had the benefit of a laboratory of experience to draw on in fashioning a thoughtful and comprehensive approach. Further, any statutory approach should not be exclusive; it should recognise and confirm, not create, rights. In this way, it will not chill further drafting experimentation. And finally, legislation should allow for changes in medical conditions and practices. The statutory law should lag, then complement social and medical developments.[168] Although our Supreme Court (viz. *Cruzan*) seems not to have trusted individual decisions, our state legislatures (viz. living wills, durable powers and family consent legislation) seem to have done so.

In sum, issues of death and disability in America are increasingly issues of choice, not fate. The durable power of attorney for health care may offer the best solution. But an expanded family consent statute, with opt-out provisions, may be needed for those who fail to consider or memorialise their choices.[169]

Notes and references

1. Generally I have cited only American or American/British authorities, on the theory that readers of this chapter will be well acquainted with the relevant British materials. Important British authorities relevant to the topics in this chapter appear to include M. Brazier, *Medicine, Patients and the Law* (1987); G. R. Dunstan and E. A. Shinebourne, *Doctors' Decisions: Ethical Conflicts in Medical Practice* ch 19 (1989); I. Kennedy, *Treat Me Right: Essays in Medical Law and Ethics* (1988); I. Kennedy and A. Grubb, *Medical Law: Text with Materials* (2nd edn, 1993); J. K. Mason, *Human Life and Medical Practice* (1988); J. K. Mason and R. A. McCall Smith, *Law and Medical Ethics* (3d edn, 1991); P. D. G. Skegg, *Law, Ethics, and Medicine* (1984).

   Most readers of this chapter will be familiar with the Law Commission's superb review of the adequacy of legal and other procedures for decision-making on behalf of mentally incapacitated adults. See The Law Commission, Mentally Incapacitated Adults and Decision-Making: An Overview (Consultation Paper No. 119, 1991) (hereinafter Consultation Paper No. 119). The Scottish Law Commission recently issued a similar study. See Scottish Law Commission, *Mentally Disabled Adults: Legal Arrangements for Managing their Welfare and Finances* (Discussion Paper No. 94, 1991).

2. See I.H. Yalom, *Existential Psychotherapy* (1980). See also E. Becker, *The Denial of Death* (Free Press edn 1975) (1973). See gener-

ally J. M. Humber and R. F. Almeder, *Biomedical Ethics and the Law* (2d edn, 1979) 489–634, especially 589–609.

3. As related in Yalom, *ibid* at 58. He attributes the line to Freud.

4. As quoted in L. Morrow, "A Dying Art: The Classy Exit Line" *Time*, (January 16, 1984) at 76.

5. "Depend upon it, sir, when a man knows he is to be hanged in a fortnight, it concentrates his mind wonderfully." Samuel Johnson, *Letter to Lord Chesterfield*, September 19, 1777, quoted in *Bartlett's Familiar Quotations*, 355 (E. Beck 15th edn, 1980).

6. See eg, L. A. Frolik and A. Barnes, *Elderlaw: Cases and Materials* (1992); L. A. Frolik and M. C. Brown, *Advising the Elderly or Disabled Client* (1992); M. Gilfix and P. J. Strauss, "New Age Estate Planning: The Emergence of Elder Law" *Tr. and Est.* (April 1988) at 15; K. Bergheim, "The Advent of Elder Law" *Lawyers Monthly* (A Supplement to Lawyers Weekly Publications, Inc.) (November 1990) at 1.

7. Two particularly useful American references on the matters considered in this chapter come not from bioethics sources but from the field of estate planning. They are D. P. Callahan and P. J. Strauss (eds), *Estate and Financial Planning for the Aging or Incapacitated Client* (1992, PLI Est. Plan. and Admin. Course Handbook Series No. 209, 1992) and S. J. Schlesinger, "Planning for the Elderly or Incapacitated Client" (1991) 16 *American College of Trust and Estate Counsel Notes* 211. The proceedings of the annual University of Miami Law Center Philip E. Heckerling Institute on Estate Planning, edited by Professor John T. Gaubatz, often contain useful articles relating to health care decisions and documents. See also, F. J. Collin Jr, "Planning and Drafting Durable Powers of Attorney" 15 *Prob. Notes* 27 (1989); and T. L. Beauchamp and J. F. Childress, *Principles of Biomedical Ethics* (3d edn, 1989).

8. F. J. Collin Jr, "Planning and Drafting Durable Powers of Attorney for Health Care" 22 *Univ. of Miami Philip E. Heckerling Inst. on Est. Plan.* paras 500, 501.2, pp. 5-6 to 5-6.

9. See J. P. Rosenfeld, "Old Age, New Beneficiaries" (1991) 16 *Prob. Notes* 260, 263.

10. F. J. Collin Jr, "Planning and Drafting Durable Powers of Attorney for Health Care" 22 *Univ. of Miami Philip E. Heckerling Inst. on Est. Plan.* paras 500, 501.1, p. 5-4.

11. *Ibid* at 5-4.

12. *Ibid* at 5-5.

13. *Ibid*.

14. *Ibid* at 5-7.

15. A. L. Otten, "People Patterns: We Can Hope It's Getting Wiser, Too" *Wall Street Journal* (February 28, 1992) at B1. This article is the source for the figures in this and the following paragraph.

15a. *Ibid*

16. E. Berendt and L. L. Michaels, "Your HIV Positive Client: Easing the Burden on the Family Through Estate Planning" (1991) 24 *John Marshall Law Review* 509.

17. R. Yates, "Estate Planning for the '90s: A Discussion" *American Bar Association Journal* (November 1991) at 60, 63 (quoting Joseph R. Baker III).

18. North Carolina Medical Society, *The Layman's Guide to Death with Dignity* 1 (1991); R. Kanigel, "New Guidelines Fuel Debate on 'Right to Die'," Raleigh, NC, *News and Observer* (February 24, 1991) at C1.

19. This factor may not be as significant in Britain. As I understand it, in Britain most patients go first to a Family Doctor or General Practitioner who provides primary care for the community. He or she then refers the patient, if necessary, to a specialist, probably practising in a hospital. C. Ham, *Health Policy in Britain: The Politics and Organization of the National Health Service* (1982) 41–59.

20. As quoted in "Britons are Urged to Save by Minding P's and Q's", *New York Times* (February 8, 1981) at A8.

21. See generally D. P. Callahan and P. J. Strauss (eds), *Health Care Proxies, Powers of Attorney, and Living Wills* (Practising Law Institute 1991); N. M. P. King, *Making Sense of Advance Directives* (1991); Schlesinger, *supra*, note 7; Alberta Law Reform Institute, *Advanced Directives and Substitute Decision-Making in Personal Health Care* (The Institute, 1991).

22. This chapter assumes that the individual has the capacity to execute the relevant document. Problems of defining or determining incapacity are beyond the scope of this chapter. Similarly, problems of potentially different standards for determining capacity (e.g. a living will compared to a durable power of attorney for health care) are not considered. Cf. P. J. Strauss, "Drafting Strategies: Some Guidelines for the Practitioner", in D. P. Callahan and P. J. Strauss (eds), *supra*, note 7, at 451, 453. For a general discussion of capacity, see T. Grisso, *Evaluating Competencies: Forensic Assessments and Instruments* (1986). The terms "capacity" and "competency" appear to be used interchangeably, despite the possible connotation of some skill in the term "competency".

23. The 1990 revision of the Uniform Probate Code relaxes this rule; death of a principal who has executed a written power of attorney, durable or otherwise, does not revoke the agency until the attorney-in-fact has actual knowledge of the death of the principal. Unif. Probate Code, section 5-504(a) (1990).

In the USA an important organisation known as the National Conference of Commissioners on Uniform State Laws (NCCUSL) seeks to prepare and secure enactment by the state legislatures of Uniform Acts for subjects in which uniformity of laws from state to state is desirable. NCCUSL submits the Uniform Acts to the American Bar Association for approval before promulgating them to the states for consideration. Prominent examples of Uniform Acts include the Uniform Commercial Code and, more closely related to the topic of this chapter, the Uniform Probate Code.

24. Prefatory Note, Unif. Durable Power of Attorney Act, 8 ULA 511, 511–12 (1983).

25. Unif. Durable Power of Attorney Act, *ibid.* See M. Fowler, "Appointing an Agent to Make Medical Treatment Choices" (1984) 84 *Columbia Law Review* 985 at 994.

26. See generally L. Griffiths, "The Enduring Power of Attorney" (1987) 17 *Family Law* 7; D. Carson, "Disabled-Enduring Powers of Attorney Act 1985" [1985] JSWL 344.

27. Consultation Paper No. 119 raises as a potential problem with durable powers of attorney for property management the lack of court supervision of the attorney-in-fact (in contrast, say, to a guardian and some trustees). See Consultation Paper No. 119, *supra*, note 1 at section 3.13. Despite this theoretical objection, American estate planners universally favour durable powers over guardianship and generally favour them over trusts. See J. N. Zartman, "Planning for Disability" (1989) 15 *Prob. Notes* 11. The lack of court supervision is seen as an advantage, not a disadvantage, of durable powers, *ibid.* This unblinking acceptance may in part be a reaction to the encrusted, expensive, and onerous aspects of court supervision of guardianships and trusts.

28. Although it is generally not advisable to do so.

   In general, a health care proxy should be separate from a general power of attorney. This seems desirable even though the principal resides in a state where a durable power of attorney statute authorises health care proxies. A client may wish to select different individuals to handle his business and financial affairs (pursuant to general power of attorney) and to make medical decisions (pursuant to a health care proxy). Use of a separate document will avoid the designation of a proxy becoming a public document (if the power of attorney has to be filed with public records), and will prevent the general power of attorney becoming part of the client's medical records. Finally, there may be different execution requirements for a health care proxy and a general power of attorney, and state law may provide for the expiration after a period of time of the health care proxy, which would not be desirable for the general power of attorney: S. J. Schlesinger, *supra*, note 7, at 16; S. Kess and B. Westlin, 1 *CCH Financial and Estate Planning* para 3295.20 (1991).

29. See generally K. L. Grice, "Advance Health Care Planning: Filling the Void" *Prob. and Prop.* (July/August 1990) at 40.

   Although the impetus for the health care proxy has been the desire of normal individuals to provide for treatment decisions if they become terminally ill, these statutes also have the potential for serving the mentally ill. The New York statute, for example, specifically includes mental health care. R. J. Isaac, "A Detour Around Crazy Mental Health Laws" *Wall Street Journal* (April 16, 1992) at A24. The health care agent may also be empowered to make ordinary treatment decisions, not just ones relating to terminal illness.

30. Consultation Paper No. 119, *supra*, note 1 at 66–7.
31. The Enduring Powers of Attorney Act 1985, section 3(1).
32. *Ibid*, section 3(2).
33. D. Carson, *supra*, note 26 at 350.
34. See Consultation Paper No. 119, *supra*, note 1 at 144. Consultation Paper No. 119 raises as a potential problem with durable powers of attorney for health care the problem of determining the time of the onset of incapacity. See Consultation Paper No. 119, *supra*, note 1 at section 3.14. American drafters have approached the problem in various ways. The typical durable power is a springing one. Some drafters prefer simply to state a general standard, for example "This power shall take effect in the event I become unable to make my own health care decisions." Other drafters prefer to specify who shall make the decision, for example, "This power shall take effect in the event I become unable, in the opinion of my attending physician, to make my own health care decisions." It does not appear that the determination of incapacity has been a problem; if the principal becomes incompetent, everyone knows it and the principal by definition lacks the capacity to take effective contrary action.
35. California Natural Death Act, Cal. Health and Safety Code sections 7185–95 (1976). See generally R. F. Weir, *Abating Treatment with Critically Ill Patients* (1989) 24. Recently the Governor of California vetoed a bill which would have expanded its Natural Death Act, *inter alia*, by adding "permanent unconsciousness" to the medical conditions under which life-sustaining treatment could be withheld and by eliminating the requirements that the living will be re-executed every 5 years. S. J. Schlesinger, *supra*, note 7 at 233.
36. N. M. P. King, *supra*, note 21 at 97–100.
37. See Consultation Paper No. 119, *supra*, note 1 at 139–43.
38. The living will was developed by Luis Kutner, a Chicago attorney, in the early 1930s in response to the medical treatment administered against the protests of a dying friend. It was called a "living will" because it sets forth the individual's decisions to take effect prior to death should the person become terminally ill. For a superb history of the development of living will legislation, see R. F. Weir, *Abating Treatment with Critically Ill Patients: Ethical and Legal Limits to the Medical Prolongation of Life* (1989).

A Uniform Rights of the Terminally Ill Act was promulgated in 1985 by the National Conference of Commissioners on Uniform State Laws (see note 23 for a brief description of the National Conference). This attempt at a uniform natural death Act, which provides for living wills and health care proxies, has not been widely adopted, probably because the Act: (1) fails to provide a mechanism for appointment of a proxy decision-maker for health care purposes; (2) lacks procedures governing non-terminal, permanently unconscious patients; and (3) fails to establish a decision-making process for abatement of medical treatment on behalf of an incompetent patient who has not executed a living will or health care proxy. M. A. Chapman, "The Uniform Rights of the Terminally Ill Act: Too Little Too Late?" 42 *Arkansas Law Review* 319 (1989). See also W. H. Pedrick, "The Uniform Rights of the Terminally Ill Act" *(Arizona Attorney)* (March 27, 1991) at 17.

39. See *Or Rev Stat* section 127.635(2) (1991).
40. It is unclear whether a health care provider who relies on a medical directive that lacks statutory sanction is protected from liability. See R. Kanigel, *supra*, note 18.
41. L. L. Emanuel and E. J. Emanuel, "The Medical Directive: A New Comprehensive Advance Care Document" (1989) 261 *Journal of the American Medical Association* 3288; E. E. Schultz, "Ruling Draws the Worried to 'Living Wills' " *Wall Street Journal* (June 29, 1990) at C1. For a study of patient attitudes towards medical directives, see L. L. Emanuel, M. J. Barry, J. D. Stoeckle, L. M. Ettelson and E. J. Emanuel, "Advance Directives for Medical Care: A Case for Greater Use" (1991) 324 *New England Journal of Medicine* 889. I am told that the Emanuels are revising their form and have reduced the number of choices the patient must make to something in the thirties. It has been questioned whether it is advisable for the patient to try to spell out the specific treatment, as opposed to the *outcome*, he desires. See R. Yates, "Estate Planning for the 90s: A Discussion" *American Bar Association Journal* (November 1991) at 60, 62 (quoting J. N. Zartmen); A. S. Brett, "Limitations of Listing Specific Medical Interventions in Advance Directives" (1991) 266 *Journal of the American Medical Association* 825. ("The focus on specific procedures may divert attention inappropriately away from treatment goals, does not necessarily enhance self-determination, and may provide a false sense of security." *Ibid*, at 827–8.)
42. See S. J. Schlesinger, *supra*, note 7 at 243.
43. One other kind of statute has been enacted in two states (New York and Georgia) to deal with the legal status of "Do Not Resuscitate" (DNR) orders. These two statutes permit the withholding of cardiopulmonary resuscitation (CPR) under certain statutory conditions. See S. J. Schlesinger and B. J. Scheiner, "Estate and Financial Planning for the Aging or Incapacitated Client" in D. P. Callahan and P. J. Strauss, *supra*, note 7 at 72–4. Many hospitals, as required by their accrediting body, have issued guidelines for DNR orders. See D. A. Smith, "Choice in Dying, Inc. Materials", in D. P. Callahan and P. J. Strauss (eds), *supra*, note 7 at 72–4. These statutes and guidelines

apparently came as a response to the informal use in some hospitals of blue dots or other cryptic notations (e.g. "Code Blue") on the patient's records, signifying to the nursing staff that a gravely ill patient was not to be resuscitated if death were imminent.

For a historical explanation and a critical review of the New York statute, see J. A. McClung and R. S. Kamer, "Implications of New York's Do-Not-Resuscitate Law" (1990) 323 *New England Journal of Medicine* 270.

For a discussion of ethical considerations in DNR orders, see C. B. Cohen and P. J. Cohen, "Do-Not-Resuscitate Orders in the Operating Room" (1991) 325 *New England Journal of Medicine* 1879.

44. I have tried nevertheless to identify the key conceptual differences.
45. *Cruzan, infra*, note 48 at 2858 note 4.
46. S. J. Schlesinger, *supra*, note 7 at 240.
47. 70 NJ 10, 355 A 2d 647, cert denied *sub nom Garger* v. *New Jersey* 429 US 922 (1976). See note 147, *infra*.
48. 497 US 261, 110 S Ct 2841, 111 L Ed 2d 224 (1990) (hereinafter cited as *Cruzan*; specific page citations are to 110 SCt).

For several thoughtful but different perspectives on the *Cruzan* case, written before the Supreme Court's decision, see "The Court and Nancy Cruzan" *Hastings Center Report* (January/February 1990) at 38–50, containing a collection of four articles: S. M. Wolf, "Nancy Beth Cruzan: In No Voice at All" *ibid* at 38; J. Bopp Jr, "Choosing Death for Nancy Cruzan" *ibid* at 42; G. Scofield, "The Calculus of Consent" *ibid* at 44; and I. M. Ellman, "Can Others Exercise an Incapacitated Patient's Right to Die?" *ibid* at 47.

For an article on *Cruzan*, arguing that American termination of treatment decisions have erroneously assumed that patient autonomy is absolute, see D. C. Blake, "State Interests in Terminating Medical Treatment" *Hastings Center Report* (May/June 1989) at 5.

There is an extensive literature on the *Cruzan* case. Leading articles appear to include: J. Bopp Jr and D. Avila, "The Due Process 'Right to Life' in Cruzan and Its Impact on 'Right-to-Die' Law" (1991) 53 *University of Pittsburgh Law Review* 193; J. Bopp Jr and D. Avila, "Perspectives on Cruzan: The Siren's Lure of Invented Consent: A Critique of Autonomy-Based Surrogate Decisionmaking for Legally-Incapacitated Older Persons" (1991) 42 *Hastings Law Journal* 779; S. R. Martyn and H. Bourguignon, "Coming to Terms with Death: The Cruzan case" (1991) 42 *Hastings Law Journal* 817; J. A. Robertson, "Cruzan and the Constitutional Status of Nontreatment Decisions of Incompetent Patients" (1991) 25 *Georgia Law Review* 1139. Leading student casenotes appear to include: J. Shur Jr, Comment: "Cruzan v. Director: Clear and Convincing Call for Comprehensive Legislation to Protect Incompetent Patient's Rights" (1991) 40 *American University Law Review* 1477; A. M. Gaudin, Note: "Cruzan v. Director, Missouri Department of Health: To Die or Not to Die: That is the

Question — But Who Decides?" (1991) 51 *Louisiana Law Review* 1307; J. E. Bennett Overton, Note: "Unanswered Implications: The Clouded Rights of the Incompetent Patient Under Cruzan v. Director, Missouri Department of Health" (1991) 69 *North Carolina Law Review* 1293; E. D. McLean, Comment: "Living Will Statutes in Light of Cruzan v. Director, Missouri Department of Health: Ensuring that a Patient's Wishes Will Prevail" (1991) 40 *Emory Law Journal* 1305.

49. Of course, one solution to the problem of termination of treatment for persons in a persistent vegetative state (PVS) would be to redefine death to include permanent loss of sentience. That is, for some patients PVS could be conceived not as the lowest-functioning phase of life but as the highest-functioning state of death. See D. Wikler, "Not Dead, Not Dying? Ethical Categories and Persistent Vegetative State" *Hastings Center Report* (February/March 1988) at 41.

For a discussion of the definition of death see M. Brazier, *supra*, note 1, ch 19; J. K. Mason and R. A. McCall Smith, *supra*, note 1, ch 13. In contrast to Great Britain, which has no statutory definition, all but one of the American states (South Dakota) have defined death by statute. *Wall Street Journal* (April 10, 1991) at B8. The usual definition is total cessation of all brain functions, *ibid*, including the automatic functions (breathing, heartbeat) controlled by the brain stem. P. J. Riga, "A Brief Life that Could Save Others" *National Law Journal* (April 27, 1992) at 15.

In 1991 New Jersey passed an unusual declaration of death law, requiring doctors to consider a patient's religious beliefs before declaring the patient "brain dead" and removing life-sustaining treatment, *Wall Street Journal, supra*. "The law states that patients who have permanently lost all brain functions are legally dead, unless there are religious objections. If objections exist death will be defined by the traditional criteria of irreversible loss of breathing and heartbeat." *Ibid*. The religious exemption likely will be copied by other states. *Ibid*.

50. *Cruzan, supra*, note 48 at 2855.

51. See "Cruzan Will Be the Last" *National Law Journal* (December 17, 1990) at 6 (quoting former Missouri Supreme court Judge Warren Welliver: "The state's just not going to be getting back in. This was an aberration. It just hit at a time when they were in desperation for something to beef up the abortion cases.")

52. 492 US 490.

53. For an excellent summary of current American cases and statutes, see D. A. Smith, "Choice in Dying, Inc. Materials" in D. P. Callahan and P. J. Strauss (eds), *supra*, note 7 at 187–273. These materials support the statements in the accompanying paragraph and the following paragraph of the text. The majority opinion in *Cruzan* contains a very good listing and discussion of state court decisions on the right to die. See *Cruzan, supra*, note 48 at 2847–51.

54. For discussions of informed consent, see P. S. Appelbaum, C. W. Lidz and A. Meisel, *Informed Consent: Legal Theory and Clinical Practice* (1987); Law Reform Commission of Victoria Symposia 1986, *Medicine Science and the Law: Informed Consent* (1986); R. R. Faden, T. L. Beauchamp and N. M. P. King, *A History and Theory of Informed Consent* (1986); and A. B. Churchward, "A Comparative Study of the Law Relating to the Physician's Duty to Obtain the Patient's 'Informed Consent' to Medical Treatment in England and California" (1990) 5 *Connecticut Journal of International Law* 483.

55. See *Cruzan, supra*, note 48 at 2846, for a summary of the trial court's decision.

56. *Cruzan* v. *Harmon* 760 SW 2d 408 (Mo 1988).

57. Missouri had not yet enacted its living will statute at the time of Nancy's accident.

58. J. E. Nowak and R. D. Rotunda, *Constitutional Law* (4th edn, 1991) 575–6.

59. American courts generally use three standards of evidence: a preponderance of the evidence (in most civil cases), clear and convincing evidence (in some civil cases), and evidence beyond a reasonable doubt (in criminal cases). It is difficult to define "clear and convincing evidence" except to say that it is a higher standard than a preponderance of the evidence but lower than evidence that is beyond a reasonable doubt. For a discussion of the standard of clear and convincing evidence, see *Cruzan, supra*, note 48 at 2853–4; G. J. Annas, "Nancy Cruzan and the Right to Die" (1990) 323 *New England Journal of Medicine* 670, 670–1.

60. Concern for Dying and Society for the Right to Die. These organisations, originally formed for the separate tasks, respectively, of disseminating information about the right to die and of advocating legislation to allow the right to die, were recently merged into one organisation, Choice in Dying, Inc.

61. National Legal Center for the Medically Dependent and Disabled, Association for Retarded Citizens of the US, and the Nursing Home Action Group.

62. 410 US 113 (1973).

63. The right to privacy was found to inhere in the United States Constitution in the case of *Griswold* v. *Connecticut*, 381 US 479 (1965), which held that a Connecticut law forbidding the use of contraceptives unconstitutionally intruded upon the right of marital privacy. In a phrase of lasting constitutional fame (or infamy, depending on one's attitude towards expansive judicial interpretation) the majority opinion by Mr Justice Douglas found the constitutional right to privacy floating somewhere in the netherworld: "specific guarantees in the Bill of Rights have penumbras, formed by emanations from those guarantees that help give them life and substance". *Ibid* at 484.

64. *Supra*, note 52.

The Supreme Court will have another opportunity to further limit or even to overrule *Roe* v. *Wade* in the closely watched case of *Planned Parenthood of Southeastern Pennsylvania Reproductive Health and Counseling Service* v. *Casey*, Nos 91-744 and 91-902, expected to be decided in the summer of 1992. *Casey* involves preabortion requirements of a 24-hour waiting period, spousal notice, parental consent for minors, and a lecture on abortion dangers. See generally D. J. DeBenedictus, "Restrictive Abortion Law Withheld", *American Bar Association Journal* (January 1992) at 16; H. J. Reske, "Playing Politics with Abortion Decision" *ibid* at 18; H. J. Reske, "Is This the End of Roe?" *American Bar Association Journal* (May 1992) at 64.; "Abortion Rights Activists See Hostile Thomas" *National Law Journal* (March 23, 1992) at 5; M. Coyle, "The Writer and the Fighter" *National Law Journal* (April 20, 1992) at 1; "The Administration Renews Call to Repeal Roe" *National Law Journal* (April 29, 1992) at 5, 10. [In late June 1992, by a five to four margin the Court upheld the Pennsylvania restrictions in *Planned Parenthood* v. *Casey* 112 SCt 2791 (1992). Nevertheless, the "joint opinion" of three Reagan appointees, Justices O'Connor, Kennedy and Souter, joined in part by two sometimes liberal Justices, Blackman and Stevens, agreed that "the essential holding of *Roe* v. *Wade* should be retained and once again reaffirmed". Justices Rehnquist, White, Scalia and Thomas dissented and would have overruled *Roe* v. *Wade*. As usual, Justice Scalia was trenchant: "The permissibility of abortion, and the limitations upon it, are to be resolved like most important questions in our democracy: by citizens trying to persuade one another, and then voting." *Ibid* at 2873.

If the Court ducks the issue in *Casey*, other cases working their way through the courts, particularly *Guam Society of Obstetricians and Gynecologists* v. *Ada*, No. 90-16706, may present a clearer challenge to *Roe* v. *Wade. Ibid*; P. M. Barrett, "Abortion Right Is Affirmed in Guam Case" *Wall Street Journal* (April 17, 1992) at B8; "Appeals Courts at Forefront of Abortion Action" *National Law Journal* (January 20, 1992) at 5. In late 1992, the court refused to hear an appeal seeking reinstatement of the criminal prohibition of abortion enacted by the territory of Guam. By declining to disturb the lower court ruling striking down the Guam law, the Court still left open the question of how courts should deal with abortion restrictions less severe than outright bans. P. M. Barrett, "Supreme Court Refuses to Hear Appeal of Ruling Against Guam Ban" *Wall Street Journal* (December 1, 1992) at A2.

65. The Justices who participated in the decision and the Presidents who appointed them are as follows. In the majority, Justices Rehnquist (Nixon), White (Kennedy), O'Connor (Reagan), Scalia (Reagan) and Kennedy (Reagan). In the minority, Justices Brennan (Eisenhower),

Marshall (Johnson), Blackmun (Nixon) and Stevens (Nixon). Justices Brennan and Marshall have since retired, being replaced by Justices Souter (Bush) and Thomas (Bush).

66. *Cruzan, supra,* note 48. For an excellent analysis of the *Cruzan* case and its relationship to the abortion decisions, see K. R. Wing, "The Supreme Court's Spring Term: Abortion, the Right to Die, and the Decline of Privacy Rights" (1990) 15 *Journal of Health Politics, Policy and Law* 919. Professor Wing compares *Cruzan* to two abortion decisions of the same term, *Hodgson* v. *Minnesota* 497 US 417 (1990) (upholding a Minnesota statute requiring an unemancipated minor to give 48 hours notice to both her parents prior to an abortion), and *Ohio* v. *Akron Center for Reproductive Health* 497 US 502 (1990) (upholding an Ohio statute requiring a physician to personally give 24 hours parental notice prior to an abortion for an unemancipated or unmarried minor). For a thoughtful exploration of the possible inconsistency between *Cruzan* (in effect denying the family a role in the decision to terminate medical treatment) and *Ohio* v. *Akron Center for Reproductive Health* (in effect requiring the family to participate in the decision to obtain an abortion), see M. Minow, "The Role of Families in Medical Decisions" (1991) *Utah Law Review* 1.

See generally G. J. Annas, *supra,* note 59; R. F. Weir and L. Gostin, "Decisions to Abate Life-Sustaining Treatment for Nonautonomous Patients" (1990) 264 *Journal of the American Medical Association* 1846.

In another widely publicised Missouri case, the issue was whether the father and guardian of a 21-year-old daughter in a persistent vegetative state could properly act by moving his daughter to another jurisdiction for the ostensible reason of finding a lower standard (than Missouri's) for decisions to remove feeding tubes. The court held the father could not move the daughter unless sufficient evidence showed it was in her best interests. *In re Busalacchi*, No. 59582, 1991 WL 26851 (Mo Ct App Eastern District, March 5, 1991).

67. US Const amend XIV, section 1.

68. The term "liberty interest" is a relatively new one in American constitutional jurisprudence. It first appeared in *Board of Regents* v. *Roth* 408 US 564, 573 (1971). See also, L. H. Tribe, *American Constitutional Law* 685–94 (1988). For some discussion of the meaning of "liberty interest" see *Cruzan, supra,* note 48 at 2851.

69. "Cruzan's Death Doesn't Still Debate" *American Bar Association Journal* (March 1991) at 26. This article is the source for the other statements in this paragraph.

70. L. Greenhouse, "Liberty to Reject Life" *New York Times* (June 27, 1990) at A16.

71. *Compare*: "The principle that a competent person has a constitutionally protected liberty interest in refusing unwanted medical treatment may be inferred from our prior decisions" and "Still other cases support the recognition of a general liberty interest in refusing med-

ical treatment." *Cruzan, supra*, note 48 at 2851, *with*:

> Petitioners insist that under the general holdings of our cases, the forced administration of life-sustaining medical treatment, and even of artificially-delivered food and water essential to life, would implicate a competent person's liberty interest. Although we think the logic of the cases discussed above would embrace such a liberty interest, the dramatic consequences involved in refusal of such treatment would inform the inquiry as to whether the deprivation of that interest is constitutionally permissible. *But for purposes of this case, we assume that* the United States Constitution would grant a competent person a constitutionally protected right to refuse lifesaving hydration and nutrition.

Ibid at 2852 (emphasis added).

72. K. Wing, *supra*, note 66 at 925–6.
73. N. Cantor, *Legal Frontiers of Death and Dying* 39 (1987) (withholding respirator suffocates as much as withholding nutrition starves), P. G. Peters Jr, "The State's Interest in the Preservation of Life: From Quinlan to Cruzan" 50 *Ohio State Law Journal* 891 at 966; R. A. Destro, "Quality of Life Ethics and Constitutional Jurisprudence: The Demise of Natural Rights and Equal Protection for the Disabled and Incompetent" (1986) 2 *Journal of Contemporary Health Law and Policy* 71 at 126 (it is not the disease that kills when nutrition is withheld).
74. F. J. Collin Jr, *supra*, note 7 at 41–2.
76. K. Wing, *supra*, note 66 at 925–6.
76. In her concurring opinion, Justice O'Connor, the only woman on the court, indicated her likely view on this issue: "I also write separately to emphasize that the Court does not today decide the issue whether a State must also give effect to the decisions of a surrogate decisionmaker . . . In my view, such a duty may well be constitutionally required to protect the patient's liberty interest in refusing medical treatment." *Cruzan, supra*, note 48 at 2857.
77. D. Orentlicher, "The Right to Die After Cruzan" (1990) 264 *Journal of the American Medical Association* 2444 at 2445. Overall the article is a thoughtful exploration of the explicit and implicit principles of the *Cruzan* opinion.
78. The logical error is known as the fallacy of denying the antecedent. M. Black, *Critical Thinking* 64 (2nd edn, 1952).
79. See P. M. Barrett, "The Loner: Despite Expectations, Scalia Fails to Unify Conservatives on Court" *Wall Street Journal* (April 28, 1992) at A1; A. Wohl, "Whose Court Is It? Conservatives in Search of their Own Brennan" *American Bar Association Journal* (February 1992) at 40.
80. *Cruzan, supra*, note 48 at 2859.
81. *Ibid* at 2858.

82. "Bioethicists' Statement on the U.S. Supreme Court's Cruzan Decision" (1990) 323 *New England Journal of Medicine* 686. The statement was drafted at the Second Annual Conference of Bioethicists, 6 days after the *Cruzan* decision.

83. The full text of the statement is as follows:

On June 25, 1990, the U.S. Supreme Court issued its long-awaited decision in the case of Nancy Cruzan, the first "right to die" case to come before it. The purpose of this statement is to clarify the meaning of that case in order to prevent misinterpretation that might lead to serious adverse consequences for hopelessly ill patients, their families, and health care professionals.

First, the Supreme Court affirmed the right of competent patients to refuse life-sustaining treatment.

Second, the Court did not treat the forgoing of artificial nutrition and hydration differently from the forgoing of other forms of medical treatment.

Third, the holding in the *Cruzan* case was only that the state of Missouri could require the continued treatment of a patient in a persistent vegetative state unless there was "clear and convincing evidence" that she had explicitly authorized the termination of treatment before losing the capacity to make decisions.

Fourth, the *Court* did not require that other states adopt Missouri's rigorous standard of proof, nor did it preclude Missouri from adopting a different evidentiary standard in the future.

Fifth, the *Cruzan* decision does not alter the laws, ethical standards, or clinical practices permitting the forgoing of life-sustaining treatment that have evolved in the United States since the *Quinlan* case in 1976.

We recommend that physicians continue to be guided by the ethics of the medical profession and accepted clinical practices concerning the forgoing of life-sustaining treatment unless and until these are affirmatively changed by their state courts or legislatures. Although advance directives are not necessary for the discontinuance of life-sustaining treatment of incompetent patients, except in Missouri and New York, they often help to resolve legally and ethically troubling cases. We urge physicians to discuss the use of life-sustaining treatments with their patients in order to discover the patient's preferences and values. Physicians should also encourage patients to discuss their preferences with their families and close friends and to prepare and sign advance directives.

84. See J. E. Nowak and R. D. Rotunda, *supra*, note 58 at 812–16. See also I. M. Ellman, *supra*, note 48.

85. 410 US 113 (1973).

86. See e.g., N. K. Rhoden, "Trimesters and Technology: Revamping Roe

v. Wade" (1986) 95 *Yale Law Journal* 639 at 639–40.
87. See text accompanying note 80, *supra*.
88. *Cruzan, supra,* note 48 at 2860–2.
89. See generally P. Katzeff, "Right-to-Die Forces See Gains" *National Law Journal* (September 2, 1991) at 15.
90. D. Kong, "Drive to Draft Living Wills" Raleigh, NC, *News and Observer* (December 16, 1990) at E1.
91. J. Sherwood, "Washington Sets Euthanasia Vote" *American Association of Retired Persons Bulletin* (November 1991) at 1. A. Griffin, "Best Seller, Michigan Suicide Machines Spark Controversy" *Daily Tar Heel* (November 4, 1991) at 2.
92. Humphry was born in England and now lives in the state of Oregon, the American headquarters of the Hemlock Society.
93. J. Keown, "Dutch Slide Down Euthanasia's Slippery Slope" *Wall Street Journal* (November 5, 1991) at A18; J. Sherwood, *supra*, note 91.
94. J. Beck, "The Question of Too Much Care" Raleigh, NC, *News and Observer* (January 10, 1991) at 15A. See also, J. Balzar, " 'Death with Dignity' on Ballot" Raleigh, NC, *News and Observer* (October 6, 1991) at 1A.
95. *Ibid.*
96. J. Gross, "Voters Turn Down Mercy Killing Idea" *New York Times* (November 7, 1991) at B16.

If I may be forgiven a bad pun, the issue of legal approval for euthanasia is not dead, even after the failure of Initiative 119. In February 1992 the American Bar Association House of Delegates defeated a resolution supporting the right of terminally ill persons to receive aid in dying from their physicians. The resolution, sponsored by the Beverly Hills, California, Bar Association, was similar to Initiative 119 and would have applied only to persons expected to live 6 months or less. Another initiative, to place on the November 3, 1992 California ballot a Death with Dignity Act similar to the Washington State Initiative 119, is expected to gain sufficient signatures. [The California measure, known as Proposition 161, was a fine-tuned version of Washington's Initiative 119. For example, euthanasia would have been allowed only when two doctors had certified that the patient was incurably ill and had a life expectancy of less than 6 months, when the patient was mentally competent, and when the patient had requested death on at least two occasions in front of disinterested witnesses. F. Jones, "Euthanasia Boosters Aim to Kill Our Compassion" *Toronto Star* (November 9, 1992) at D1. Proposition 161 failed by the same margin as the Washington Initiative, 54% to 46%. *Ibid*; G. de Lama, "States Take Pulse on Morality" *Chicago Tribune* (November 5, 1992) at 7. See also, D. J. Saunders, "Pull the Plug on California Initiative" *Wall Street Journal* (October 29, 1992) at A15. Reportedly, similar measures have been introduced in the legislatures of Maine, New Hampshire, Iowa and Michigan. S. B. Goldberg, "Assisted

Suicide Resolution Defeated" *American Bar Association Journal* (April 1992) at 107; J. Podgers, "Matters of Life and Death: Debate Grows Over Euthanasia" *American Bar Association Journal* (May 1992) at 60; "Section News: ABA Mid-Year Meeting" *Prob. and Prop.* (May/June 1992) at 6; "Quayle Spices Up ABA Meeting" *National Law Journal* (February 17, 1992) at 1, 55. The ABA has formed a Commission on Legal Problems of the Elderly, *see* Goldberg, *supra*, as well as a Coordinating Group on Bioethics and the Law. "Around the ABA: New Group Will Coordinate ABA's Efforts in Bioethics" *American Bar Association Journal* (May 1992) at 107. For general discussions of euthanasia, see J. K. Mason and R. A. McCall Smith, *supra*, note 1, ch 15; G. Grisez and J. M. Boyle Jr, *Life and Death with Liberty and Justice: A Contribution to the Euthanasia Debate* (1979); J. Rachels, *The End of Life: Euthanasia and Morality* (1986).

Controversy about the role of the doctor in possibly ending a person's life has been sharpened by frequent news accounts of the activities of Dr Jack Kevorkian. He has been involved in the suicides of four women in Michigan in the past 2 years. The women were not terminally ill, although all had painful or debilitating diseases. Dr Kevorkian apparently provided the devices that allowed the women to die, although the women activated them personally. Michigan has no law against this sort of assisted suicide, although legislation is under consideration. However, prosecutors have charged Dr Kevorkian with homicide for his involvement in two of the deaths, and a trial is possible. In addition, the latest woman's death has been ruled a homicide rather than a suicide. "Death at Kevorkian's Side Is Ruled Homicide" *New York Times* (June 6, 1992) at A10.

On the other hand, in *McKay* v. *Bergstedt*, 801 P2d 617 (Nev 1990), a 31-year-old quadriplegic had been sustained on a respirator for over 20 years. He was cared for by his father, a cancer-stricken amputee with a pension of only $1100 per month. The son petitioned for a ruling that he had a right to remove the respirator and for immunity for anyone who helped him. A few weeks after his death, Nevada's high court affirmed the lower court decision in favour of the quadriplegic. By then, the father also was dead. The Nevada court cited a landmark 1986 "quality of life" case from California, *Bouvia* v. *Superior Court*, 179 Cal App 3d 1127, 225 Cal Rptr 297 (Ct App 1986), *review denied* (Cal June 5, 1986), which allowed a paralysed woman unilaterally to refuse intubation and thereby to starve herself to death. G. D. Cox, "Right-to-Die Cases Raise Questions on Quality of Life" *National Law Journal* (December 17, 1990) at 3.

For a statement against euthanasia and Initiative 119, issued by 13 Jewish and Christian theologians and philosophers, under the auspices of the Ramsey Colloquium of the Institute on Religion and Public Life, see "Always to Care, Never to Kill" *Wall Street Journal* (November 27, 1991) at A8. For letters to the editor responding to the statement, see "'Living Will' and the Will to Die" *Wall Street Journal* (December 19, 1991) at A15.

97. 579 NE2d 32 (Ind 1991).

98. 411 Mass 512, 583 NE 2d 1263, *cert denied*, 112 S Ct 1512 (1992).

99. The court also held, consistently with *Cruzan*, that artificial nutrition and hydration are medical treatment that a patient or her surrogates may refuse. *In re Sue Ann Lawrance, supra,* note 97 at 39–40. *Lawrance* was followed in the April 1992 Wisconsin case of *In re Guardianship of L.W.*, 482 NW 2d 60 (Wis 1992), also holding that a surrogate (in this case a court-appointed guardian rather than the parents) of an elderly incompetent in a persistent vegetative state (1) could refuse artificial nutrition and hydration where refusal was in the best interests of the ward, (2) without prior approval from the court.

100. Two months later, in the March 1992 case of *Care and Protection of Beth*, 412 Mass 188, 587 NE 2d 1377 (1992) (six to one decision), the Massachusetts Supreme Judicial Court approved a trial judge's Do Not Resuscitate order for the 5-year-old child in an irreversible coma. The child's parents were unmarried, separated minors. The theory of the decision was substituted judgment.

101. See *Wall Street Journal* (September 17, 1991) at B8.

Most cases concerning termination of treatment involve a fight by the patient or the patient's surrogates to refuse treatment. The recent American case of Helga Wanglie is unusual because Mrs Wanglie's husband would not abide by the wishes of the doctors in the hospital caring for his wife and allow the removal of her life-sustaining treatment. After a heart attack, Mrs Wanglie, 87, suffered severe brain damage that left her in a persistent vegetative state. She was completely unresponsive and dependent on a respirator and feeding tube with no hope of recovery. Nevertheless, Mr Wanglie insisted that his wife had told him she would want to be kept alive even in such a situation, based on her strong religious convictions. After determining that further treatment was futile, the hospital went to court in an attempt to obtain appointment of an independent conservator who would agree to termination of treatment. The judge rejected the hospital's arguments and determined that Mr Wanglie was the best judge of what his wife would have wanted. Mrs Wanglie died of pneumonia 3 days after the decision, still receiving treatment. "Brain-Damaged Woman at Center of Lawsuit Over Life-Support Dies" *New York Times* (July 6, 1991) at A8; "Doctors Assert Patient's Right to Die" *American Bar Association Journal* (October 1991) at 26. See also M. Angell, "The Case of Helga Wanglie: A New Kind of 'Right to Die' Case" (1991) 325 *New England Journal of Medicine* 511.

102. Omnibus Budget Reconciliation Act of 1990, Pub. L. No. 101-508, at 4206 (1990). The law took effect in December 1991, 1 year after

Congress passed it. It is codified as 42 USC section 1396A (1991). See generally M. Gates, "Patients Due Facts on Treatment Rights" *AARP Bulletin* (November 1991) at 1; K. C. Mulholland, "Protecting the Right to Die: The Patient Self-Determination Act of 1990" (1991) 28 *Harvard Journal on Legislation* 609.

103. Home of *Webster* and *Cruzan*.

104. M. Lavelle, M. Coyle and F. Strasser, "Living Wills Get Boost from the Lawmakers" *National Law Journal* (October 29, 1990) at 5, 33.

105. M. Coyle and M. Lavelle, "Quietly, A Tougher, Less Gentle EPA Emerges" *National Law Journal* (December 3, 1990) at 5.

106. R. Kanigel, "Every Patient to Face Issue of Right to Die" Raleigh, NC, *News and Observer* (December 1, 1991) at C1 (quoting Larry Churchill, a medical ethicist at the University of North Carolina at Chapel Hill).

107. See generally A. J. Diosegy, "Advance Care Directives: May the Force Be With You" *The Will and the Way* (January 1991) at 1; N. M. P. King, "The Natural Death Act: A Philosophical Context for a Practical Problem" *North Carolina State Bar Quarterly* (Winter 1992) at 12; C. A. Schwab, "Advance Directives: North Carolina's Response to Cruzan" *The Will and the Way* (November 1991) at 1; B. Tillman, "Exercising the Right to Die: North Carolina's Amended Natural Death Act and the 1991 Health Care Power of Attorney Act" (1992) 70 *North Carolina Law Review* 2108.

108. Act of June 29, 1977, ch 815, sections 1–2, 1977 NC Sess Laws 1101 (codified at NC Gen Stat section 90-321 (Supp 1991).

109. Act of July 11, 1991, ch 639, section 3, 1991 NC Sess Laws 486, 494 (codified at NC Gen Stat section 90-321 (Supp 1991).

110. J. Diosegy, *supra*, note 107 at 3.

111. Act of July 11, 1991, ch 639, section 4, 1991 NC Sess Laws 486 (codified at NC Gen Stat section 90-322 (Supp 1991)).

112. Act of June 27, 1983, ch 626, sections 1–3, 1983 NC Sess Laws 563 (codified at NC Gen Stat sections 32A-8 to -14 (1991).

113. NC Gen Stat section 32A-2(9) (1991).

114. J. Diosegy, *supra*, note 107 at 3.

115. Act of July 11, 1991, ch 639, sections 1–2, 1991 NC Sess Laws 486, 486 (codified at NC Gen Stat sections 32A-15 to -26 (1991)). See generally J. B. Tillman, *supra*, note 107.

116. The North Carolina durable power of attorney statute expressly recognises springing powers as of 1983. Act of 1983, ch 626, section 1, 1983 NC Sess Laws 563 (codified at NC Gen Stat section 32A-8 (1991). The new health care power of attorney may also be in springing form. Act of July 11, 1991, ch 639, sections 1–5, 1991 NC Sess Laws 486 (codified at NC Gen Stat section 32A-20 (1991)).

117. The Society for the Right to Die Materials presented at the February 7–8, 1991 conference on Estate and Financial Planning for the Aging or Incapacitated Client and dated August 3, 1990 listed 27

states as having durable power of attorney statutes that permit agents to make medical decisions, 20 of them specifically including decisions to withhold or withdraw life support and seven not specifically addressing the issue. See F. Rouse, *Society for the Right to Die Materials*, Estate and Financial Planning for the Aging or Incapacitated Client 1991 at 449 (1991). A somewhat similar summary for the February 6–7, 1992 conference and dated September 25, 1991 listed 39 states as having legislation that authorises both living wills and the appointment of a health care agent and four states with legislation that authorises only the appointment of a health care agent (the major states of Massachusetts, Michigan, New York and Pennsylvania). See D. A. Smith, *Choice in Dying, Inc. Materials*, Estate and Financial Planning for the Aging or Incapacitated Client 1992 at 259 (1992).

The legislature of the state of New York has been skittish about advance directives. No New York statute yet sanctions living wills, although several cases approve the device. See e.g., *In re Westchester County Medical Center on behalf of O'Connor*, 72 NY 2d 517, 534 NYS 2d 836, 531 NE 2d 607 (1988). New York did recently enact a health care proxy statute. New York Health Care Proxy Act [1990], NY Pub Health Law sections 2980–94 (McKinney Supp 1991). See generally S. J. Schlesinger, *supra*, note 7 at 233–5, 238–9.

The *ABA Journal* reported in May 1992 that 42 states now have living will statutes and 36 have durable health care power of attorney statutes. J. Podgers, *supra*, note 96 at 63. In 1991, four states passed living will laws and seven others created laws authorising health care proxies. *National Law Journal* (December 30, 1991 to January 6, 1992) at S10.

118. B. A. Rich, "The Values History: A New Standard of Care" (1991) 40 *Emory Law Journal* 1109, 1132.

119. The observer may be struck by the primary role played by American courts in the right-to-die debate, but there seemingly is a unique American ethos that looks to the courts to decide social as well as legal issues. See J. Podgers, *supra*, note 96 at 60.

Indeed, the National Center for State Courts has issued a report entitled *Guidelines for State Court Decision Making in Authorizing or Withholding Life-Sustaining Medical Treatment*. "Excerpts: Guidelines for Life-Sustaining Medical Care Cases" *National Law Journal* (January 13, 1992) at 9. This report, prepared by a 12-member group that included prominent state court judges, practitioners and a biomedical ethicist, was prepared to give state judges some guidance in response to the apparent frequency of litigation over life-sustaining medical treatment (LSMT). The report found over 100 published LSMT decisions in the period from *Quinlan* in 1976 to April 1991 (shortly after *Cruzan*). Opinions were published in 23 states, five federal courts, and the District of Columbia.

Extrapolating from a survey of state trial judges, the report estimated that about 2400 trial judges currently on the bench have heard at least one LSMT case and altogether trial judges have heard over 7000 LSMT cases. For further data from this survey, see T. L. Hafemeister and D. M. Robinson, "A Survey of Judges About Life-Sustaining Medical Treatment" (1991) 324 *New England Journal of Medicine* 1673.

120. *Cruzan, supra*, note 48 at 2874–5.

121. *Ibid* at 2875, note 21. Apparently even fewer have designated a person to make medical decisions for them if they become incapacitated. R. Kanigel, "Every Patient to Face Issue of Right to Die" Raleigh, NC, *News and Observer* (December 1, 1991) at C1.

122. *Ibid* at 2877.

123. J. Beck, "The Question of Too Much Care" Raleigh, NC, *News and Observer* (January 10, 1991) at 15A.

124. *Cruzan, supra*, note 48 at 2878.

125. *Ibid*.

126. *Ibid* at 2864. One out of four Americans over age 65 will enter a nursing home during his lifetime. F. J. Collin Jr, "Planning and Drafting Durable Powers of Attorney for Health Care" 22 *Univ. of Miami Philip E. Heckerling Inst. on Est. Plan.* paras 500, 507.7, p. 5–12 (1988).

127. *Cruzan, supra*, note 48 at 2864.

128. Unif. Probate Code section 2-102, Comment (1990).

129. 22 and 23 Chas II, ch 10 (1670).

130. See generally P. J. Strauss, "The Geri-Hat-Truck: Three Goals of Estate Planning for the Elderly" (1990) 14 *Univ. of Miami Philip E. Heckerling Inst. on Est. Plan.* paras 1300, 1302.5; J. N. Zartman, "Planning for Disability" 15 *Prob Notes* 11, 12–13 (1989); D. P. Callaghan and P. J. Strauss (eds), *Estate and Financial Planning for the Aging or Incapacitated Client* (1990) at 134 (Practicing Law Institute 1990).

There has been periodic American advocacy of reform of the law of guardianship, particularly to place more procedural safeguards, on behalf of the allegedly incapacitated person, around the decision that the person is incapacitated. There has even been advocacy for a federal law of guardianship, overriding the traditional reservation of the law of property, wills and trusts to the states. See C. A. Collier and J. W. McCue, "Regents Oppose Imposition of Federal Standards for Guardianships and Conservatorships" 17 *ACTEC Notes* 16 (1991); Zartman, *supra*, at 15–16 (1989). The North Carolina law of guardianship recently received a comprehensive rewrite by the state legislature. Act of July 6, 1987, ch 550, 1987 NC Sess Laws 891 (codified at NC Gen Stat ch 35A (1991). See generally R. A. Bigger Jr, "Simplifying Guardianship: The New North Carolina Incompetency and Guardianship Act" *The Will and the Way* (February 1988) at 1.

131. Zartman, *ibid* at 18.

132. US Congress, Office of Technology Assessment, OTA-BA-306, Life Sustaining Technologies and the Elderly 53 (US Government Printing Office, 1987); M. W. Riley and J. W. Riley Jr, "Longevity and Social Structure: The Potential of the Added Years" in *Our Aging Society: Paradox and Promise* 53 A. Pifer and L. Bronte (eds) (1986); L. L. Emanuel, M. J. Barry, J. D. Stoeckle, L. M. Ettelson and E. J. Emanuel, "Advance Directives For Medical Care: A Case for Greater Use" (1991) 324 *New England Journal of Medicine* 889; M. Danis *et al.*, "A Prospective Study of Advance Directives for Life-Sustaining Care" (1991) 324 *New England Journal of Medicine* 882. A potentially provocative finding of the Danis study was that, in response to hypothetical questions, the family members of incompetent patients consistently preferred to have life-sustaining treatments withheld more frequently than the competent patients did for themselves. *Ibid* at 883–4.

For other data on likely patient desires, see L. L. Emanuel *et al.*, *supra.*

133. *Ibid.*

134. See "Do We Own Our Bodies? A Symposium" (1991) 1 *Health Matrix* 1, especially M. J. Mehlman, "Presumed Consent to Organ Donation: A Reevaluation", *ibid* at 31.

135. See, e.g., OR Rev Stat section 127.635(2) (1991), *supra*, note 39.

136. See Ark Code Ann section 20-17-214 (Michie Supp 1987); Conn Gen Stat section 19a-571 (Supp 1989); Fla Stat Ann section 765.07 (West 1990); Haw Rev Stat section 327D-21 (Supp 1988), as interpreted by *In re Guardianship of Crabtree*, No. 86-0031 (Hawaii Fam Ct 1st Cir, April 26, 1990) (Heeley J); Il Rev Stat ch 110 1/2, para 851-25 (1991); Indiana Health Care Consent Act, Ind Code Ann section 16-8-12-2 (West 1990), as interpreted by *In re Lawrance*, No. 29504-9104-CV-00460 (Ind September 17, 1991); Iowa Life Sustaining Procedures Act, Iowa Code Ann section 144A.7 (West 1989); Louisiana Life-Sustaining Procedures Act, La Rev Stat Ann section 40:1299.58.5 (West Supp 1989); Maine Uniform Rights of the Terminally Ill Act, Me Rev Stat Ann tit. 18a, section 5-707 (West 1990); Montana Rights of the Terminally Ill Act, Mont Code Ann section 50-9-106 (1991); Nevada Uniform Act on the Right of the Terminally Ill (SB 442, signed June 6, 1991); New Mexico Right to Die Act, NM Stat Ann section 24-7-8.1 (Michie 1986); North Carolina Right to Natural Death Act, NC Gen Stat section 90-322 (1985); Ohio Modified Uniform Rights of the Terminally Ill Act, Ohio Rev Code Ann section 2133.08(B) (Page Supp 1991); Oregon Rights with Respect to Terminal Illness Act, Or Rev Stat section 127.635(2) (1984); Texas Natural Death Act, Tex Rev Civ Stat Ann, sections 672.006 and 672.009 (Vernon Supp 1989); Utah Personal Choice and Living Will Act,

Utah Code Ann section 75-2-1105(2) (Supp 1988); Virginia Natural Death Act, VA Code section 54:1-2986 (Michie 1988); Substituted Consent Act, VA Code section 37.1-134.4 (Michie Supp 1989); District of Columbia Health Care Decisions Act, DC Code Ann section 21-2210 (1989).

137. *Ibid.*

138. For examples of this ranking provision see, e.g., Ark Code Ann section 20-17-214 (Michie Supp 1987), Conn Gen Stat section 19a-570 (Supp 1989) (definition of "next of kin" specifies family members), and District of Columbia Health Care Decisions Act, DC Code Ann section 21-2210 (1989).

139. See, e.g. NC Gen Stat section 90-322 (1985).

140. E.g., Minn Stat section 144.651 (Supp 1991), cited in M. Minow, *supra*, note 66, at 21–2 notes 93–94.

141. See text accompanying note 106, *supra.*

142. By determining which services are compensated or not compensated, national policy can affect the doctor's willingness to devote time to discussion of living wills and other health care documents with patients. It is not clear whether Medicare, the federal system of payment of hospital and doctor bills, will reimburse the doctor's charges for time and advice about living wills. See M. Freudenheim, "Physicians Refuse Medicare Patients" *New York Times* (April 12, 1992) at 1.

143. See note 133, *supra.*

144. See note 123, *supra.*

145. As pointed out by Professor Brock in his chapter, this is a separate issue of distributive justice, reached only after it has been decided that a person has properly evidenced his desire to be kept alive. For a discussion of the ethical considerations in rationing health care, see T. L. Beauchamp and J. F. Childress, *Principles of Biomedical Ethics* 290–301 (3d edn, 1989). For an examination of the issue from economic and other perspectives, see R. M. Veatch, "Justice and the Economics of Terminal Illness" *Hastings Center Report* (August/September 1988) at 34. See generally "Health Care Symposium: Health Care in America: Armageddon on the Horizon?" (1991) 3 *Stanford Law and Policy Review* 16-215, especially R. A. Epstein, "Rationing Access to Medical Care: Some Sober Second Thoughts" *ibid* at 81.

Consultation Paper No. 119 discusses possible differences in situation resulting from the fact that the American health care system is more profit-oriented than the British. See Consultation Paper No. 119, *supra*, note 1 at paragraph 6.9. It does not appear that American doctors have been quick to terminate life support of the terminally ill, despite the high costs of care. See note 163, *infra.* Nevertheless, one should be sensitive to ask whether more procedural safeguards on the decision to terminate treatment are required in the USA than in Britain, due to the possibly greater financial incentive to terminate treatment in the USA than in Britain. As the chair of the ABA's Commission on Legal Problems of the Elderly, John Pickering, has said, "We must recognize that as long as there is no universal health insurance, families and health-care institutions can exert a subtle pressure on patients to terminate their lives because of the costs involved in life-sustaining treatment." See S. B. Goldberg, "Assisted Suicide Resolution Defeated" *American Bar Association Journal* (April 1992) at 107.

146. As pointed out by Professor Brock in his chapter, this is not a random menu of standards from which a drafter or legislator will choose only one. Rather, there should be an ordering among the standards. Reflecting the principle of patient autonomy, the patient's desires should control if there is sufficient evidence of them. Absent a clear expression of the patient's intent, the substituted judgment standard should be used: the surrogate should seek a decision consistent with the patient's known beliefs, values and other subjective criteria. Failing sufficient evidence to allow substituted judgment, the surrogate should decide on the basis of the patient's best interests. See also A. Buchanan, M. Gilfix and D. W. Brock, *Surrogate Decision Making for Elderly Individuals Who Are Incompetent or of Questionable Competence*, Office of Technology Assessment, Congress of the United States (November 1985); F. J. Collin Jr, *supra*, note 7 at 43–6; *In re Conroy*, 486 A 2d 1209 (NJ 1985) (albeit using somewhat different terminology, *viz* "limited objective test", "pure objective test").

147. See note 47, *supra*. *Quinlan* held that there would be no criminal liability for withdrawing mechanical ventilation from a comatose young woman in a persistent vegetative state. Her family and guardian were allowed to make the decision to withdraw treatment, on a theory of substituted judgment. See generally M. Brazier, *supra*, note 1 at 316–18. It was predicted that Karen Quinlan would quickly die if removed from the respirator, but in fact she lived 9 years after removal from the respirator, eventually dying from an infection. R. F. Weir, *supra*, note 38, at 164 note 5.

Actually, the living will statutes passed in the aftermath of *Quinlan* dealt with a different scenario (removal of extraordinary means of support from a terminally ill and likely aged person) than *Quinlan* (removal of mechanical ventilation from a PVS and young person). Nevertheless, it appears that publicity given to the *Quinlan* case led the state legislatures to consider the general subject of care of persons with no hope of recovery, the result being the enactment of living will legislation.

In fact, it appears that the drafters of the original living will statutes were aware of the need for broader legislation. However, in order to gain support from, or at least to weaken the opposition to living will legislation from right-to-life advocates, the reach of the statutes had to be circumscribed. R. F. Weir, *supra*, note 38 at 197.

148. The drafters of the first living will statutes were aware of many of these questions, but were unable to secure enactment of more far-reaching statutes. R. F. Weir, *supra*, note 38 at 197. It was hoped that later "clean-up" legislation would be able to remove some of the restrictions, *ibid*, but it appears that substantial changes were not possible until *Cruzan* again focused public attention on the right to die. The first statute, that of California enacted in 1976, was amended five times in the state assembly and four times in the state senate; the final version became the model for other states, *ibid*, suggesting that legislators should be sensitive to possible shortcomings of early statutes borrowed from other sates.

149. Curiously, the amended North Carolina health care power of attorney statute adds "severe dementia" and permanent "coma" to the standard list of conditions ("terminally ill" or "persistent vegetative state") that can trigger the withholding or withdrawing of consent, while the living will statute mentions only terminal illness and PVS. It is unclear whether this lack of parallelism was accidental or deliberate. N. M. P. King, *supra*, note 107 at 13.

150. While I accept the medical usage of the term "hydration", it has always seemed lugubrious to me, invoking, as it were, images of the watering of a potted plant. The attorney for Lt. Col. Oliver North, one of the principal Iran/Contra hearing figures, was Brendan Sullivan, partner in a prominent Washington firm headed by Edward Bennett Williams. At one point in the Congressional hearings, Sullivan uttered the famous line to an indifferent panel of Congressmen: "I am not a potted plant!" E. Magnuson, "Not Yet a Potted Plant: Despite His Iranscam Wounds, Reagan is Hardly a Pushover" *Time* (August 1987) at 12.

151. It has been questioned whether there is an appropriate distinction between ordinary and extraordinary methods of treatment. See T. L. Beauchamp and J. F. Childress, *supra*, note 7 at 151–69; R. F. Weir, *supra*, note 38 at 216–8, 233–5. The *Quinlan* case accepted the distinction, which has a prominent history in certain religious traditions. R. F. Weir, *supra*, note 38 at 110.

152. Generally the courts and legislatures have not found any legal difference between withholding and withdrawing treatment. They have recognised that if the law made it impossible to withdraw treatment once started, doctors and families might be discouraged from even attempting treatment, lest it prove unsuccessful but legally not be terminable. D. A. Smith, *supra*, note 43 at 193–4. See also G. Scofield, *supra*, note 48 at 45.

It has been suggested that more procedural safeguards might be needed on a decision to terminate treatment made by a nursing home as opposed to one made by a hospital. See J. K. Mason and R.

A. McCall Smith, *supra*, note 1 at 342.
153. 1976 Cal Stat ch 1439, p 6480, formerly codified as Cal Health and Safety Code section 7188. See S. J. Schlesinger, *supra*, note 7 at 233. The statute was amended in 1991, *inter alia*, to delete the 5-year requirement. 1991 Cal Stat ch 895, section 2, now codified as Cal Health and Safety Code section 7186.5 (West Supp 1992).
154. See, P. G. Haskell, *Preface to Wills, Trusts and Administration* (1987) 39.
155. This tendency reflexively to use old concepts brings to mind F. Scott Fitzgerald's peroration in *The Great Gatsby*: "and so we beat on, boats again the tide, borne back ceaselessly into the past." F. Scott Fitzgerald, *The Great Gatsby* 182 (Charles Scribner & Sons, 1953) (1925).
156. S. Kess and B. Westlin, 1 *CCH Financial and Estate Planning* para 3295.25 (1991).
157. P. G. Haskell, *supra*, note 154 at 61.
158. See S. J. Schlesinger, *supra*, note 7 at 233–5; P. G. Haskell, *supra*, note 154 at 164–5.
159. The traditional test for wills of property is the capacity to (a) know the nature of the testator's property, (b) know the natural objects of this bounty, (c) be capable of forming an orderly plan of disposition, and (d) understand the disposition being made by the will. P. G. Haskell, *supra*, note 154 at 36.
160. See generally I. Kennedy, *supra*, note 1 at chs 1, 16–18.
161. S. M. Wolf, *supra*, note 48 at 39.
For a suggested one-page health care proxy form, prepared in response to the growing complexity of these forms, see G. J. Annas, "The Health Care Proxy and the Living Will" (1991) 324 *New England Journal of Medicine* 1210.
162. Dr Donald Murphy, Speech at the Association of American Law Schools Annual Meeting, Washington, DC (January 5, 1991).
Recently the Royal Society for Mentally Handicapped Children and Adults (MENCAP) and the British Medical Association separately published proposals for procedures for decision-making by the attending physician and the most appropriate relative. For patients lacking a suitable relative, an ethics committee composed of persons from diverse backgrounds would be available. See Consultation Paper No. 119, *supra*, note 1 at sections 6.28–6.29, 6.41–6.43. These proposals seem based on the same notions as the American family consent statutes. Procedures for persons lacking a suitable relative would bring a latent issue to the fore: should decision be made by a jury of the patient's peers or by a jury of persons from diverse backgrounds? The jury of peers approach would resemble a substituted judgment standard of the patient's likely subjective desires, while the diverse background approach would resemble a "best interests" standard or perhaps a "reasonable person" stand-

ard. The choice of jury again highlights the question of how and by whom these decisions should be made.

163. M. Danis, L. J. Southerland, J. A. M. Garrett, J. L. Smith, F. Hielema, C. G. Pickard, D. M. Egner and D. L. Patrick, "A Prospective Study of Advance Directives for Medical Care" (1991) 324 *New England Journal of Medicine* 882. See also West, *Practical Experience With Durable Powers of Attorney for Health Care*, 1986 UCLA/CEB Estate Planning Inst, ch 2, 50 (1987). D. L. Redleaf, S. B. Schmidtt and W. C. Thompson, "The California Natural Death Act: An Empirical Study of Physicians' Practices" (1979) 31 *Stanford Law Review* 913. For a doctor's argument that physician discretion must be preserved because "Patients and families trying to figure out in advance how best to handle all potential life-threatening events often say what they do not mean and vice versa," see P. R. Alper, "A Living Will Is a Bloodless Document" *Wall Street Journal* (January 11, 1991) at A10.

165. See, e.g., Ill Stat Ann section 851-20(f) (1991); Iowa Code Ann section 144A.9(2) (West 1989); La Rev Stat Ann section 40:1299.58.8 (West Supp 1989); Me Rev Stat Ann tit. 18a, section 5-709 (West 1990); NM Stat Ann section 24-7-7(D) (Michie 1986); Or Rev Stat section 127.625(2) (1984).

165. One question posed by Consultation Paper No. 119 was whether any reform should take a minimalist approach (a general "tidying up" to remove the main anomalies), an incremental approach (to update or reform particular kinds of problems), or an overall approach (the creation of a comprehensive code governing all aspects of decision-making for mentally incapacitated adults). See Consultation Paper No. 119, *supra*, note 1 at sections 4.10–4.16, 7.5. The American approach, so far, has been the incremental one.

166. Oliver Wendell Holmes, *The Common Law* 1 (1881).

167. *New York Trust Co.* v. *Eisner* 256 US 345, 359 (1921).

168. See I. Kennedy, *supra*, note 1 at 4–5.

169. The Guidelines for State Court Decision Making in Authorizing or Withholding Life-Sustaining Medical Treatment, *supra*, note 119, recommended the development of family consent laws as one of several innovative non-judicial alternatives worthy of study.

The National Conference has created a drafting committee for a Uniform Health-Care Decisions Act. Letter from Professor David M. English, Reporter for the committee, to the author (November 16, 1992) (on file with author).

It appears that existing family consent statutes limit the family's decision-making authority to conditions described by the statute (e.g. terminal illness, persistent vegetative state). D. P. Callahan and P. J. Strauss (eds), *supra*, note 7 at 193. Consideration should be given to removal of statutory limitations or at least to expansion of the statutory sphere of decision-making. M. D. A. Freeman (ed), *Medicine, Ethics and the Law* 103–20 (1988).

The Patient Self-Determination Act: the medical Miranda!

Maureen A. Eby

A 65 year old South Carolina man who had suffered from hypertension, diabetes, kidney failure, and a variety of other diseases collapsed on the kitchen floor of his home after supper. His wife called the emergency number 911, paramedics arrived at the home and began resuscitating the gentleman. The time between his collapse and the attempt at resuscitation exceeded 12 minutes, in itself an indication that extensive brain damage had already occurred. With some luck he was resuscitated, intubated, and rushed to the hospital emergency room. Over the next 11 days his health deteriorated dramatically, there was never any hope that he would regain consciousness, be able to breathe on his own, or overcome the numerous maladies that affected him. There was uncertainty as to what he wanted for himself, he had never taken the opportunity to fill out a living will or to document any other wishes. Through all communications he indicated to his wife and his family that he did not want to be a vegetable but reports of family conversations were not acceptable to the physician to withdraw the ventilator upon which the gentleman had become dependent and allow him to die.[1]

An 83 year old St Louis woman was admitted to hospital for complications that developed because of respiratory distress and pneumonia. After several tests and a bronchoscopy it was decided that the advanced respiratory disease from which she was suffering was irreversible. It was foreseen that she would have to be placed upon a ventilator eventually in order to assist her in breathing, otherwise she would die. In this case, the patient had executed a living will according to the laws of the state of Missouri and had numerous family

Decision-Making and Problems of Incompetence. Edited by A. Grubb.

discussions with her sons about what she wanted for herself should she ever suffer from a life threatening illness and be in a terminal condition. Both the documented evidence in the living will and the discussions with her family were accepted as a reasonable indication of her desires. She died some days later comfortably without a ventilator and not in pain.[2]

What is the difference between these two cases? In the first scenario the gentleman was clearly suffering from a variety of diseases, any one of which could have been terminal. At no time did he, his family, or more importantly his physician ever think to encourage him with his family to consider completing an advance directive — either a living will or a durable power of attorney for health care.

That in itself is not unusual for there have been several studies looking at this phenomenon. Two studies found that both physicians and providers felt that it was the patient's responsibility to inform them of either a living will or a durable power of attorney or even to bring up the topic for discussion in the first place.[3] However, patients when asked felt the opposite, that it was the physician's responsibility to initiate discussions on this subject. From the provider's perspective, even in hospitals with advance directive policies, only 4% asked patients whether they had either a living will or a durable power of attorney, while the other 96% felt that the patient would inform the hospital of such a directive.[4] Studies looking at the "Do Not Resuscitate" order found that as many as 70% of hospitalised patients have this order written before their death, and in 60% of these orders it was written only 3 days before the patient's death.[5] Other studies have found that only 14% of hospitalised patients had discussion with their physicians before the order was written and in many cases the patient had lost their decision-making capacity by the time a "Do Not Resuscitate" order was contemplated.[6]

In the wake of these studies and the *Cruzan* case,[7] Senators Danforth and Moynihan introduced the "Patient Self-Determination Act" (Senate Bill 1766) "a bill to amend titles XVIII and XIX of the Social Security Act to require providers of services under such titles to enter into agreements assuring that individuals receiving services from such providers will be provided an opportunity to participate in and direct health care decisions affecting such individuals".[8] In the bill's introduction, Senator Danforth goes on to state:

This bill accomplishes a critical goal. It ensures that people are informed of their rights, under State law, to control decisions about their own health care — even when they are no longer able to voice their wishes — through the use of advanced directives for medical care . . . Common law dictates that competent patients always have a right to refuse any and all treatment for themselves, even if doing so would certainly hasten death . . . A patient should not lose that right if he or she becomes comatose or unconscious and terminally ill or otherwise unable to make decisions. But that, Mr. President, is in effect what happens today. Our bill seeks to protect that right . . . Our health care system has become obsessed with extending life, at times neglecting the caring component of medicine and trampling on the rights of patients . . . Our bill only begins the process of bringing those concerns to the forefront. What it accomplishes, though, is really very simple. It encourages people to at least start thinking about planning ahead. It does so by requiring Medicare and Medicaid providers to inform patients of a vehicle for doing that: advance medical directives.[9]

Nearly 1 year later, President Bush signed into law the "Patient Self-Determination Act" (*Omnibus Budget Reconciliation Act of 1990*, Public Law No. 101–508) which took effect on 1st December 1991. This law was designed to increase the patient's involvement in his own health care decision-making by ensuring that his advance directive was made available to his physician at the time medical decisions were being made and that if the patient had not made an advance directive, that he be aware of his right to do so.

As a condition of Medicare and Medicaid reimbursement, this Act requires health care providers, i.e. hospitals, skilled nursing facilities, home health agencies, hospice programmes and health maintenance organisations, to:

- develop written policies concerning advance directives;
- ask all new patients whether they have prepared an advance directive and include this information in the patient's medical record;
- give patients written materials regarding the facility's policies on advance directives and the patient's right under applicable state law to prepare such documents; and
- educate staff and the community about advance directives.[10]
- Furthermore, health care facilities cannot condition treatment or discriminate against individuals that have not executed any form of an advance directive.[11]

In other words, if a health care establishment fails to fulfil the above then its reimbursement for medical services rendered from Medicare (medical aid for the elderly) and Medicaid (medical aid for the poor) will not be denied. That is quite an incentive for compliance and in some cases there is a considerable amount of work to be done before a health care establishment can comply.

In a study conducted in 1989 prior to the Act becoming law, a survey of 400 hospitals (with a 56% return response rate) selected at random found only 146 hospitals (67%) had some formal policy regarding advance directives. Only 46% of the responding hospitals reported having an ethics committee; however, the presence of an ethics committee was not significantly associated with the presence of a formal policy. Of the 69 hospitals that had both a formal policy and an ethics committee, only 30 hospitals or 43% stated that their policy on advance directives had been reviewed by their ethics committee. But more importantly for compliance with this Act only nine of the 219 responding hospitals or 4% reported having a formal policy to ask all patients or a selected subgroup of patients whether they had ever completed an advance directive.[12] Thus, regardless of the amount of work needed for compliance, all four areas of the Act — patient information, documentation, education and non-discrimination — must be met prior to reimbursement from federal funds.

However, there are limitations to this Act that need to be examined.

Clinical barriers

The Act assumes that receiving written information about advance directives will automatically ensure that individuals will complete one. In Hare and Nelson's study, this was not the case.[13] In addition studies of informed consent forms indicate that these forms generally do not provide patients with a clear understanding of the contemplated procedures. In fact a review of the readability of consent forms used in paediatric medical research found that to understand these forms required reading skills at the advanced college level, and the forms' readability compared with that of the *New England Journal of Medicine*.[14]

Furthermore, even though this information needs to be given to patients on admission, at what point in the admission procedure will it be given and by whom? In some cases, this information will be given during the initial admitting procedures conducted by the admitting clerk. It is also at this time that patients are now asked to sign forms for authorization for treatment; release of information; authorization for assignment of benefits, personal property, coordination of benefits, and a Medicare second payer form; and finally before the admitting procedure is completed patients are asked to read an important message about Medicare and their rights in the hospital.[15] For the patient to receive yet another piece of paper with further instructions and advice to read at the same time as all these other forms will mean that probably this information on advance directives will go unread and astray. This was not what the Act meant to accomplish. Should this mean that the patient's primary nurse or the patient's physician take on this role? Again, hospitals are deciding as to whose role this task should become, with some clearly delineating it as a nurse's role.[16]

Legal barriers

First of all, this Act does not create any new patient rights. It only requires that hospitals in order to continue to receive Medicare and Medicaid reimbursements inform patients of their existing rights currently available under their state law, and these laws vary from state to state, sometimes with disastrous consequences. In Chicago, a father disconnected his 2-year-old son from the ventilator while holding the intensive care staff at gunpoint until his child died.[17] The father was frustrated that the physician and hospital attorney would not intervene even though his child would never regain consciousness despite the fact that the hospital could have invoked the Federal "Baby Doe" law.

In other examples based on incorrectly interpreting these laws, a dying woman was resuscitated 70 times in 24 hours; placement of a pacemaker was planned in a brain-dead patient; and family members had to bar the door of a patient's room to prevent unwanted resuscitation.[18] In each case, the treatment was recommended by the hospital's counsel.

As the Act requires that patients be informed of their rights under the relevant state law, it may well be that their rights under state law may be less than their rights under the United States Constitution: many existing statutes limit the kinds of directives that patients can give and the conditions under which patients can give directives. For example, a state's living will statute may apply only to terminally ill patients or may exclude feeding tubes.[19]

The Patient Self-Determination Act requires that not only the health care facility develop and maintain written policies regarding advance directives, but also that each state with the assistance of the Department of Health and Human Services develop written materials describing that state's laws concerning advance directives. Hopefully, through both sets of initiatives scenarios such as previously described will become tales of the past.

However, if the law of the state where the health care is provided does not recognise a particular type of advance directive, i.e. the living will or the durable power of attorney, then this Act does not grant these legal options if they are not already available in that state's law. Likewise, the Act does not create a legal duty for the health care provider to comply with any advance directive provision that does not already exist under the state's law.

The Act does require that patients be informed of the hospital's written policies on complying with advance directives. For example, most state laws that recognise living wills do not require health care providers always to comply with a patient's directives. Some facilities have policies that suspend the directives of the living will during intraoperative care. If a hospital policy providing for suspension of the living will during intraoperative care is legal in a particular state, then the Patient Self-Determination Act does not make this practice illegal. This Act does, however, require that patients be informed of that policy at the time of admission. Most states also require physicians or facilities unwilling to honour an advance directive to cooperate with the transfer of the patient to a facility that will honour it and this Act will ensure that patients are informed of this obligation.[20]

Ethical barriers

Ethical questions have arisen out of this Act with regard to cost containment.[21]

The cost of prolonged medical care is prohibitively expensive. It was estimated that the cost of Nancy Cruzan's care was $112000 per year,[22] with the predicted cost of care for the estimated 10000 patients in a persistent vegetative state currently in the USA over a 10-year period to be in excess of $15 billion. In 1988, Medicaid paid for almost half of that skilled nursing care but the rest of it was paid for by the patients themselves or their relatives.[23]

The Patient Self-Determination Act was part of the Omnibus Reconciliation Act of 1990, which is expected to reduce or limit payments to Medicare reimbursed providers, including hospitals, nursing homes, hospices and health maintenance organisations. In the words of LaPuma *et al.*, "Six percent of Medicare enrollees die annually; their care amounts to 28% of the annual Medicare expenditures. The Act is expected to decrease provider costs, assuming that many patients — especially the elderly — will opt to limit the expensive, intensive treatment they may receive in hospitals."[24] These authors go on further to state ". . . Persuading disadvantaged patients to sign advance directives for institutional financial reasons is reprehensible.[25]

What checks and balances can be put in place to prevent this from happening? Primarily this is where the role of the nurse is crucial to the monitoring of the performance of this Act. Patient education has always been one of the prime duties of the nurse, and informing patients under this new Act falls well within these parameters, especially within the health maintenance organisations. Making patients aware of their options is also a nursing responsibility. Doing so with a supportive attitude so patients can make their own treatment decisions would be upholding the nurse's role as patient advocate.[26] In that sense then this Patient Self-Determination Act would indeed become a "medical Miranda"!

References

1. Fr. Brodeur "On the Patient Self Determination Act" *Congressional Record-Senate* (October 17, 1989) s 13570.
2. *Ibid*, at s 13571.
3. B. Lo, G. McLeod and G. Saika, "Patient Attitudes to Discussing Life-Sustaining Treatment" (1986) 146 *Archives of Internal Medicine* 1613; M. Kohn and G. Menon, "Life Prolongation: Views of Elderly Outpatients and Health Care Professionals" (1988) 36 *Journal of American Geriatric Society* 840.
4. J. LaPuma, D. Orentlicher and R. Moss, "Advance Directives on Admission: Clinical Implications and Analysis of the Patient Self Determination Act of 1990" (1991) 266 *Journal of the American Medical Association* 402.
5. P. Jonsson, M. McNamee and E. Campion, "The 'Do Not Resuscitate' Order: A Profile of its Changing Use" (1988) 148 *Archives of Internal Medicine* 2372.
6. T. Finucane *et al.*, "Planning with Elderly Outpatient for Contingencies of Severe Illness" (1988) 3 *Journal of General Internal Medicine* 322; R. Fairman, "Withdrawing Life-Sustaining Treatment" (1992) 152 *Archives of Internal Medicine* 25; K. Gleeson and S. Wise, "The Do-Not-Resuscitate Order: Still too Little too Late" (1990) 150 *Archives of Internal Medicine* 1057.
7. *Cruzan* v. *Director, Missouri Department of Health* (1990) 497 US

261 (US Sup Ct).

8. J. Danforth, "Patient Self Determination Act" *Congressional Record-Senate*, October 17 (1989), s 13566.

9. *Ibid.*

10. P. Greco *et al.*, "The Patient Self Determination Act and the Future of Advance Directives" (1991) 115 *Annals of Internal Medicine* 639.

11. E. Murphy, "OR Nursing Law: Advance Directives and the Patient Self Determination Act" (1992) 55 *AORN Journal* 270.

12. S. Van McCrary and J. Botkin, "Hospital Policy on Advance Directives: Do Institutions Ask Patients about Living Wills?" (1989) 262 *Journal of the American Medical Association* 2411.

13. J. Hare and C. Nelson, "Will Outpatients Complete Living Wills?" (1991) 6 *Journal of General Internal Medicine* 41.

14. K. Tarnowski *et al.*, "Readability of Pediatric Biomedical Research Informed Consent Forms" (1990) 85 *Pediatrics* 58.

15. See J. LaPuma, D. Orentlicher and R. Moss, *supra*, note 4 at 403.

16. L. Belkin, "Hospitals Will Now Ask Patients if They Wish to Make Death Plan" *The New York Times Metro*, (Sunday, December 1, 1991), 1, 47; "Law Enlarges Caregiver Role in End-of-Life Decisions" (1992) *American Journal of Nursing* (January) 85; P. Greve, "Legally Speaking: Advance directives — What the New Law Means for You" (1991) *RN* (November), 63.

17. *New York Times*, (May 1, 1989) at A1, 3.

18. G. Annas, "Reconciling Quinlan and Saikewicz: Decision Making for the Terminally Ill Incompetent" in A. Doudera and J. Peters (ed), *Legal and Ethical Aspects of Treating Critically and Terminally Ill Patients*, (1982, Ann Arbor, MI: AUPHA Press), 28–62.

19. See J. LaPuma, D. Orentlicher and R. Moss, *supra*, note 4 at 404.

20. See E. Murphy, *supra*, note 11 at 272.

21. D. Murphy, "Improving Advance Directives for Healthy Older People" (1990) 38 *Journal of American Geriatric Society* 1251; A. Capron, "The Patient Self Determination Act: Not Now" (1990) 20(5) *Hastings Center Report* 35; J. LaPuma and D. Schiedermayer, "Ethics Consultation: Skills, Roles and Training" (1991) 114 *Annals of Internal Medicine* 155; J. LaPuma, D. Orentlicher and R. Moss, *supra*, note 4 at 404; P. Greco *et al.*, *supra*, note 10 at 642.

22. T. Lewin, "Nancy Cruzan Dies, Outlived by a Debate over the Right to Die" *New York Times*, Section A (December 27, 1990) 1, 15.

23. P. Greco *et al.*, *supra*, note 10 at 642.

24. *Supra*, note 4 at 404.

25. *Ibid.*

26. M. DeWolf-Bosek and J. Fitzpatrick, "Legal Speaking: Finding the Right Words" (1991) *RN* (November), 66–67.

The right to die: withdrawal of tube feeding in the persistent vegetative state in Canada

H. E. Emson

In this chapter I shall try to cover, from the perspective of current practice in Canada, the generally accepted ethical beliefs and the state of the law on withdrawal of tube feeding from a patient in a persistent vegetative state (PVS) and to combine this with comments on advance directives.

For those who are not familiar with Canada, I must remind readers that it is a medium-sized country in population (about 25 million) spread over a huge area, with a great diversity of climate, physical geography, ethnic variety and regional interests which are usually conflicting. Geographically, most Canadian regions have closer affinities with the corresponding part of the USA to the south, than laterally. Nevertheless, ethically and legally there are significant differences between us and the USA. Superimposed is a federal system of government divided uneasily between Ottawa, and the provinces and territories, and at present ravaged by the problem of Quebec. Oddly enough, running through all this confusion there is a Canadian ethos.

I shall divide my discussion under the major headings of ethics, law and practice.

Decision-Making and Problems of Incompetence. Edited by A. Grubb.
© 1994 John Wiley & Sons Ltd.

Ethics

One fundamental consideration is the patient's right to *autonomy*, expressed as the right to consent to, or more importantly, to refuse proposed treatment. In the competent, adult patient (and this may be hard to define) the right to autonomy is established and accepted and buttressed by law, although difficulties with it still surface in individual situations. The notion of *advance directives* is more recognised by many lay people and organisations than it is in some of the determinedly retrospective bastions of legal and medical paternalism. It is minimally supported in law, but is seeping into public consciousness to the extent that doctors will take note of it. In general we are told what most people believe, that advance directives represent a legitimate ethical extension of the autonomy principle, and should be honoured as such.[1] Just how much this is honoured in the breach rather than the observance, no one knows.

Artificial feeding and hydration, hereafter termed "tube feeding", has its tremendous symbolic importance recognised in the recent British report;[2] in my experience, this is more often significant for nursing than for medical staff. It would be wrong to say that a general consensus has been consciously reached that it is a form of treatment rather than something else, but when the discussions are concluded this is where we arrive. I do not know of a nationally accepted statement so defining tube feeding; the best I can say is that there is no denial, and that codes of ethics such as that of the Canadian Medical Association (CMA), while silent on specifics, are so interpreted. Working papers developed by individual institutions can be more specific; they do on occasion define tube feeding as treatment, and state that circumstances exist in which ethically it may be withdrawn.[3] Sometimes the religious foundations seem rather clearer than the lay ones on this.

Life support of various kinds is withdrawn each day, either on the authority of the expressed wish of a then competent adult patient, or relying upon an advance directive, or as a decision made by a surrogate for the irreversibly incompetent.[4] It is in the last instance that most problems arise. One typical case with which I am familiar was referred to the consultation service of a hospital's ethics committee at the unanimous request of the 93-year-old patient's children, all themselves over 60 years old. The patient was in a PVS from multiple strokes and had been tube fed for more than a year. While there was no adversarial situation, the physician was uncertain of his ethical and legal position, and there was some uneasiness in the nursing staff. The chairman of the ethics committee set out the relevant factors in the situation as he perceived them to be, in a position paper given to the doctor and the family members, and then led a discussion with them and members of the committee. No advice was given; the best word I can find for the process is "facilitation". The participants were satisfied, and by common agreement the physician withdrew the tube; the patient died a few days later.

I think that most decisions of this type are arrived at between the physician, other health care workers and the family members. Few are publicised. As the situation becomes more defined, the process more familiar and the decision more commonly accepted, an ethics consultation service in such cases will be needed less often. Most large hospitals in Canada do have such a service, although communication between them is poor, and we have not developed mechanisms for sharing our common problems. There is no provincial or federal, consultative or decision-making body, in contrast to the area of ethics in research on human subjects.

We are not, however, one big happy family. Individuals and organisations, generally characterised as the "right to life" movement, disagree with such decisions and try to influence them in various ways. In an intensely pluralistic society this poses ongoing problems.

Law

As regards law, Canada tends to sit uneasily upon a fence between the English and American systems. There is an ooze of legal ideas northwards across the undefended border — which in some ways helps and in others handicaps us. We have the problems of multiple provincial jurisdictions and a federal Charter of Rights and Freedoms to contend with which is essentially interpreted by the Supreme Court. Again, sometimes this helps; sometimes as in *Re Eve*, the British House of Lords commented that it just does not make sense. Some of the court's decisions seem to fly in the face of common public perception of the right and good, but our legal system is not unique in this regard.

To deal with the easy bit first, *advance directives* have minimal legal force in Canada. They fall under provincial jurisdiction, only Manitoba has legislated for the "living will", and only in Nova Scotia is there specific provision for durable power of attorney in decisions on health care. A Bill which would establish advance directives is before the House in Ontario, and the Law Reform Commission of Saskatchewan, my own province, has very recently drafted a recommendation for one.

However, compared with the USA, Canadians are very bad at making both statute and case law in health care — perhaps for "bad", I should substitute "inactive". Our practice in health care changes without waiting for legal authority, which is just as well, because the law generally lags behind public perception by a matter of 50 years or so. Advance directives are commonly drafted by individuals, using various sources of advice and standard forms, and by lawyers at the request of persons who may become patients. It is hard to imagine a charge being brought, and even harder of one being sustained, against a physician for acting in accordance with an advance directive that was not in itself illegal (and even on what is lawful, the law is unclear). The situation in the USA might be regarded as persuasive, where most states have legislated for advance directives and it is mandatory to instruct a patient on their existence and effect upon admission to hospital.[5] Advance directives are reported not to work very well in the USA, but my own opinion is that this is more likely due to the national obsession with adversarial litigation rather than because of an intrinsic defect in the notion of advance directives. There is some medical opposition to them, but on other grounds. We shall likely see the statutory establishment of advance directives in a Canadian province within the next few years.

Our rights of *consent and refusal* are well established in case law, notably by *Reibl* v. *Hughes*,[6] which deals with the standard of information and more recently by the case of *Nancy B*. This established the right of a quadriplegic patient to have her respirator turned off, and I think emphasises three points in relation to the right to refuse treatment: the right to do so even if death is sure to follow; the right to withdrawal of treatment already in progress; and the right to have this withdrawal effected by a surrogate. On one view, the *Nancy B* case was unnecessary because such practice, while not commonplace, is accepted and performed, and has never previously been the subject of suit. However, the fears of the physician and hospital which led to the judicial ruling have underlined the rights which we had assumed to apply. The case also established the principle in Quebec, which uniquely among Canadian jurisdictions has a civil code.

Even in the absence of statutory support, I think it is safe to assume, and to act, as if this expression of autonomy may be effected via an advance directive. A limited precedent was set in a case in Ontario, which involved the duty of a physician to honour a card carried by a Jehovah's Witness, incompetent as a result of accident, prohibiting blood transfusion.[8] As I said earlier, it is hard to conceive of a case being brought or sustained against a doctor for acting in accordance with an advance directive, and many hospital policies emphasise this as a doctor's duty. In decisions made by surrogates the law is unclear. There are many sections of the Criminal Code[9] which *might* be invoked against a doctor. For example, section 215 involves responsibility to provide the "necessaries of life", which includes health care, to dependants. Sections 219, 220 and 221 concern criminal negligence, and section 222 homicide. Section 226 defines "acceleration of death": sections 229, 230 and 231 murder and sections 232, 233 and 234, manslaughter. Section 241 is important in that it makes it an offence "to counsel, aid or abet suicide", terms virtually undefined in the contexts I have discussed. Physicians labour under the concern that any or all of these might be invoked against them; this is one of the areas where the technology and practice of health care have most notably outstripped recognition by the law. A charge under the criminal code may only be laid by, or with the consent of the provincial Attorney-General, or upon the order of a judge. So far these persons have acted reasonably in the eyes of physicians. Nevertheless, statutory as opposed to discretionary protection might be thought more appropriate.

Finally, what happens in *practice*? Advance directives are increasingly a matter of public awareness but are becoming accepted rather more slowly by physicians. When we rewrite hospital policies, such as those for do-not-resuscitate (DNR, no. 99) orders, we try to take them into account. However, I am still asked to attend ward conferences where physician unwillingness to discuss advance directives, or to honour their expression of patients' wishes is a source of tension and open disagreement. Statutory legislation would help, and I think is likely to come soon. Withdrawal of life support is practised routinely, if not commonly, and most decisions by surrogates are accepted routinely. One area in which they are not is for persons made formal wards, in which legislation commonly denies this authority. This is a source of problems, particularly with children made wards of such persons as a Minister of Social Services.

One way in which we may infer that we are doing the right things is by *absence* of litigation. Recently I tried to find cases involving negligence in research procedures upon human beings, and we seem to have only two in the last 30 years. We scoff at American practice, where virtually every decision seems to be referred to a court, but we do seem to rely to a significant extent upon the precedents they set, mostly without formal acknowledgment. On occasion we oppose statutory changes, ostensibly designed to tidy things up; some of those proposed by our Federal Law Reform Commission, recently disbanded by the government, seemed to us to verge upon the imbecilic. The same applies to a Bill on consent before the Ontario House in 1992, which appeared to doctors totally unworkable. We tend to function in a limbo, hoping that what we think is moral, is not illegal, but we fear from bitter experience that formal legal remedy for such uncertainty might be worse than the disease.

This is par excellence an area in which the exponential expansion of technological possibilities forces upon us the necessity of making moral decisions for which we may have no precedent in ethics or law. This is why what has come to be called "bioethics" is a growth industry, and why even those of us who practise on the edges of civilisation have to try to keep up with its development.

References

1. "Advance Directives: Are Thay an Advance?" (1992) 146 *Canadian Medical Association Journal* 127 (Advance Directives Seminar Group, Centre for Bioethics, University of Toronto).
2. "Withdrawal of Life-Support from Patients in the Persistent Vegetative State" (1991) 337 *Lancet* 96 (Institute of Medical Ethics Working Party on the ethics of prolonging life and assisting death).
3. "A Working Paper on Ethical Guidelines for Decision Making in Regard to the Introduction and Maintenance of Medically Provided Hydration and Nutrition" (St Joseph's Hospital, Hamilton, Ontario (undated)).
4. "Hospitals Routinely Withdraw Life Support", *Medical Post* (21 January 1992) 18.
5. "Searching for Death with Dignity" (1991) *Bulletin of Medical Ethics* (February) 3–4; S. Wolf *et al.*, "Sources of Concern about the Patient Self-Determination Act" (1991) 325 *New England Journal of Medicine* 1666.
6. *Reibl* v. *Hughes* (1980) 114 DLR (3d) 1.
7. *Nancy B* v. *Hôtel-Dieu de Québec* (1992) 86 DLR (4th) 385 (Que Sup Ct).
8. *Malette* v. *Schulman* (1990) 72 OR (2d) 417 (Ontario CA).
9. Martin's Annual Criminal Code (Canada Law Book Inc., Aurora, 1991).

Advance directives
and AIDS

The Terrence Higgins Trust
Living Will Project

Introduction

The problems of decision-making on behalf of mentally incompetent
adults in general, and the possible development of living wills in particular, have been the subject of increasing attention in the UK. The
Law Commission have recently published a Consultation Paper on
the former,[1] and Age Concern together with the Centre of Medical
Law and Ethics at King's College London have published a study of
the latter.[2]

In early 1991 the Terrence Higgins Trust[3] established a Project
Group[4] to determine whether there was a demand for living wills
among people with human immunodeficiency virus (HIV) and ac-
quired immunodeficiency syndrome (AIDS) in the UK, and if there
was, to try to find a way of meeting it. Coincidentally, at the same time
Ms Charlotta Schlyter, a research fellow at the Centre of Medical Law
and Ethics, King's College London was embarking on a study of advance directives and AIDS. She contacted the Trust and it was agreed
to work in cooperation. Ms Schlyter joined the Trust's Project Group
and participated in its work until the completion of her own project
and her departure in February 1992 for another job abroad.[5] In turn
the Trust was able to help her in the collection of some of the data for
her own research. Ms Schlyter has written a report about her research,
and the Trust's project has culminated in the production of a living
will form for use by people with HIV and AIDS.[6] We should like to

Decision-Making and Problems of Incompetence. Edited by A. Grubb.
© 1994 John Wiley & Sons Ltd.

take this opportunity to record our pleasure that the Centre and the Trust have been able to cooperate in this way on a subject of so much importance to so many people.

This chapter seeks to raise some of the issues (both legal and non-legal) we have had to consider.

Terminology

The term "living will" is used in a number of ways, but it is used here to mean a document one of whose purposes is to enable a person to write down his wishes about life-sustaining medical treatment, so that those wishes can be made known to and relied upon by doctors if the person then becomes terminally ill, and unable to communicate or otherwise unable to participate in decisions about his or her medical care. Such written wishes are often known as "advance declarations" or "advance directives". Often the wishes expressed by the maker of such a document are to the effect that in any of certain stated cases his or her life is not to be prolonged by medical treatment, which is rather to be confined to keeping the patient comfortable and free from pain.

The living will document prepared by the Trust, in cooperation with the Centre, also includes a section for appointing another person, sometimes known as a "health care proxy", to participate in medical decisions on the person's behalf if he or she becomes unable to do so.

Living wills and AIDS

The Terrence Higgins Trust is, of course, an HIV and AIDS organisation, and is not directly concerned with other conditions. However, the Centre of Medical Law and Ethics also thought that in any event AIDS was a particularly appropriate background against which to examine interest in advance directives.

Those with HIV and AIDS in the UK are, so far, predominantly young people. As a group they have demonstrated a high level of awareness about their condition and its treatment and prognosis. An AIDS diagnosis does not mean the person with AIDS is permanently ill. On the contrary, many people with AIDS are perfectly well at any given moment, and quite capable of thinking through the issues raised by a living will. Although the incidence of AIDS-related dementia is low, there is a great fear of it, but any period of mental incompetence is likely to be relatively short (in which it is to be contrasted with, say, Alzheimer's disease) and therefore the problems associated with relying upon wishes recorded a long time ago are much reduced. It was also thought that a living will could benefit people with HIV and AIDS by increasing the control they exercise over their treatment, by promoting consideration of and discussion about the deeply difficult subject of terminal care, and thereby also by increasing the psychological well-being of the patient. In addition it was thought that a living will might help to resolve disputes about a patient's medical treatment which, sadly, arise on occasion between a patient's family, on the one hand, and his or her partner, on the other. Such disputes of course occur in the context of any condition, but can occur with especial frequency and rancour in the AIDS context since so far in England and Wales so many with the condition have been young gay men.

Assessment of demand for and interest in advance directives in the HIV and AIDS field

The Trust's Living Will Project was of course charged first with trying to decide whether people with HIV and AIDS in the UK *wanted* living wills, and also with the attitudes of doctors to them. The Centre's research project dealt with the same questions. The initial task, therefore, was clearly to try to determine the demand. This was done initially by sending out a questionnaire to some 39 AIDS service organisations and hospices caring for people with AIDS, and also (through the Trust's internal mechanisms) to the Trust's Buddy Group leaders,[7] asking whether the people they represented would find a living will useful. Those who responded were uniformly favourable.

This questionnaire was followed by a more detailed one intended for completion by individuals represented by the organisations to whom the original questionnaire was sent and who agreed to participate in this further stage. (We did not think it proper to approach such people directly.) Many hundreds of these questionnaires were distributed, including one to each Trust Buddy (themselves totalling 389). The results of this exercise are described in the report published by the Centre of Medical Law and Ethics. In addition comments were invited from the public by means of letters and short articles in certain publications. It was clear (at least from this self-selecting sample) that those responding were in favour of a living will document being made available in the UK.[8]

The Trust had decided at an early stage that, if an effective living will form was to be introduced, it was essential that doctors and other health carers supported the idea and helped ensure that what it said made medical sense. Here our view was that a living will could be of great help, not only to people with AIDS, but also to their doctors when it came to making difficult treatment decisions at a difficult time. The Centre was also interested in the attitudes of doctors and nurses to terminal care and discussions about life-sustaining treatment. Accordingly the Trust's project and Ms Schlyter together embarked upon an extensive programme of consultations with doctors and other health care professionals in the AIDS field, primarily in London (although we have also established contact with some doctors in Edinburgh, where the demography of the condition is rather different from that in London, affecting as it does a much higher proportion of drug-users and proportionately fewer gay men). In addition we have kept bodies such as the British Medical Association informed of our projects and their progress, and have had informal contacts with a number of other bodies.

The results of all this research are reflected in Ms Schlyter's report, but it may be interesting to make a few observations here. It is, in particular, interesting to discover that while fewer than half of those with AIDS who responded said they had had an opportunity to have a discussion with a doctor about life-sustaining treatment, *all* of those with AIDS who had not had such an opportunity, and more than four-fifths of those with HIV infection, said that they would like to have such a discussion with a doctor if given an opportunity. But fewer than half of the doctors responding said that they normally had such a discussion with people with AIDS, although nearly all of them did so at least in some cases. It may be that both patients and doctors find it difficult to know how to raise the subject, with the result that in some cases a matter which both would privately prefer to discuss is insufficiently explored. Another interesting observation is that while almost all of those asked said they would consider appointing a health care proxy, most would not appoint a family member;[9] and over half the doctors responding said it was not always obvious whom to turn to for the purpose of consultations. Yet the use of the term "next of kin" (which in this context has no legal definition) in hospital forms may suggest to a patient that he or she is supposed to record the name of a family member. But the most striking feature of the responses has been the almost universal level of support for the availability of living wills.

Legal issues

Living wills have so far been more common in other countries than in the UK. In particular, following the case of Karen Quinlan,[10] many of the United States have introduced legislation governing their terms and giving them binding force,[11] and there is also legislation and discussion in (for example) Canada and Australia. In Switzerland the medical profession itself has been responsible for formulating such a document.

In the UK the general principle is that a person who is capable of giving or withholding consent to medical treatment cannot be treated without his or her consent.[12] A living will records a person's wishes about medical treatment in case in the future he becomes unable to express his consent. The question which arises is whether those wishes are legally enforceable and indeed whether giving effect to them could give rise to any legal liability.

Although the legal effect of advance directives has not yet been expressly determined in court, it has for some time been argued that such declarations are legally enforceable in the UK. For example, it has ben suggested that:

> [i]f the patient has foreseen the circumstances which have since arisen and there is no reason to believe that he would have changed his mind if still capable of doing so, the doctor should only be justified in proceeding to the same extent as he could if the patient were still capable of consenting.[13]

In Canada, in a decision of persuasive authority, a court held that a doctor was liable in battery for ignoring an incompetent patient's expressions of her wishes before the onset of incompetence.[14]

Although these questions will not be finally resolved in the UK until the courts have had an opportunity to consider them in terms, developments in 1992 suggest that a court is likely to find that an advance refusal of consent to treatment will be binding provided it complies with certain conditions. The first development was the publication in May 1992 of a Statement on Advance Directives by the British Medical Association. This statement supported the use of advance directives and said that doctors should normally comply with them. The next development was the case of _Re T_. That case confirmed the general principle that an adult patient was entitled to refuse consent to treatment irrespective of the wisdom of that decision,[15] but said that for a refusal to be effective the patient's doctors must be satisfied that at the time of refusal the patient had capacity to make that decision, that he or she was not under any undue influence, that he or she had considered the situation in which it would become relevant and knew the consequences of the decision in that situation, and that it had not been arrived at as a result of misinformation or false assumptions. The court clearly contemplated that provided these conditions were satisfied a refusal of consent expressed in advance would be legally binding. The court also contemplated that such a refusal might be expressed by way of a form or some other written document.[16]

The legal effect of appointing a health care proxy has also never been tested in the courts in the UK, but it is thought that making medical decisions on behalf of a principal is probably not within the powers of an attorney under the Enduring Powers of Attorney Act 1985. Those powers are confined to dealing with the principal's "property and affairs".[17]

So far as legal liability on the part of a doctor giving effect to wishes expressed is concerned, it seems unthinkable that any liability in negligence would ensue,[18] and equally it does not seem reasonable to suppose that there could be any criminal liability. The latter would presumably have to be based either on manslaughter or on assisting a suicide. To regard the refusal, by a person who is going to die soon in any event, of medical treatment designed to prolong life does not easily fall within any commonly accepted concept of "suicide", and indeed the Crown Prosecution Service are reported as having indicated that:

> [i]t is unlikely that a solicitor who is professionally instructed to draw up a living will, which merely sets out an exhortation . . . as to what should occur given certain physical or mental incapacity, commits an offence under the Suicide Act 1961.[19]

It seems clear also that a doctor giving effect to such wishes is not doing so with the intention of accelerating the patient's death, and indeed such a doctor may prove to be legally bound by the wishes expressed. In short, a doctor is under no duty to treat a patient who is unable to communicate in the face of previously expressed contrary wishes which the doctor does not believe to have changed.[20]

The living will form

In the light of research conducted by the Centre and the Trust together, the next step for the Trust was to formulate a draft living will document for consultation purposes. That was completed late in 1991 and about 120 consultation documents were sent out, each with one of two alternative questionnaires (one for the general run of consultees and a specialised one for doctors and health care workers). The final task was to consider the responses and to prepare a final version of the living will form, which was published in September 1992.

We decided at an early stage that the lack of express authority on advance directives and the uncertain legal effect of appointing a health care proxy need present no obstacle to developing a form of living will provided doctors were in practice prepared to give effect to the wishes expressed. This was one reason motivating the extensive consultation with the medical and health care professions which the Trust and the Centre have undertaken. Any change in the law would require legislation and it was thought that any attempt to crystallise in statutory language the exact circumstances in which a living will was to have compulsory effect would be a very difficult task indeed. The matter is ideally suited to development by the common law.

AIDS doctors and other health professionals consulted proved to be favourable to the introduction of living wills. Although this has been with different degrees of enthusiasm, nobody has opposed them in principle and indeed some have been strongly supportive. But it is clear that any form must navigate carefully between some very real problems. The main difficulty is, of course, that of determining what the patient's wishes actually are — or would have been had he or she been able to express them — and whether these wishes are the same as, or different from, wishes expressed in a living will which may have been signed some time earlier. A patient who has changed his or her mind should clearly be entitled to have his or her latest wishes respected. In this respect AIDS is, perhaps, an easier field in which to introduce the idea of the living will, as periods of mental incompetence are unlikely to be very prolonged (and much less so than, for example, with Alzheimer's disease). There are also questions concerning the burden which might be placed on a health care proxy, and some have voiced fears that a living will form might become a substitute, rather than a catalyst, for doctor–patient discussions. It is clear that the introduction of a living will form is not to be undertaken lightly. But our hope is that living wills made by people with AIDS are going to be a valuable factor in decisions concerning their medical care and will stimulate greater discussion and sensitivity about these issues. At the same time the knowledge that their wishes have been recorded in a way that doctors will pay the utmost respect to will give people with AIDS much-needed peace of mind and will leave them with the confidence that when they die they will do so with dignity and in accordance with their own decisions (perhaps expressed through a trusted person close to them), and not those of any other person.

Acknowledgements

The author would like to acknowledge that this chapter includes material derived from the work of Ms Charlotta Schlyter, lately Research Fellow at the Centre of Medical Law and Ethics, King's College London, and of Mr Wesley Gryk, solicitor. This work was prepared initially as a paper for a Workshop held at King's College, London in April 1992, and has subsequently been updated to December 1992.

Notes and references

1. Law Commission Consultation Paper No. 199, *Mentally Incapacitated Adults and Decision-Making: An Overview* (March 1991). See especially Part VI, which contains among other things a discussion of living wills.
2. *The Living Will· Consent to Treatment at the End of Life— A Working Party Report* (Edward Arnold, 1988).
3. The Trust is one of the foremost HIV and AIDS voluntary organisations in the UK.
4. The members of the Project Group are currently: Mr Robin Dormer, Mr Wesley Gryk, Mr Paul Meadows (all solicitors and volunteer members of the Trust's Legal Services Group), and Ms Simmy Viinikka (solicitor, Advice Centre, Terrence Higgins Trust).
5. Her departure unfortunately prevented her from participating in the workshop for which this chapter was prepared.
6. Both the report (*Advance Directives and AIDS*) and the living will form were published in September 1992.
7. The idea of the "buddy" comes originally from the USA. The Trust has several hundred volunteer buddies. Each buddy befriends a person with AIDS and provides him or her with such support as he may need, whether this be practical or emotional. They are expected to be non-judgmental and to complement rather than replace existing support from partners, families, friends and others. The role of the buddy is always determined by the wishes of the person they work with, their individual needs and the level of support they are already receiving. The Trust's buddies are organised into a number of groups for administrative purposes.
8. The response rate cannot be calculated meaningfully because the

questionnaires were distributed only indirectly to those who were intended to complete them, and the proportion which reached their destination cannot be ascertained.

9. "Family member" did not here include a spouse or partner; in any event, the partner of an unmarried person would not in normal usage count as "family".

10. *In the Matter of Karen Quinlan* 335 A 2d 647 (1976) (New Jersey Supreme Court). In *Cruzan* v. *Director, Missouri Department of Health* 110 S Ct 2841 (1990), the US Supreme Court held that a competent person may refuse medical treatment and an incompetent person may have that right exercised by a proxy, but that individual states may legitimately require "clear and convincing evidence" of the incompetent patient's wishes.

11. In all, 48 states of the USA have legislation on the subject. The Patient Self-Determination Act now also requires that upon admission to hospital all patients must be told of their rights under state law to consent to or refuse medical treatment, and to make a living will or appoint a health care proxy.

12. This proposition was recently confirmed in *Re T (adult: refusal of treatment)* [1992] 3 WLR 782 but is, of course, much simplified. In particular, it needs qualification in relation to children. See *Gillick* v. *West Norfolk and Wisbech Area Health Authority* [1986] AC 112 (HL) and *Re R (wardship: medical treatment)* [1991] 3 WLR 592 (CA). The Family Law Reform Act 1969, section 8 provides that the consent of a child aged at least 16 to surgical, medical or dental treatment is as effective as that of a person of full age. There is also authority about how much information a patient needs to be given before the consent is effective: see, in particular, *Bolam* v. *Friern Hospital Management Committee* [1957] 1 WLR 582 and *Sidaway* v. *Board of Governors of the Bethlem Royal Hospital and the Maudsley Hospital* [1985] AC 871.

13. P. D. G. Skegg, *Law, Ethics and Medicine* (Oxford, 1984) at 116.

14. *Malette* v. *Shulman* (1990) 72 OR (2d) 417, [1991] 2 Med LR 162 (Ontario Court of Appeal). In that case the patient was an unconscious Jehovah's Witness who carried a card indicating that she did not wish to have any blood transfusion. See also Malcolm Hurwitt, "The Right to Die", *Law Society's Gazette* (10 July 1991) at 20; cf D. A. Lush, "Living Wills", *Law Society's Gazette* (22 March 1989) at 21.

15. A later case, *Re S (adult: refusal of treatment)* [1992] 3 WLR 806 appears to contemplate an exception to the principles expressed in *Re T. Re S* involved a woman who refused a Caesarean section; the court held that the operation could be performed lawfully despite her refusal if the lives of mother and child were at risk if it were not performed. *Sed quaere.*

16. While the case of *Airedale NHS Trust* v. *Bland* [1993] 1 All ER 820 (HL) (the case of Hillsborough victim Tony Bland) does not raise the

issue directly since Tony Bland had made no advance directives, it seems clear from the speeches in that case that a refusal of consent to treatment expressed in advance by way of living will is legally binding.

17. See, for example, *Re W (EEM)* [1971] Ch 123, 142–3, per Ungoed-Thomas J for a discussion in a different context of the meaning of a patient's "affairs".

18. Given that a patient can validly refuse consent to treatment when capable of expressing such consent, a doctor can hardly be accused of negligence by reason of giving effect to wishes expressed before the onset of incompetence and which he or she has no reason to suppose have been altered subsequently. It would, of course, be different if the doctor did have reason to suppose that the patient's wishes were no longer as stated in any living will document.

19. Hurwitt, *op cit* at 20.

20. In the light of the BMA Statement on Advance Directives, it is at least clear that there is a responsible body of medical opinion to this effect. The case of *Tony Bland*, the Hillsborough victim in a persistent vegetative state, although not directly relevant to the question of advance directives as he had not made one, is relevant in that it seems that artificial nutrition and hydration could be the subject of an advance directive, and has clarified the duties of doctors to keep such patients alive despite a hopeless prognosis in a situation where there is no dispute that the patient should be allowed to die. The House of Lords held that Tony Bland need not be kept alive by means of artificial nutrition and hydration. As noted above, it now seems clear that an advance refusal of consent expressed by way of a living will would be binding.

Index

*Index compiled by
Campbell Purton*

"... A series stemming from lectures given at the centre of Medical Law and Ethics at King's College, London. The contributors include both members of the Centre and visiting lecturers, and the topics covered range over a wide spectrum. I would recommend it strongly for the libraries of educational institutions".

Physiotherapy

Volume 7 ...

■ CHOICES AND DECISIONS IN HEALTH CARE

Edited by A. GRUBB, School of Law and Centre of Medical Law and Ethics, King's College London, UK

The seventh volume in the series of King's College Studies, while maintaining the theme of diversity of coverage, focuses on one important issue for medical law and ethics, namely that of decision-making and the incompetent patient whether child or adult. The right-to-die litigation in the USA, and the wider question of patients' rights and the role of society in making decisions about their medical care, is discussed in depth.

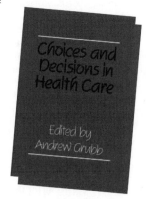

CONTENTS: Medical Ethics in Islam ■ Euthanasia ■ Treatment Decisions: Keeping it in the Family ■ Autonomy in the Company of Others ■ The Persistent Vegetative State - Medical, Ethical and Legal Issues ■ Geriatric Medicine: Some Ethical Issues Associated with its Development ■ The Development and Future of Research Ethics Committees in Britain ■ Innovations in Procedure and Practice in Multiparty Medical Cases ■ The Medical and Legal Response to Post-Traumatic Stress Disorder.

0471936219   258pp   1993   £28.95

Volume 6 ...

■ CHALLENGES IN MEDICAL CARE

Edited by A. GRUBB, School of Law and Centre of Medical Law and Ethics, King's College London, UK

The sixth volume in this series takes a reflective view of medical law and ethics, the health care system and challenges raised by modern technology.

CONTENTS: HIV and AIDS: Discrimination and the Challenge for Human Rights ■ Ethics and Regulation in Randomized Controlled Trials of Therapy ■ Legislative Criteria: The Human Fertilisation and Embryology Bill ■ The Legal Status of the Frozen Human Embryo ■ Maternal-Fetal Conflict: Reformulating the Equation ■ Medical Accountability: A Background Paper ■ Does the National Health Service Have a Purpose? ■ Inequality Among Health Care Professionals: Ethical Dimensions of their Relationship ■ Is there a Future for a National Health Service?

0471931020   206pp   1991   £32.50

Volume 5 ...

■ ETHICS AND LAW IN HEALTH CARE AND RESEARCH

Edited by P. BYRNE, Department of Theology and Religious Studies, King's College, London, UK

The aim of this volume is to provoke thought on fundamental questions - legal, political, and philosophical - arising out of the nature and delivery of medical care and medical research in the 1990s.

CONTENTS: The Ethics of Clinical Research ■ Equipoise, Consent and the Ethics of Randomised Clinical Trials ■ Some Ethical Aspects of Current Fetal Usage in Transplantation ■ Child Abuse and the Role of the Courts in its Control ■ Infertility Treatment: A Selective Right to Reproduce? ■ Making Public Policy on Medical - Moral Issues ■ AIDS: Some Civil Liberty Implications ■ Resource Allocation in the National Health Service ■ Homicide, Medical Ethics and the Principle of Double Effect ■ A Woman, and her Unborn Child: Rights and Responsibilities.

0471928062   204pp   1990   £28.95

Volume 4 ...

■ MEDICINE, MEDICAL ETHICS AND THE VALUE OF LIFE

Edited by P. BYRNE, Department of Theology and Religious Studies, King's College, London, UK

CONTENTS: Euthanasia in the Netherlands ■ The BMA on Euthanasia: The Philosopher versus the Doctor ■ The Value of Human Life ■ Abortion, Embryo Research and Fetal Transplantation: Their Moral Interrelationships ■ Can Medical Ethics be Taught? ■ Teaching Medical Ethics: Impressions from the USA ■ The Allocation of Scarce Medical Resources: A Democrat's Dilemma ■ AIDS and Tolerance ■ The Ethics of Sex Selection.

0471925160   172pp   1989   £28.95

Wiley books are available through your bookseller. Prices may vary and are subject to change. Alternatively order direct from Wiley (payment to John Wiley & Sons Ltd). Credit card orders accepted by telephone - 0243 829121 or dial FREE on 0800 243407 (UK only). Fax your order on 0243 539132.

JOHN WILEY & SONS LTD, BAFFINS LANE, CHICHESTER, WEST SUSSEX, PO19 1UD, UK

WILEY